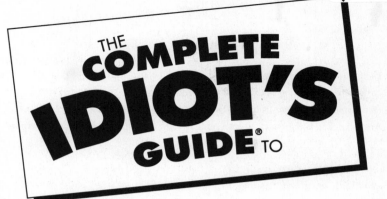

THE
COMPLETE
IDIOT'S
GUIDE® TO

World Conflicts

Second Edition

by Steven D. Strauss

ALPHA

A member of Penguin Group (USA) Inc.

For Bruddie, who likes political stories more than anyone.

ALPHA BOOKS

Published by the Penguin Group

Penguin Group (USA) Inc., 375 Hudson Street, New York, New York 10014, U.S.A.

Penguin Group (Canada), 10 Alcorn Avenue, Toronto, Ontario, Canada M4V 3B2 (a division of Pearson Penguin Canada Inc.)

Penguin Books Ltd, 80 Strand, London WC2R 0RL, England

Penguin Ireland, 25 St Stephen's Green, Dublin 2, Ireland (a division of Penguin Books Ltd)

Penguin Group (Australia), 250 Camberwell Road, Camberwell, Victoria 3124, Australia (a division of Pearson Australia Group Pty Ltd)

Penguin Books India Pvt Ltd, 11 Community Centre, Panchsheel Park, New Delhi—110 017, India

Penguin Group (NZ), cnr Airborne and Rosedale Roads, Albany, Auckland 1310, New Zealand (a division of Pearson New Zealand Ltd)

Penguin Books (South Africa) (Pty) Ltd, 24 Sturdee Avenue, Rosebank, Johannesburg 2196, South Africa

Penguin Books Ltd, Registered Offices: 80 Strand, London WC2R 0RL, England

International Standard Book Number: 1-59257-511-0
Library of Congress Catalog Card Number: 2005937491

08 07 06   8 7 6 5 4 3 2 1

Interpretation of the printing code: The rightmost number of the first series of numbers is the year of the book's printing; the rightmost number of the second series of numbers is the number of the book's printing. For example, a printing code of 06-1 shows that the first printing occurred in 2006.

Printed in the United States of America

Note: This publication contains the opinions and ideas of its author. It is intended to provide helpful and informative material on the subject matter covered. It is sold with the understanding that the author and publisher are not engaged in rendering professional services in the book. If the reader requires personal assistance or advice, a competent professional should be consulted.

The author and publisher specifically disclaim any responsibility for any liability, loss, or risk, personal or otherwise, which is incurred as a consequence, directly or indirectly, of the use and application of any of the contents of this book.

Most Alpha books are available at special quantity discounts for bulk purchases for sales promotions, premiums, fund-raising, or educational use. Special books, or book excerpts, can also be created to fit specific needs.

For details, write: Special Markets, Alpha Books, 375 Hudson Street, New York, NY 10014.

Publisher: *Marie Butler-Knight*
Editorial Director: *Mike Sanders*
Acquisitions Editor: *Tom Stevens*
Development Editor: *Michael Thomas*
Senior Production Editor: *Billy Fields*
Copy Editor: *Keith Cline*

Cartoonist: *Richard King*
Book Designer: *Trina Wurst/Kurt Owens*
Cover Designer: *Bill Thomas*
Indexer: *Heather McNeill*
Layout: *Brian Massey*
Proofreading: *Mary Hunt*

Contents at a Glance

Contents

Foreword

Followers of world news might rightly conclude that neither evolution nor intelligent design could possibly account for mankind's penchant to kill, often in great numbers. It's not survival of the fittest out there. It's just madness. From Rwanda to North Korea, Colombia to Somalia, the value of human life at times seems no greater than a can of soda pop; something you hold for a few minutes only to consume and discard.

But of course it's not just random, when seen through the eyes of a keen observer. There are histories to the world's conflicts and personalities that drive them. Some conflicts can be counted on to provide steady carnage and last almost forever, like the Middle East, because of competing claims for holy lands. Others are more unpredictable, such as India and Pakistan, a long fault line that could quake the planet to its core should a violent shift result in a nuclear confrontation.

No one has time to thoroughly understand all of the world's conflict zones, if that were even possible, not even those who make a living in this line of study. As a journalist who has covered Afghanistan, Iraq, the Balkans and other war zones, I can say that even my fleeting flashes of insight were quickly followed by reminders of how little I truly knew. Other times, I faced situations that no rational human could explain, such as gravesites with torsos without heads.

Yet author Steven D. Strauss manages in this volume to provide a thoroughly understandable survey of the world's trouble spots. The book is a challenge to the old adage that "a little knowledge is a dangerous thing." Novices to the world of foreign affairs and national security will find insights that compel them to look further into, say, why trouble in Azerbaijan could affect people in Des Moines. And they might be surprised to learn that the nation that goes to war more than any other is the United States of America. Others, who have developed an interest or expertise in a particular region or conflict, will find quickly that, while every place is unique, in a way no place is completely different. Hatred and violence have common themes including the thirst for power, greed, corruption, and sadly, religious competition.

Immersion in the world's troubles is a sobering thing. But Strauss takes pains to point up examples of hope, too. There's Northern Ireland and the countries that have emerged successfully from Soviet domination after the fall of the Berlin wall. Egypt and Israel have coexisted peacefully for a generation now due to the bravery of their leaders including Anwar Sadat, who was assassinated after signing the peace treaty.

Strauss thoughtfully includes a lengthy catalogue of resources, including web sites, for those who want to dive more deeply into the world's conflicts. Even by itself, this book provides a valuable survey. Busy folks need never go beyond its pages.

As they listen to, watch, or read the news and hear America's leaders, they'll have an extra bit of understanding and interest—exactly the kind of knowledge that, if the whole world had it, might make a future edition of a book like this a lot shorter.

—Steven Komarow

Steven Komarow is a national security and foreign policy correspondent for *USA Today*. Komarow was an embedded reporter with the U.S. Army during the 2003 invasion of Iraq and since has covered post-invasion developments. He is a graduate of George Washington University with a degree in political science.

Introduction

Although September 11 changed America forever, the rest of the world has, for many years, been engaged in conflicts that dwarf the destruction of the Twin Towers. In Africa alone, civil wars have killed literally millions of civilians, and made refugees of millions more. In the Middle East, terrorism is a way of life. So you may excuse the rest of the world if they think that the death of 3,000 Americans is not the worst tragedy they have ever witnessed, because it's not.

But even beyond the sheer numbers of these conflicts, it is the tales of war and peace that are so fascinating. From the old—the Cuban missile crisis, for example—to the new—the War on Terror—learning what happened and why they happened makes for some great reading.

The good news is that although conflict and war abound, peace still finds a way. Israel and Egypt, the most bitter of enemies, have forged a delicate peace. Protestants and Catholics in Northern Ireland found a peaceful solution to their age-old conflict. The former Warsaw Pact countries of Hungary, Poland, and Czechoslovakia threw off their Soviet master and have, amazingly, since joined NATO. The United Nations says that armed conflicts around the globe have declined 40 percent in the past decade. There is reason to hope.

What's in It for Me?

The Complete Idiot's Guide to World Conflicts, Second Edition, is your chance to learn the facts. Why is it that the rest of the world seems to hate the United States? After reading this book, you will see why America is often perceived by others as a big bully. By the same token, you will also see how the United States has often made the world a safer, better place. This book allows you to understand the whole world, not just your own.

The Complete Idiot's Guide to World Conflicts, Second Edition, is intended to make these sometimes complicated matters (just who are the bad guys in the Balkans, anyway?) easy to understand and interesting to read. As such, the book is divided into geographic regions so that you can grasp an entire continent's issues easily and quickly.

Is war inevitable? Is peace possible? Read on, and decide for yourself.

How This Book Is Organized

This book is divided into seven parts or geographical regions:

Part 1, "Wars of the World," begins with a broad overview of the state of conflict in the world today. Analyzing war in general, and the War on Terror between East and West in particular, this section helps you understand the big picture.

Part 2, "The Middle East and North Africa," analyzes that most problematic of places, the Middle East. Here you will see that, although peace is possible, the likelihood of further conflict is even more probable.

Part 3, "Central and Southern Africa," might be the most gruesome part of this book. It is simply unbelievable how widespread, how redundant, and just how wanton the violence in this part of the world can be. With civil wars that seemingly never end and mayhem as a tool of destruction, Africa has been devastated by conflict.

Part 4, "Asia and the Pacific," not only recounts some of the largest conflicts of our time (Korea, for example), but it also examines the likelihood of further conflict in the region, and what might set those conflicts off. With China growing as it is, and as repressive as it remains, the chance for even more conflict in Asia grows daily.

Part 5, "Europe," examines the continent that was the cause of the most war, grief, and destruction during the twentieth century. Besides looking at historical conflicts, this section explains in an understandable way more modern conflicts: the breakup of the Soviet Union, what happened in the Balkans, and the chances for a lasting peace in Northern Ireland.

Part 6, "South America and Latin America," looks at the long-running war in Columbia and analyzes the prospects for peace there. It also looks at the terrible tragedy that Papa Doc and Baby Doc Duvalier brought to Haiti, as well as smoldering conflicts in Peru, Ecuador, and Paraguay.

Part 7, "North America," looks at the many conflicts that the world's last superpower, America, has been and is currently involved in. It also looks at problems in Mexico and Canada, and then concludes with the prospects for an overall more peaceful world.

Extras

Throughout the book, you will also encounter many more tidbits of information that have been highlighted by friendly icons. Here's what to expect:

def•i•ni•tion

The jargon of war and peace can often be confusing. This section translates it into plain English.

Landmine!

Especially gruesome facts, or problems to be on the lookout for, are discussed in this sidebar.

Reliable Resources

Insider information, facts, knowledge, and quotes of interest can be found here.

Peacekeepers

Tips and hints can be found here.

Acknowledgments

A special thanks to Shirley Goodblatt for her assistance in the preparation of this book. I would also like to thank Mara, Sydney, Jillian, Maria, Spencer, and Larry.

Special Thanks to the Technical Reviewer

The Complete Idiot's Guide to World Conflicts, Second Edition, was reviewed by an expert who double-checked the accuracy of what you'll learn here, to help us ensure that this book gives you everything you need to know about world conflicts. Special thanks are extended to Connie Robinson, who also provided guidance on the scope and coverage of the second edition.

Connie Robinson is a Ph.D. candidate in Sociology at New School University in New York, New York. Her research focuses on nationalism, state formation, and democratization in the former Yugoslavia. She has taught at Eugene Lang College, Fairleigh Dickinson University, and Westchester Community College.

Trademarks

All terms mentioned in this book that are known to be or are suspected of being trademarks or service marks have been appropriately capitalized. Alpha Books and Penguin Group (USA) Inc. cannot attest to the accuracy of this information. Use of a term in this book should not be regarded as affecting the validity of any trademark or service mark.

Part 1

Wars of the World

September 11 crystallized just how much the world has changed since the Soviet Union fell and the Cold War ended. Back then, U.S. politicians debated what should be done with the ensuing "peace dividend." September 11 changed all that. It may be that the War on Terror is in fact World War III; it just looks different from what we expected.

Why does humankind have so much conflict? Why is the current conflict between the West and radical Islam so intractable? And just what is the War on Terror? In this part, the big questions are examined.

Chapter 1

The World at War

In This Chapter

◆ The world is getting smaller

◆ The state of things today

◆ Why people go to war

◆ The potential for peace

The world is a crazy place, and it seems to get crazier by the moment. If Islamic extremists aren't attacking the United States, then the Serbs are attacking Kosovo, the Palestinians and Israelis are killing each other, or Protestants are blowing up Catholics. North Korea is digging what former President Clinton has called "a big hole in the ground," supposedly to hold nuclear weapons intended for use against their estranged brethren in the south.

Many of these conflicts are well-known: India hates Pakistan, China has it in for Taiwan. Many more are not: the Tutsi and the Hutu in Rwanda have been at it for years. (Almost one million Tutsi were murdered in 1994 alone.) Did you know that Iraq made its first claim to annex Kuwait in 1961 but was rebuffed by the presence of British troops? Who hates whom?

In this chapter, I explain the state of conflict in the world today, examine who goes to war the most and why, and conclude by analyzing the potential for peace.

The world is getting smaller.

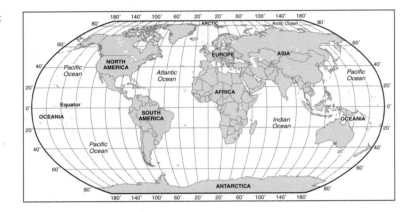

It's a Small World After All

The attacks on New York City by Osama bin Laden exemplify how these festering animosities around the globe can suddenly erupt, seemingly without notice. Take for example, the surprising subway bombings in London in July 2005.

On July 7, 2005, a coordinated series of four bomb attacks struck London during rush hour. Three bombs exploded almost simultaneously on three different London Underground trains, and a fourth blew up a double-decker bus about an hour later. The attacks were the result of Islamic suicide attackers and were the worst bombings in London since World War II. Two weeks later to the day, four more explosions occurred, but apparently due to mistake, only the detonators of the bombs went off, and no one was hurt. All four suspected bombers were subsequently arrested by Scotland Yard.

Reliable Resources

In August 2004, an Islamic terrorist cell was uncovered in Luton, England. The cell was discovered after an al-Qaeda operative in Pakistan had been arrested and his laptop computer seized. That computer is said to have contained plans for attacks on the London Underground and New York financial institutions.

After the Luton cell was broken up, British agents held and interrogated Mohammad Sidique Khan. Kahn was subsequently released and not followed. Almost a year later he became one of the four London suicide bombers.

Not only is the world getting crazier, but it is also getting smaller; thus the need to understand it is ever increasing. The Internet and the advent of instantaneous global communications, when combined with more and more economic interdependence, have made the earth a very small place indeed.

A few years ago, Thailand made some economic mistakes that affected the entire Southeast Asian economy. The entire Pacific Rim was then jarred, and for a while, the whole world was on the verge of recession. The downturn in the Asian economy then caused an already hurting North Korea to become even more aggressive toward its rival South Korea. Conflict in the twenty-first century is sure to hit closer to home as the world becomes an ever-smaller place.

By the way, it is important to understand that conflict and war are not necessarily the same thing, although they sure are close. For example, when the United States attacked the Taliban in Afghanistan after the attacks on September 11, 2001, no formal declaration of war was ever passed by the United States Congress; but that the conflict was a war is no surprise. A formal declaration of war is not necessary for a war to be a war.

Even so, there are conflicts that are not wars. For example, although the Armenians and Azerbaijanis are still in conflict to this day, they are not now at war; however, they could be at any time. Therefore, throughout this book, I use the terms *conflict* and *war* interchangeably.

The challenge is to understand why conflict and war seem so inevitable, so commonplace, as well as how they might be reduced.

War Today

There are 192 countries on Earth, and in the past half century, almost every one of them has been involved in more than one conflict. Some have had many.

Which country do you think has had the most wars and conflicts in the past 50 years? The answer is—the United States. Not only has it engaged in six wars (Korea, Vietnam, the Cold War, Iraq, Afghanistan, and Iraq II), but it has also been involved in three incursions and invasions (Laos, Cambodia, and Libya), two liberations (Grenada and Bosnia), six peacekeeping operations (Dominican Republic, Lebanon twice, the Gulf, Somalia, Kosovo), two rescue missions (the SS Mayaguez in Cambodia and American hostages in Iran), and one ouster (Panama).

Who's next? If you guessed Israel, you would be right. Since the end of World War II, the tiny Jewish state has been involved in no fewer than seven wars:

- The War of Independence (1948)
- The Suez War (1956)
- The Six-Day War (1967)
- The War of Attrition (1967–70)
- The Yom Kippur War (1973)
- The War in Lebanon (1982)
- The Palestinian Intifada (1987–?)

Peacekeepers

Israel is the only democracy in the Middle East. It proclaimed Jerusalem to be its capital in 1950, but the United States, like nearly all other countries, maintains its embassy in Tel Aviv. The Israeli president is elected by the 120-member Knesset for a 5-year term, but the real power lays with the prime minister, who traditionally was elected by popular vote for a 4-year term. In 2001, however, the Knesset voted to restore the previous method under which the legislators will choose the prime minister.

But the United States and Israel are not the only countries that have been heavily involved in armed conflict during the past half century. Not surprisingly, the next two most warring countries also hail from the Middle East. The first is Israel's one-time enemy, Egypt. In the past 50 years, Egypt has been involved in …

- Six wars (five with Israel and one with Yemen)
- Three international events (Cyprus, Malta, and Western Sahara)
- One border incident (Libya)

The parade of warring Middle East countries continues, with Iraq tying with Egypt in the most number of conflicts, with six major wars (three with Israel, one with Iran, one with Kuwait and the United States, and another with the United States and its allies), several border incidents (with Iran, Syria, and Turkey for example), and an internal battle against the Kurds and Shiites.

Pakistan is the next most warring nation, with four major wars (three with India and one with Bangladesh), several incidents with bordering neighbors (Afghanistan being but one example), and numerous internal security problems (Islamic fundamentalists, for instance).

India is tied with Pakistan, having had four wars (three with Pakistan, one with China), numerous problems with its island neighbor Sri Lanka, numerous annexations (Kashmir), and a multitude of internal security problems.

Landmine!

In 2000, India's population topped the one billion mark.

Russia (and the old Soviet Union) has had three wars (Hungary, the Cold War, and Afghanistan), numerous incidents and problems with her old Warsaw Pact allies (Czechoslovakia, Poland, and Berlin), several internal "wars" (Chechnya, for example), numerous border incidents with China, and a few problems with foreign airliners (e.g., KAL 007).

A Global Perspective

In short, war and conflict are part of modern life. This is made all the more obvious in the following table, provided by the United Nations. It examines conflicts in the world at the dawn of the twenty-first century.

Conflicts in the Twenty-First Century

Region	Number of Countries in Region	Conflicts (in %)	Countries with Conflicts (in %)	Percent of World Conflict
Africa	50	13	26	36
Asia	42	13	26	36
Europe	42	1	2	3
Americas	44	2	5	6
Middle East	14	7	43	19
Totals	192	36	16	100

What does this tell us?

◆ Not surprisingly, the region hosting the most conflicts was the Middle East, with fully 43 percent of its countries at war.

◆ The most stable region was Europe, accounting for only 3 percent of all conflicts, followed by North and South America, with only 6 percent of all conflicts.

◆ A quarter of both Africa and Asia was at war.

The real question, though, is not how many conflicts there are at any given time around the globe, but rather, why are there so many conflicts?

Johnny Got His Gun

Although reading this list of recent wars might be depressing, it surely is not surprising, given just how much money is spent on arms shipments every year, as shown in the following table.

Annual Arms Shipments

Biggest Exporters of Arms (in Billion Dollars/Year)		Biggest Importers of Arms (in Billion Dollars/Year)	
United States	$18	Iraq and Iran	$6
Russia	$4.5	Saudi Arabia	$3
France	$4	India	$3
Cuba	$2	Vietnam	$2
China	$2	Angola	$2
Czechoslovakia	$1	Libya	$2
Poland	$1	Egypt and Syria	$2
Germany	$1	Australia and Japan	$1

War is big business. With countries around the world importing more than $30 billion worth of arms every year, it is no wonder that so much armed conflict exists around the globe.

Moreover, with technology increasing as rapidly as it does these days, industrialized countries such as the United States are inventing ever more sophisticated ways to kill human beings. And the military in those countries importing these weapons are anxious to try them out on their alleged enemies. Thus there are both financial and military reasons behind war.

> **Landmine!**
>
> According to the Council for a Livable World, by the late 1990s, "The United States spent, yearly, approximately $2.50 per person (non-U.S. residents) on foreign aid. Of this, military and security assistance totaled $1.25 per person (non-U.S. residents), while peacekeeping and humanitarian intervention accounted for another $0.40 per person. The remainder, approximately $0.85 per person, was spent on development aid. Meanwhile, in the same time period, the United States exported weapons worth more than $2 for every person on Earth. This is based on conservative estimates of total weapons transferred in that year."

Yet, although the manufacture and selling of arms is undoubtedly a large reason why there seems to be so much conflict in the world today, it is by no means the only reason.

War—What Is It Good For?

War has been around as long as humans have been alive. If you've ever seen the movie *2001: A Space Odyssey*, you will recall that the prehumanoids in that film fought a war, with the ones who used bones as tools being the winner. It isn't hard to imagine that something similar occurred time and again in real life. Man has always fought and has always looked for better ways to kill his fellow man.

Mankind fights for many reasons: survival, hate, anger, greed, need, miscalculation, power, freedom, insecurity—the list is probably as lengthy as the list of human emotions.

However, just as long as man has been at war, so, too, has he been trying to understand and end it. Woodrow Wilson said that World War I

> **Landmine!**
>
> War has been waged against us by stealth and deceit and murder. This nation is peaceful, but fierce when stirred to anger. This conflict was begun on the timing and terms of others. It will end in a way, and at an hour, of our choosing.
>
> —President George W. Bush, speech at National Cathedral, September 14, 2001

would be the "war to end all wars." George W. Bush said that the purpose of the War on Terrorism was to "wipe out evil."

Indeed, mankind has been discussing the causes of war from a very early date. For instance, one of the first great works of history, Thucydides's *History of the Peloponnesian War,* written in the fifth century B.C.E., is an analysis dedicated to discussing why men fight.

Certainly, as researcher Walter Fritz points out in his online article "Peace Between Nations," beyond emotion and survival, there are other subjective reasons for war, including …

◆ The belief that the war will be beneficial to society in the long run.

◆ Errors of appreciation of the political, economic, and social situation of its own society and of the adversary.

◆ Accidents in which a critical situation gets out of hand.

◆ A fight over resources.

Maybe more than anything else, war is seen as a means to achieve an end, the end being the perceived betterment of the nation. Maybe that is why capitalistic democracies do not go to war *against one another*.

Democracy and capitalism are shared values, and, when combined with an ever-increasing interdependent economic system, it is rarely in the interest of one such country to harm another because the net result will be a diminution of both. As such, one of the best things that can be done to promote world peace is to promote capitalistic democracies. Far from being jingoistic, this is simply a conclusion drawn from the facts: democracies don't go to war against one another.

Reliable Resources

It will not be quick and it will not be easy. Our adversaries are not one or two terrorist leaders, or even a single terrorist organization or network. It's a broad network of individuals and organizations that are determined to terrorize and, in so doing, to deny us the very essence of what we are: free people.
—Secretary of Defense Donald Rumsfeld, press briefing, September 18, 2001

As R. J. Rummel, professor of political science at the University of Hawaii, observes, "[T]he [statistical] probability of any [two democracies] engaging in war from 1946 to 1986 was 32/6876 or .0047." The probability of two democracies "not engaging in war was .9953." He concludes, "The probability of this lack of war between democracies being by chance is virtually 100 to 1."

War and Poverty

According to a report by Radio Free Europe journalist Anthony Georgieff, the Center for War and Peace Research in Uppsala, Sweden, issued a report that stated that most armed conflict today occurs within a country's own borders, whereas in years past, most wars were fought *between* different countries.

What is even more interesting, according to the report, is that poverty was the major cause of about 80 percent of today's wars. Poorer countries were found to be three times at greater risk of war than richer countries. Indeed, throughout the decade of the 1990s, most wars were fought by countries with severe economic problems.

Yes, ethnicity was a factor, but not as big a factor as you may believe. It is when ethnicity is tied to poverty that war often results. In richer countries, those ethnic divides are more easily breached without violence and war.

War According to the United Nations

United Nations Secretary-General Kofi Annan has another idea when it comes to the causes of war. In an article summarizing Annan's annual report to the fifty-fourth session of the U.N. General Assembly InterPress journalist Thalif Deen characterized Annan's stance as follows. Although Annan acknowledges that poverty does play a role in many contemporary standoffs, he would like us to shift our focus of attention to the lack of equality and power many domestic social groups face in the world today: "It is this [inequality], rather than poverty, that seems to be the critical factor."

Regardless whether the inequality is based on ethnicity, religion, national identity, or economic class, according to Annan, "it tends to be reflected in unequal access to political power that too often forecloses paths to peaceful change." Another factor that fuels the fires of violent conflict today, according to the United Nations, is the disturbing rise in ethnic, or so-called "identity politics." According to the United Nations, "fewer than 20 percent of its 185 member states are ethnically homogeneous." This diversity can easily cause friction within a country, and political demagogues thus have little difficulty finding targets of opportunity and mobilizing support for bigoted causes. Says Annan, "The upsurge of ethnic cleansing in the 1990s provides stark evidence of the appalling human costs that this vicious exploitation of identity politics can generate."

The good news from the United Nations is two-fold. First, it is apparent that peace agreements are on the rise. In the 1990s, three times as many nations signed peace agreements than in the previous three decades, reflecting, as Deen reports, " a more than 30 percent decline in the overall number and intensity of armed conflicts worldwide from 1992 to 1997."

The second piece of good news is even better: According to the U.N.'s first-ever Human Security Report, published in October, 2005, armed conflicts around the globe have plummeted by more than 40 percent since 1992, and genocide and human rights abuses declined even more. According to the study, the break-up of the Soviet Union was the main cause for this dramatic development as it reduced the number of "proxy wars" around the globe. According to the study, the only type of conflict that is presently getting worse is terrorism.

> **Landmine!** _____
>
> According to *New York Times* journalist Barbara Crosset's summary of the U.N. Human Development Report 1998 (September 27, 1998): "The richest fifth of the world's people consumes 86 percent of all goods and services, while the poorest fifth consumes just 1.3 percent. Indeed, the richest fifth consumes 45 percent of all meat and fish, 58 percent of all energy used and 84 percent of all paper, has 74 percent of all telephone lines and owns 87 percent of all vehicles."

War and Resources

It is common knowledge that the first Gulf War was a war over oil, and who would control it. The United States was loathe to cede that power to Saddam Hussein. So clearly, resources are another reason that countries go to war.

Similarly, wars on a much smaller scale are often fought over specific areas, areas that are usually rich in resources. After this land has been conquered, resources such as oil, diamonds, and timber can be looted and sold for hard currency. Be that as it may, most states at most times get the natural resources they need by means other than war.

As such, fighting over resources is a relatively rare reason for countries to go to war. As in the case of the Gulf War, it is the power to control the resource, and not the resource itself, that is usually the reason for war.

Freedom

Needless to say, one of the oldest reasons for war is that it allows a people to free themselves from what they consider to be tyranny. Consider these words:

> When in the Course of human events, it becomes necessary for one people to dissolve the political bands which have connected them with another, and to assume among the powers of the earth, the separate and equal station to which the Laws of Nature and of Nature's God entitle them, a decent respect to the opinions of man-kind requires that they should declare the causes which impel them to the separation.

> We hold these truths to be self-evident, that all men are created equal, that they are endowed by their Creator with certain unalienable Rights, that among these are Life, Liberty and the pursuit of Happiness. That to secure these rights, Governments are instituted among Men, deriving their just powers from the consent of the governed, That whenever any Form of Government becomes destructive of these ends, it is the Right of the People to alter or to abolish it....

Those revolutionary words, from the Declaration of Independence, might be the most elegant ever put to paper explaining why men sometimes feel the need to take arms against other men.

In the world today, there are many such people who feel similarly: Palestinians, young Chinese, Cubans. One side's freedom fighter is another side's terrorist. Who is to say which is which?

In the end, history determines who was right and who was wrong. As they say, the winner writes the history books. But if one thing is clear, it is this: freedom usually finds a way. The forces of oppression are mighty indeed, but the yearning of a people to be free is a force difficult to stop.

Reliable Resources

The actual day of American independence is July 2, 1776, when the Continental Congress passed the resolution for independence. Congress approved the declaration two days later.

All We Are Saying

Whatever the cause, one thing is certain: The twentieth century was the bloodiest, most violent century in recorded history. It is estimated that World War I caused more than 30 million deaths. World War II caused about 60 million deaths, almost half of which were civilians.

Something must change. The means of killing other people are becoming so sophisticated that whereas a conflict 100 years ago might have caused 10,000 deaths, the weapons of mass destruction that are so readily available today could cause 10 times the deaths for the same conflict. As technology advances, the potential for devastating destruction accelerates.

To paraphrase the late Israeli Prime Minister Yitzhak Rabin, "You don't make peace with your friends. You make peace with your enemies." It's not easy, but it is possible. Catholics and Protestants in Northern Ireland proved it is possible. Israelis and Egyptians proved it is possible. Eastern Europe proved it is possible.

If the twenty-first century is to differ from the one preceding it, bravery will be required. It used to be that going to war was considered courageous. Yet today, with the stakes ever increasing, with lethality ever growing, the courage not to fight might be what will be required; the new badge of honor.

The Least You Need to Know

- The world is getting smaller and weapons are getting deadlier.
- More than 33 percent of the world is usually engaged in conflict at any one time.
- War serves many purposes, some noble, some not.
- You don't make peace with your friends. You make peace with your enemies.

2

East Is East and West Is West

In This Chapter

- ◆ Understanding Islam
- ◆ The Afghan connection
- ◆ The roots of jihad
- ◆ Terrorism against the United States
- ◆ The culture clash between East and West

Like December 7, 1941, September 11, 2001, is a day that will live in infamy. On that day, 19 fanatical terrorist followers of Osama bin Laden hijacked 4 American jumbo jetliners, flying 2 into the towers of the World Trade Center in New York City and 1 into the Pentagon, while another crashed into a deserted field in Pennsylvania.

The shock from those events changed the way America sees itself and its place in the world. A seemingly once-lightweight President George W. Bush found his *raison d'être*. Transformed into a man of purpose, he was determined to root out terrorism wherever it could be found. The United States discovered patriotism again for the first time in two generations, and the world will never be quite the same.

How this conflict will end is difficult to say. Without a doubt, there will be more bloodshed and many more lives lost before this suicidal, militant form of Islamic terrorism is thwarted, if ever. Although the outcome is not certain, how we got to this point most certainly is, as you'll learn in this chapter.

Islam is the world's fastest-growing religion.

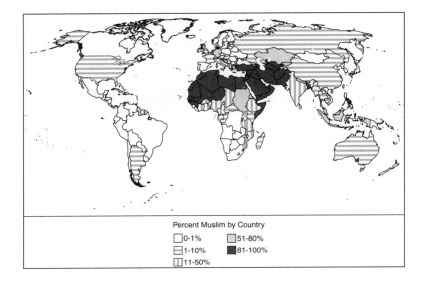

Percent Muslim by Country

☐ 0-1%	51-80%
1-10%	■ 81-100%
11-50%	

Reliable Resources

Six to seven million Americans consider themselves Muslim, and they worship in 1,209 mosques from coast to coast. African Americans are the dominant Muslim population in the United States, accounting for 27 percent of the religion. Arab Americans account for only 15 percent.

Islam

The word *Islam* is an Arabic word, the root of which is *Silm* and *Salam*. Among other things, it means peace, greeting, salutation, obedience, loyalty, allegiance, and submission to the will of the Creator of the Universe. The religion was begun by the prophet Muhammad in sixth-century Arabia. A Muslim (that is, a self-surrendered one) is a follower of this faith, and nearly one in every seven persons alive on Earth today is a Muslim. It is among the fastest-growing religions in the United States.

Islam has two basic foundations: The holy book, or *Qu'ran* (or Koran, from the Arabic word for "recitation"), and reports about Muhammad's life and work called the *Hadith* (from the Arabic word for "report"). The Koran as a book is comparable in length to the Gospels of the Christian Holy Bible.

According to religious scholar Karen Armstrong, when the prophet Muhammad brought the Koran to the Arabs, a major part of his mission was devoted to bringing an end to mass slaughter. Pre-Islamic Arabia was caught up in a vicious cycle of warfare in which tribe fought tribe in a pattern of vendetta and counter vendetta. Muhammad had to fight a deadly war in order to survive, but after achieving victory, he then devoted himself to building a peaceful coalition of tribes. By the time of his death in 632, he had almost single-handedly brought peace to war-torn Arabia.

By and large then, Islam teaches peace. Yet part of the problem in the modern world is that Islamic fundamentalists have been using a term found in the Koran—*jihad*—to justify murder. A jihad is supposed to be a holy war, an oxymoron if ever there was one, raising the question: Just what does the Koran say about jihad?

The Koran and Jihad

As Armstrong points out in her essay "The True, Peaceful Face of Islam," the only permissible war in the Koran is one of self-defense. Muslims may not begin hostilities (2:190), but may fight in self-defense (2:191; 2:217) or to preserve decent values (4:75; 22:40). (For those of you who are unfamiliar with the preceding notation, the first number notates the chapter, and the second number notates the verse in the Koran where the teaching can be found.)

Accordingly, the Arabic word *jihad* does not mean "holy war," but rather, "struggle." Even so, Islamic scholars have even been divided on how the word *struggle* should be interpreted. According to Middle East analyst Fiona Symon, "For some, it means the struggle to defend one's faith and ideals against harmful outside influences. For others, it has come to represent the duty of Muslims to fight to rid the Islamic world of Western influence in the form of corrupt and despotic leaders and occupying armies."

Under modern Islamic thought, there are in fact three levels of jihad:

◆ **Personal jihad.** This jihad is the struggle to purify the soul of negative influences; to cleanse one's spirit of sin. This is typically the most important level of jihad.

- ◆ **Verbal jihad.** Mohammed encouraged raising one's voice in the name of Allah on behalf of justice, stating, "The most excellent jihad is the speaking of truth in the face of a tyrant."

- ◆ **Physical jihad.** This is the type of jihad that is at issue today. This jihad refers to combat waged in defense of Muslims by the enemies of Allah. This "jihad with the hand" is the aspect of jihad that has come to be widely accepted among the more militant Muslim groups, although most would not agree with the methods adopted by Osama bin Laden and his al-Qaeda movement.

Modern Jihad

For much of its history, Islam was not interpreted to allow this last form of jihad as an excuse to wage war and kill innocent people. Jihad as a tool for terror is not part of historic Islam. As such, the origins of bin Laden's radical concept of jihad is a recent phenomenon that must be traced back to two early-twentieth-century figures who started powerful Islamic revivalist movements in response to colonialism and its aftermath: Hassan al-Banna's Muslim Brotherhood in Egypt and Syed Abul Ala Maududi's Jamaat Islami in Pakistan.

In Symon's analysis, these men blamed the Western idea of the separation of church and state for the decline of Muslim societies, believing that in Muslim societies, church and state should not be separate entities. Thus, they thought, the negative effects of colonialism could be corrected through a return to Islam in its traditional form—in which society was governed by a strict code of Islamic law. This belief would later form the basis of Afghanistan's Taliban.

In addition to promoting the creation of pure Islamic states, these two men also instigated a new concept of jihad, proffering the theory that "holy war" was a viable Muslim method for ending foreign occupation of Muslim lands.

def•i•ni•tion

In the Islamic culture, an **infidel** is an unbeliever.

This idea was taken a step further in the 1950s, In Symon's analysis, when a man by the name of Sayed Qutb, a prominent member of Egypt's Muslim Brotherhood, theorized that all non-Muslims were *infidels*. Qutb predicted an eventual clash of civilizations between Islam and the West.

Qutb's words struck a chord with an Islamic populace that was increasingly ready to rid themselves of Western influence. Indeed, his radical notion of Islam inspired a whole generation of Muslims, including Ayatollah Khomeini, who developed an Iranian version of fundamental Islam in the 1970s. In 1966, Qutb was executed by Egyptian President Gamal Abdel Nasser.

Peacekeepers

During the ninth month of the lunar Islamic calendar, Ramadan, Muslims who are old enough and healthy enough fast for 29 or 30 days from sunup to sundown.

Jihad and bin Laden

Osama bin Laden would be introduced to the radical ideas of Qutb and the growing Islamic fundamentalist movement by Abdullah Azzam. Azzam was a Palestinian scholar who had fought with the Palestinian Liberation Army (P.L.O.) in the 1970s, but became disillusioned with the PLO leadership because of its secular outlook.

Azzam had studied Islamic law in Cairo, where he met the family of Sayed Qutb. He then went on to teach in Saudi Arabia. It was there that he met and taught a sharp university student named Osama bin Laden, who quickly became enamored of this emerging fundamentalist philosophy.

Reliable Resources

Osama bin Laden was born in Saudi Arabia in 1957 to a father of Yemeni origins and a Syrian mother. His father, Mohammed bin Laden, founded a construction company and with royal patronage became a billionaire. The company's connections won it important commissions such as rebuilding mosques in the holy cities of Mecca and Medina. Osama was the seventeenth son, and he studied management and economics at King Abdul Aziz University in Jedda, Saudi Arabia. The bin Laden family's construction business is worth $5 billion.

Afghanistan Ho!

In 1979, the Soviet Union invaded its neighbor Afghanistan. The Afghans, long accustomed to invasions and intruders, began to actively resist the mighty Soviet army. This battle to liberate the predominantly Muslim Afghanistan from Soviet occupation gave Abdullah Azzam an opportunity to put his revolutionary Islamic ideals into practice. Dubbed the "emir of jihad," he was one of the first Arabs to join the Afghan *mujahedeen*, along with Osama bin Laden.

def•i•ni•tion

A **mujahedeen** is someone who actively fights for Islam.

Together they set up a base in the country, where they recruited and housed Arabs who had come to join the jihad. Azzam taught that it was the moral duty of every Muslim to undertake jihad, and he traveled the world calling on Muslims to join the fight.

The ruling family of Saudi Arabia, which had long been criticized for its pro-Western views, seized the occasion of the Soviet invasion of Afghanistan to deflect internal criticism. The kingdom threw its political and financial weight behind the Afghan jihad—which was also backed by Pakistan and the United States under the apparent premise that the enemy of my enemy is my friend—against the Soviet Union.

Osama on the Move

The upshot of the decade-long war in Afghanistan was that a mentality of jihad emerged that many mujahedeen found difficult to abandon. Followers of the Egyptian Islamic Jihad movement, an extremist offshoot of the Muslim Brotherhood, believed that Afghanistan should be a template for the liberation of the entire Muslim world.

After the victory in Afghanistan, Osama bin Laden returned to his native Saudi Arabia to continue the fight against the government there. The Saudis were not disposed to tolerate his calls to insurrection, and in April 1994, his Saudi citizenship was revoked for "irresponsible behavior," and he was expelled from the country.

Reliable Resources

Centuries before the women's movement in the West, Islam granted women the right to own property, to be educated, and the right to inherit. In the West, in many instances, women did not receive these rights until centuries later.

Together with his immediate family and a large band of followers, bin Laden moved to the Sudan where he set up several businesses to help continue to fund his war against the West. Among bin Laden's numerous Sudanese commercial interests were a factory to process goatskins, a construction company, a bank, a sunflower plantation, and an import-export operation.

However, Sudan was on the U.S. State Department's list of state sponsors of terrorism, making it an outlaw nation. Because the country was in much need of help, it decided that the United States would be a better friend than Osama bin Laden could ever be. So, as a gesture toward the United States, the Sudanese government requested that bin Laden depart. In May 1996, running out of places to go, the terrorist moved back to Afghanistan.

The Gulf War and Its Aftermath

In the meantime, the 1991 Gulf War had brought U.S. troops to Saudi Arabia. After devoting their lives to the liberation of Muslim territory, this was a bitter blow for bin Laden and his Arab brethren, seeing the land they regarded as sacred being occupied by American infidels.

For bin Laden, the continuing presence of American troops so close to the Islamic holy sites of Mecca and Medina was the last straw. So, in February 1998, he announced the formation of an umbrella organization called "The Islamic World Front for the struggle against the Jews and the Crusaders."

He then issued a *fatwa*, and declared war on the United States, though few knew of the declaration. It was this so-called fatwa that paved the way for the terrorist attacks on American targets that followed.

def•i•ni•tion

A **fatwa** is a legal opinion or decree on a specific issue.

Fatwa This!

On February, 23, 1998, Osama bin Laden, his top aide, Egyptian Ayman al-Zawahiri, and his group, al-Qaeda, issued the following proclamation:

> Praise be to Allah…. The Arabian Peninsula has never … been stormed by any forces like the crusader armies spreading in it like locusts, eating its riches, and wiping out its plantations. All this is happening at a time in which nations are attacking Muslims like people fighting over a plate of food. In the light of the grave situation and the lack of support, we and you are obliged to discuss current events, and we should all agree on how to settle the matter.

> No one argues today about three facts that are known to everyone; we will list them, in order to remind everyone:

> First, for over seven years the United States has been occupying the lands of Islam in the holiest of places, plundering its riches, dictating to its rulers, humiliating its people, terrorizing its neighbors, and turning its bases in the Peninsula

into a spearhead through which to fight the neighboring Muslim peoples. The best proof of this is the Americans' continuing aggression against the Iraqi people.

Second, despite the great devastation inflicted on the Iraqi people by the crusader-Zionist alliance, and despite the huge number of those killed, which has exceeded 1 million … despite all this, the Americans are once again trying to repeat the horrific massacres, as though they are not content with the protracted blockade imposed after the ferocious war or the fragmentation and devastation.

Third, if the Americans' aims behind these wars are religious and economic, the aim is also to serve the Jews' petty state and divert attention from its occupation of Jerusalem and murder of Muslims there.

All these crimes and sins committed by the Americans are a clear declaration of war on Allah, his messenger, and Muslims. And ulema have throughout Islamic history unanimously agreed that the jihad is an individual duty if the enemy destroys the Muslim countries.

On that basis, and in compliance with Allah's order, we issue the following fatwa to all Muslims:

The ruling to kill the Americans and their allies—civilians and military—is an individual duty for every Muslim whoterrorist can do it in any country in which it is possible to do it.

Reliable Resources

In 1989, Ayatollah Khomeini issued a fatwa against British author Salman Rushdie for his book *The Satanic Verses*. A multimillion-dollar bounty was offered for the author's death (talk about your bad review!), and Rushdie went into hiding. Britain spent years trying to get the fatwa revoked, and finally succeeded in 1998.

Understanding bin Laden and Al-Qaeda

Al-Qaeda is a terrorist network of many different organizations in diverse countries that are willing to use terrorism for the attainment of their political goals. Those goals include the overthrow of governments in their respective countries, and the establishment of Islamic governments in their place.

According to the International Policy Institute for Counter-Terrorism, much of the philosophy behind al-Qaeda was formed during the Afghan war when bin Laden came to see the world in black or white. You were either a believer or a heretic. Here, "heretics" includes pragmatic Arab regimes (including his homeland, Saudi Arabia), as well as the United States.

So bin Laden's fatwa was no idle threat. By the time he issued it, he and al-Qaeda had already proved to be deadly serious. Indeed, according to the U.S. State Department, prior to 1998, bin Laden and his groups were responsible for, among other things …

- ◆ Conspiring to kill U.S. servicemen in Yemen who were on their way to participate in the humanitarian mission "Operation Restore Hope" in Somalia in 1992.

- ◆ Plotting the deaths of American and other peacekeepers in Somalia who were there to deliver food to starving Muslims.

- ◆ Assisting Egyptian terrorists who tried to assassinate Egyptian President Mubarak in 1995 and who have killed dozens of tourists in Egypt in recent years.

- ◆ Bombing the Egyptian embassy in Pakistan in 1995; a blast that killed more than 20 Egyptians and Pakistanis.

- ◆ Conspiring to kill the pope.

- ◆ Bombing a joint U.S. and Saudi military training mission in Riyadh, Saudi Arabia, in 1995.

> **Landmine!**
> Proof of just how much the United States underestimated its foe can be seen in a 1998 statement by Clinton National Security Advisor, Sandy Berger: "Osama bin Laden *may* be the most dangerous nonstate terrorist in the world."

Then, in May 1998, soon after his fatwa was issued, bin Laden stated at a press conference in Afghanistan that the world would see the results of his latest threats "in a few weeks."

The Embassy and *Cole* Bombings

On August 7, 1998, American embassies in Nairobi, Kenya, and Dar es Salaam, Tanzania, were bombed, killing many civilians in the process. Although bin Laden was the prime suspect, conclusive proof was hard to come by until a cohort,

Mohammed Sadiq Odeh, was arrested at Karachi International Airport in Pakistan. Odeh spilled the beans, describing in detail bin Laden's international network and his role in the bombing of the American embassies.

With conclusive proof that bin Laden was the culprit, the United States struck back against him and al-Qaeda on August 20, 1998. The targets included six training camps belonging to al-Qaeda and a pharmaceuticals factory in Sudan that intelligence sources suspected of producing components of chemical weapons.

These counterattacks by the Clinton administration were mostly seen as a little more than a gesture. Critics complained that they would do little to deter bin Laden, and they were right. In fact, this limited retaliation likely encouraged the terrorists, giving them reason to conclude that the United States did not have the stomach for a "real fight."

On October 12, 2000, a small boat pulled up alongside the USS *Cole* while it was refueling in Yemen. Witnesses said they saw two men in the boat stand at attention, and then an explosion ripped a hole in one of the most advanced destroyers in the U.S. Navy, killing 17 sailors and injuring 39. What few realized at the time was that even if no one else was taking bin Laden's fatwa seriously, he certainly was.

The next year, 2001, a videotape began to circulate around the Middle East. The tape represented the clearest public link between bin Laden and the *Cole* bombing. In the tape, bin Laden's masked men are seen training in an Afghan terrorist training camp (since destroyed by the U.S. military) and singing a song that says in part: "We thank God for granting us victory the day we destroyed *Cole* in the sea." In the tape bin Laden appears repeatedly preaching at a mosque and talking to his men in the field. In an address to Palestinians at the end of the tape, bin Laden calls for "blood, blood and destruction, destruction."

September 11, 2001, was the day when that desire came to fruition.

So if the United States was unprepared for the September 11 attacks, it certainly wasn't because it hadn't been put on notice; bin Laden had loudly declared jihad against the United States and was steadily escalating his side of the war.

Indeed, al-Qaeda soon took its jihad to Europe. On March 11, 2005, a train in Spain was blown up, killing 191 people and wounding more than 2,000. Then came the pair of London transportation system bombings. A war by a rogue band of terrorists against the United States had grown into a jihad against Western countries that had participated in the Iraq War and occupation.

Never the Twain Shall Meet?

The West remained oblivious to the actual nature of the threat it faced until September 11, 2001, when it learned the hard way that many of the world's more than one billion Muslims intensely disliked America and its Western way of life.

Certainly these animosities are not one-sided. Westerners, too, have long not understood Muslim extremists: fanatical followers, suicide bombers, and undemocratic regimes. As such, the question becomes: Can East and West live in peace?

Samuel Huntington is a Harvard professor and was part of the National Security Council during the Carter administration. Huntington says that "the clash of civilizations will be the battle lines of the future" and will result in decades of conflict and violence. "Ultimately the West can prevail," he predicts, "but the outcome is not a forgone conclusion."

A significant reason for this conflict is that the Eastern and Western cultures are so very different. The West upholds values such as a free press, freedom of religion and assembly, and open thought; ideas that are not part of the Eastern way. In Muslim countries, values such as tradition, respect, and religion are far more important.

Undoubtedly, much of this Arab anger stems from American foreign policy. Middle Easterners greatly resent the United States' unswerving support of Israel and the resulting repression of the Palestinians, the stationing of U.S. troops in Saudi Arabia, the wars against Iraq, and America's previous support of the shah of Iran. They also resent and find hypocritical the American tendency to trumpet democracy, all the while supporting corrupt or oppressive governments in Egypt, Bahrain, Pakistan, the United Arab Emerites, and Saudi Arabia.

Arab Muslims also resent having, from their perspective, unwanted American values and materialism shoved down their throat. Billboards, television, and magazines in their own countries often are full of Western culture and the American way of life, lifestyles that are usually at odds with Muslims' more traditional values. Many Muslims are unhappily forced to constantly deal with the unwanted intrusion of western commercialism and its values in their traditional, everyday lives.

With all this mutual animosity, it might be hard to see how East and West can ever meet in peace. But maybe they can; hate is not a foregone conclusion for several reasons.

First, not all Muslims are created equal. Even though a few support bin Laden, the vast majority do not. Like Americans, most Muslims have a deep respect for life.

def•i•ni•tion

The **Crusades** were a series of wars begun in 1095 by Christians to take back the Holy Land from the Muslims who had come to control it.

Indeed, Islam is not so different from Christianity and Judaism. All three religions began in the Middle East, all three are monotheistic, and Islam sees itself as linked to Christianity and Judaism. It recognizes all the Old and New Testament texts and prophets, and both Jews and Muslims recognize Jesus as an important prophet. Moreover, Christians, Jews, and Muslims all consider themselves to be children of Abraham. All three religions place great emphasis on piety, kindness, and peace. In essence, they are three spokes on the same wheel, all leading to the center (God) in their own way.

Is there an answer? Certainly in the post September 11–world, it might behoove the United States to examine how there came to be such hatred for it, however misguided, and why much of the world thinks that America acts like a big bully.

By the same token, if there is to be peace, Muslim clerics and leaders must also do their part. They must loudly, and often, decry the violence wrought by those who murder innocents in the name of Allah. They must remind their flock that Islam does not condone such actions.

Part of the problem as well is simply systemic. Little can change the fact that as long as the United States is the sole superpower, there will be people who will resent that. That is the nature of people and politics.

In the end, the best hope seems to be twofold. First, the United States needs to make friends, not just attack enemies. But by the same token, Muslim nations need to publicly decry their most extremist elements and teach respect and tolerance for those with whom they disagree. Maybe then, the root causes of terrorism can be reduced.

The Least You Need to Know

- Islam is a religion of peace.
- The Soviet invasion of Afghanistan gave rise to Osama bin Laden.
- Jihad is not traditionally thought of as a "holy war."
- Osama bin Laden declared war on the United States in 1998.
- The culture clash between East and West is not insurmountable.

The War on Terror

In This Chapter

- ◆ Reactions to September 11
- ◆ Afghanistan
- ◆ Allies and enemies in the Global War on Terror
- ◆ Global war on terror strategies
- ◆ The War on Terror in review

Although Osama bin Laden, with his virulent form of fundamental Islamic radicalism, made his hatred for the West clear via his fatwa and increasingly bold surprise attacks, the response to the September 11 attacks by the West in general, and by the United States in particular, should have come as no surprise.

September 11 and Its Aftermath

Not long after the World Trade Centers were destroyed by suicidal terrorists, President Bush traveled from Washington, D.C., to New York to survey the wreckage and cleanup. It was there that he borrowed a bullhorn from one of the rescue workers and said, "I can hear you. The whole world can hear you. And the people who knocked down these buildings will hear all of us soon."

Little did anyone know how prophetic that statement was.

On September 18, 2001, a week after September 11, the United States Congress passed a resolution that would lay the legal foundation for what soon would become known as the War on Terror. The Congress authorized the president to ...

> use all necessary and appropriate force against those nations, organizations, or persons he determines planned, authorized, committed, or aided the terrorist attacks that occurred on September 11, 2001, or harbored such organizations or persons, in order to prevent any future acts of international terrorism against the United States by such nations, organizations, or persons.

Two days later in a speech before a historic joint session of Congress, President Bush laid out a comprehensive strategy to fight this new sort of war. The goal was certainly impressive: Said the President, "Our war on terror begins with al-Qaeda, but it does not end there. It will not end until every terrorist group of global reach has been found, stopped, and defeated."

Landmine! _____

Every nation, in every region, now has a decision to make. Either you are with us, or you are with the terrorists.

—President George W. Bush, September 20, 2001

The president's strategy came to be known as the "Bush doctrine." It was based on his statement that the United States would "make no distinction between the terrorists who committed these acts and those who harbor them." That is, the president asserted that it would now be the policy of the United States that any nation that refused to cooperate with the American war against terrorists would be considered an enemy.

The Afghan War

When it became clear that the September 11 attacks were perpetrated by Osama bin Laden and al-Qaeda, it also became obvious that the country that supported, trained, and sheltered al-Qaeda—Afghanistan—would be the first target in the War on Terror and the Bush doctrine.

Afghanistan Primer

From 1933 to 1973, Afghanistan was a peaceful monarchy ruled by Muhammad Zahir Shah. During the Cold War, countries fell into one of two spheres of influence: either that of the United States or the Soviet Union. Because Afghanistan's neighbor Pakistan was increasingly siding with the West, Afghanistan turned to the U.S.S.R. for support during this time.

In 1973, a coup by the cousin of Zahir Shah overthrew the king. Daoud Khan came to power in 1973, and allied himself with the Marxist-Leninist party of Afghanistan. But even so, there remained a split in the country between the urbanites in places such as Kabul, and the more rural people in the rest of the country.

> **Reliable Resources**
>
> Afghanistan is made up primarily of an ethnic group known as Pashtuns, who dominated the country and political life for centuries. The other major ethnic groups in Afghanistan are the Tajiks, Uzbeks, and Hazaras.

In 1978, Daoud was killed in a coup, beginning what would become a long, sad series of wars (civil and otherwise) and seemingly never-ending violence and instability in this once-harmonious country. The new government began a campaign of land reform, repression, and execution of thousands, causing mass uprisings throughout the country.

But because Afghanistan was a pawn in the Cold War, the problems in the country did not go unnoticed by its superpower sponsor, the Soviet Union. On December 24, 1979, the Soviets invaded Afghanistan, overthrowing the government and installing its own puppet regime with Babrak Karmal as the president.

> **Reliable Resources**
>
> There was a time, before 1978, when Afghanistan and its capital of Kabul were peaceful places. To learn more about life there before war ravaged the country, read *The Kite Runner* by Khaled Hosseini.

In what would come to be known as the "Soviet Vietnam," Russia's Afghan adventure was an unmitigated disaster. An occupation force of more than 100,000 troops attempted without success to crush the homegrown uprising that was now exclusively focused on ridding the country of its unwelcome imperial occupier.

The resistance was joined by thousands of Muslim radicals from throughout the region. It was here that Osama bin Laden first learned about fighting superpowers. It is estimated that more than 1 million Afghans died during this era, and another 5 million (out of a population of 16 million) became refugees who left the country.

The Geneva Accords

Negotiations to end the occupation finally came to fruition in the 1988 Geneva Accords, whereby the Soviet Union agreed to withdraw its troops from the country. Yet even as the Soviets left, the old factions within the country began to fight each other once again, and civil war once more erupted.

In 1992, a group known as the Northern Alliance took marginal control of the country, but fighting continued unabated. By 1995, it is estimated that fully one third of Kabul had been completely destroyed and lay in rubble. In the meantime, out in the countryside, radical Muslims ensconced themselves as local warlords.

Emergence of the Taliban

The chaos throughout the country was disheartening, and a group of fundamental Muslims joined a mullah known as Mohammad Omar to try and restore stability. This new group, known as the Taliban, wanted to create a fundamental Islamic state. The Taliban took control of the government in September 1996, and the Northern Alliance fled and became a guerilla group in opposition to the Taliban.

The Taliban version of Islam was strict indeed:

◆ Women were forbidden to work outside the home in any activity other than health care.

◆ Schools in Kabul forbade girls to attend.

◆ Men had to have beards.

◆ The most powerful government ministry was the "Ministry of Promotion of Virtue and Prevention of Vice."

The United States Begins to Target Afghanistan

Osama bin Laden returned to Afghanistan in 1996 and set up camp. (He had left in 1990). After American embassies in Nairobi, Kenya, and Dar es-Salaam, Tanzania, were bombed by al-Qaeda in 1998, the United States launched air strikes against al-Qaeda training camps in Afghanistan. The next year, the United Nations demanded that the Taliban turn over bin Laden, but it refused, so the U.N. imposed sanctions on the Islamic regime.

At the same time, the Northern Alliance had carved out a sanctuary in the northern part of the country, effectively running its own state. It and the Taliban continued to vie for supremacy in the war-torn country.

So it came as no surprise that after the United States targeted Afghanistan as the first enemy in the War on Terror, Washington would team up with the Northern Alliance in an effort to overthrow the Taliban. The Alliance knew the terrain, the enemy, and the language.

In early October 2001, U.S. and British forces began an onslaught of airpower against the Taliban. According to CNN, "The first strikes began about 8:45 p.m. Sunday (12:15 p.m. EDT) [October 7, 2001] and targeted the Taliban's air defense installations, defense ministry, airport-based command centers, airfields, electrical grids, and other energy production facilities."

At the same time, U.S. and Northern Alliance forces attacked on the ground. On November 9, 2001, they had their first major victory, capturing the northern city of Mazar-e Sharif, and setting in motion a domino effect of Taliban military defeats. A month later, the Taliban fled their last remaining stronghold, Kandahar, and a new U.S.- and U.N.-backed government took power. On December 22, Harmid Karzai became the head of the new Afghan government. The first victory in the War on Terror had been won.

Postscript: On November 3, 2004, Harmid Karzai was officially declared the winner of the Afghan elections, thereby becoming the first democratically elected president in the history of Afghanistan.

Allies and Enemies

As you well know, the next front in the War on Terror was Iraq, an issue covered in detail in Chapter 7. But the War on Terror goes well beyond Iraq and Afghanistan. There are many other countries involved in this worldwide fight against radical Islamic terrorists.

Allies

It may be hard to remember now, but there was a time, shortly after September 11 and long before the war against Iraq, when the United States received almost universal support as a result of the terrorist attacks it sustained.

The most immediate act of support came from the North Atlantic Treaty Organization, *NATO*. The day after the attacks on New York City and Washington, D.C., NATO invoked—for the first time in its history—Article V, which states, in pertinent part, "The Parties agree that an armed attack against one or more of them in Europe or North America shall be considered an attack against them all."

def•i•ni•tion

NATO was established by western democracies a few years after the end of World War II as a mutually supportive defense organization. It is also sometimes known as the Atlantic Alliance or the Western Alliance. The original members were Belgium, Canada, Denmark, France (although it withdrew from the integrated command of NATO in 1966), Iceland, Italy, Luxembourg, Netherlands, Norway, Portugal, the United Kingdom, and the United States.

Countries throughout the world were almost universally united in both their support of the United States and its nascent War on Terror and revulsion at the barbaric acts perpetrated by al-Qaeda. But after the Afghanistan war removed the Taliban, support for the War on Terror generally, and President Bush specifically, declined in almost inverse proportion as the drumbeat for war against Iraq grew louder.

When it became obvious that the next front in the War on Terror would indeed be Iraq, the number of countries willing to support the United States diminished greatly. But even so, allies remained. Spain and Australia continued to support the U.S. position. New allies joining the so-called "coalition of the willing" included Poland, Romania, and Mongolia. Conspicuous by their absence were former partners such as Germany and France.

Most significantly, America's oldest and staunchest ally, Great Britian, and its Prime Minister Tony Blair, once again saddled up next to the U.S., both in the War on Terror generally, and the war in Iraq specifically. Blair undertook his contoversial support of President Bush at great political risk at home, but in the end, he won a third term in May of 2005.

Enemies

If in fact the War on Terror is a war against terrorist organizations and countries that support them, then there is no shortage of countries to which the war is applicable. For example:

- **Iran.** Iran could well be the next major front in the War on Terror. It is a fundamental Islamic country that has a history of supporting terrorists. It funds and trains such terrorist organizations as Islamic Jihad, Hezbollah, and Hamas. Indeed, the State Department says that Iran is the "most active state sponsor of terrorism" on the planet. And if that were not enough, Iran's nuclear ambitions alone are cause for great concern to the West.

- **Syria.** Syria strongly supports Islamic terrorist organizations such as Hamas, Hezbollah, and Islamic Jihad.

- **Yemen.** Al-Qaeda has bases in Yemen, and the United States has sent special ops forces to the country.

- **Pakistan.** Although Pakistani President Musharraf has been a supporter of the U.S. War on Terror (he opened up three air bases to the United States for the Afghan war), he faces two problems on that front. First, it is in the mountainous netherland region between his country and Afghanistan that much of al-Qaeda, and Osama bin Laden, are said to reside. Second, the populace of his country, by and large, agrees with al-Qaeda ideals far more than they do with Western ones.

- **The Philippines.** The radical Muslim terrorist organization Abu Sayyaf is based here, and in 2003, the United States sent 1,700 troops to fight them.

- **Indonesia.** Indonesia is home to the largest Muslim population in the world. The terrorist Islamic organization Jemaah Islamiyah (responsible for the Bali terrorist attack) is based here.

- **The West Bank.** The following terrorist organizations have a strong presence along the West Bank of the Jordan River in Israel: Hamas, the People's Front for the Liberation of Palestine, Islamic Jihad, Hezbollah, the Al-Aqsa Martyrs Brigade, and the Popular Resistance Committees.

- **Saudi Arabia**: 19 of the 20 September 11th hijackers were Saudis.

So no, there is no shortage of places where the War on Terror may turn next.

Understanding the War on Terror

The War on Terror is unlike any war the West has ever fought. Traditional wars are between individual nations. World Wars I and II were between groups of nations. Even the Cold War was between blocks of nations.

But the War on Terror is between a group of nations (Western democracies, essentially) and Islamic countries and rogue terrorists and terrorist groups. Some of the groups, such as al-Qaeda, have no set boundaries and are dispersed throughout the world. The War on Terror is, therefore, as much a massive police action as it is a traditional war.

But although this is a different sort of war, it is similar to previous wars in that it is as much a war of ideas as anything else. As Thomas Friedman, the foreign affairs columnist for *The New York Times*, puts it …

> What you are witnessing is why Sept. 11 amounts to World War III—the third great totalitarian challenge to open societies in the last 100 years. As the long-time Middle East analyst Abdullah Schleiffer once put it to me: World War II was the Nazis, using the engine of Germany to try to impose the reign of the perfect race, the Aryan race. The cold war was the Marxists, using the engine of the Soviet Union to try to impose the reign of the perfect class, the working class. And 9/11 was about religious totalitarians, Islamists, using suicide bombing to try to impose the reign of the perfect faith, political Islam.

It might be like World War III in some regards, the War on Terror is more akin to the Cold War insofar as tactics and strategies go. During the Cold War, waging an all-out offensive was impossible because doing so would likely trigger a nuclear reprisal. And because both sides adhered to a philosophy called *mutually assured destruction*, neither was willing to take that risk.

def•i•ni•tion

Mutually assured destruction (MAD) is a military doctrine that assumes that a full-scale nuclear attack by one side would result in both sides being obliterated because the recipient would launch a full-scale counterattack before the initial weapons hit. It is a theory of deterrence.

By the same token, the number and types of enemies in the War on Terror precludes the ability of the West to launch an all-out attack. This is not the kind of war where Washington can simply send in a battalion and expect to win. To where would such a battalion be shipped? Against whom would they fight? How many other enemies are there and where are they?

Winning the War

But that does not mean that victories cannot be had; they can. According to Jonathan Stevenson, a senior fellow for counterterrorism at the International Institute for Strategic Studies, the West can do several things to win this war (*Toronto Star,* January 3, 2005):

- Isolate al-Qaeda's global leadership—financially, geographically, and politically.

- Minimize the ability of local jihadists to engage in terrorism by cutting off their funding, training, support, and equipment.

- Deny Islamic terrorists any safe havens by making it politically and militarily too costly for countries to provide such support.

- Detain and arrest known terrorists, interrogate them and thereby uncover other terrorists, organizations, funding sources, training locations, and terrorist methods.

Insofar as the state sponsors of terrorism goes, dealing with them is more problematic. As the war in Iraq proved, there is a finite number of resources, military personnel, money, and political capital available for war. It is simply not feasible that the West will attack every country listed above.

However, if the wars in Iraq and Afghanistan did anything, they will likely prove to be a deterrent, forcing other countries to think twice before continuing to aid terrorist organizations. This certainly seems to be what happened in the case of Libya.

In the 1980s and 1990s, Libya and its leader, President Momar Khadafi, were among the leaders in state-sponsored terrorism. Thus, for example, in 1992, Libyans blew up Pan Am flight 103 over Lockerbie, Scotland.

But in December 2003, after engaging in secret negotiations with the United States and Great Britain, Libya admitted it had weapons of mass destruction, and agreed to destroy such weapons, including nuclear-related materials. In addition, Libya agreed to pay $2.7 billion to the flight 103 families. In return, the United States lifted its travel ban to Libya, as well as its economic sanctions.

Although the reason Libya agreed to change its ways remains hidden, it is not a big leap to conclude that watching its neighbor Iraq get pummeled was probably a fairly strong cautionary tale that Khadafi wanted his country to avoid. The moral is that there are ways to deal with terror states in the War on Terror without resorting to full-scale war.

Losing the War

Despite several successes (ousting Saddam Hussein, attempting to bring democracy to the Middle East), there has also been heavy criticism related to the War on Terror. Not an insignificant number of people worry that various governments are exploiting the situation to crack down on civil liberties and human rights. To win the war but lose sight of a country's ideals is to not win the war at all to these folks.

For example:

◆ After September 11, suspected Muslims the world over were rounded up and sent to a U.S. facility at Guantanamo Bay, Cuba. There they stayed—for years—unable to meet with a lawyer; not charged with any crime; subject to search, seizure, and interrogation; perpetually detained; and labeled "enemy combatants" so that basic U.S. Constitutional rights would not apply to them. ("Prisoners of war," on the other hand, are subject to the protections of the Geneva Convention.)

def•i•ni•tion

The old Soviet Union had a series of forced-labor internment camps where political prisoners were sent to rot. These were known as **gulags**.

◆ Because torture is illegal under U.S. law, it is alleged that the United States sends terror suspects to other countries to be interrogated, using methods that would not pass muster in America. Amnesty International calls this system the "*gulag* of our times."

◆ At the Abu Gharib prison in Iraq, the place where Saddam Hussein tortured his enemies, repugnant photographs of U.S. soldiers abusing prisoners came to light.

So Who Is Winning the War?

The difficulty with the War on Terror is that it is not just a war against Iraq, or Afghanistan, or whomever. Rather, it is an undeclared war (in the traditional sense) against a shadowy enemy occurring in clandestine places using stealth methods at unidentified times. And because much of it is done in secret, it is also difficult to really say how the war is going.

If a terrorist with a bomb is secretly apprehended, and the bomb never goes off, it is a victory in the war to be sure, but one that no one ever hears about. How is the war going? Who knows?

The other difficulty with such a war is figuring out when and where and how will it end. The Cold War was said by Winston Churchill to be a "long, twighlight struggle" against communism. Like the War on Terror, victories were not always easy to see, and defeats were often obscure and secret.

How will this war end? When is a twighlight struggle over? Will there ever really be a time when there are no more terrorists? And are not some people's terrorists other people's freedom fighters? If wiping out terrorism is an unrealistic goal, what is the real goal, when will it be reached whatever it is, and how will we know when we reach it?

Maybe a quote from Martin Luther King is applicable here:

> The ultimate weakness of violence is that it is a descending spiral, begetting the very thing it seeks to destroy. Instead of diminishing evil, it multiplies it … Through violence you may murder the hater, but you do not murder hate. In fact, violence merely increases hate. … Returning violence for violence multiplies violence, adding deeper darkness to a night already devoid of stars. (*Where Do We Go From Here: Chaos or Community*? Beacon Press, 1967, page 62)

The Least You Need To Know

◆ The Bush doctrine states that "either you are with us, or you are with the terrorists."

◆ The first country attacked in the War on Terror was Afghanistan.

◆ Iraq was the second country attacked in the War on Terror.

◆ Traditional allies and enemies are not to be found in this war.

◆ The War on Terror is as much a shadowy police action as it is a traditional war.

Part 2

The Middle East and North Africa

Of all the conflicts in the world today, the ones raging in the Middle East are both the most publicized and the most dangerous, if not the bloodiest. The possibility of major escalation rightly keeps the problems in the Middle East on the front pages.

Israel's long conflict with her neighbors is just the tip of the iceberg. Two wars in Iraq have changed the entire complexion and stability of the Middle East. Throw in the growing threat of radical Islamic fundamentalism, and all the necessary ingredients for setting off a world war are present.

Chapter 4

The Middle East Mess

In This Chapter

◆ Sharing a small plot of land

◆ The birth of Zionism

◆ War and more war

◆ The Oslo Peace Accords

Of all the conflicts affecting the world today, none is more problematic, more irreconcilable, and likely more difficult to solve than the one in the Middle East. It combines high emotion with limited territory and years of bloodshed with sworn enemies.

Yet, there is also reason to hope. Israel and Egypt, countries that have gone to war too many times, found a way to put their animosities aside and make peace. Israel has been able to do the same thing with Jordan. The Israelis and the Palestinians were almost able to create peace in 2000, and still might do so.

But to truly comprehend the complexity of this regional conflict, one must go way, way back. Understanding why every party thinks it is right requires a bit of a history lesson, for if anything is true in the Middle East, it is that the past is prologue.

The Middle East: Fighting over a small plot of land.

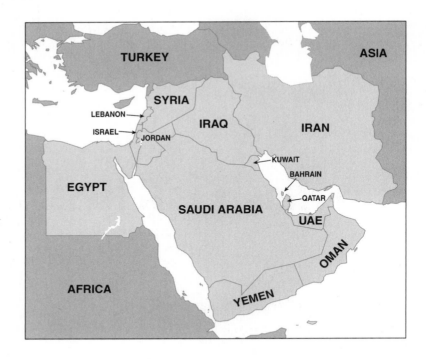

A Long Time Ago, in a Land Far, Far Away

The area fought over by Israel and the Palestinians is only 10,000 square miles. Today, the state of Israel formally occupies all the land from the Jordan River to the Dead Sea, bound by Egypt in the south, Lebanon in the north, and Jordan in the east.

However, these officially recognized borders of Israel constitute only about 78 percent of the land that today makes up all of Israel proper, as noted by Ami Isseroff in an article on mideastweb.org. The other 22 percent consists of land occupied by Israel since the 1967 Six-Day War (the so-called "occupied territories") and the Gaza Strip, which consists of 141 square miles.

Judging by fossil remains that have been found in the area, this land, which has been variously called Israel and Palestine, has been lived in for tens of thousands of years. Jericho has been identified as one of the oldest sites of agricultural activity, based on archaeological findings of hybrid wheat dating back

Landmine!

To get an idea of just how small Israel is, consider that it is about half the size of Maine, a quarter of the size of New Zealand, and about the same size as Vancouver Island.

to 8000 B.C.E. According to anthropologists, Amorites, Canaanites, and other Semitic peoples entered the area about 2000 B.C.E. Subsequently, the area became known as the Land of Canaan.

Canaan, Shmaanan

According to the Bible, Moses led the Israelites out of Egypt and into Canaan. King David of the Jews conquered Jerusalem around 1000 B.C.E. and established an Israelite kingdom over much of Canaan. The kingdom was later divided into Judah in the South and Israel in the North.

Thereafter, war became standard operating procedure in this part of the world:

◆ The Assyrians conquered Israel in 722 or 721 B.C.E.

◆ The Babylonians conquered Judah in 587 or 586 B.C.E., destroyed Solomon's Temple in Jerusalem, and exiled a large number of Jews.

◆ The Persians then conquered Babylonia about 50 years later, and they ruled the area from about 530 to 331 B.C.E.

◆ The Seleucids later ruled the area around 200 B.C.E.

When in Rome ...

About 61 B.C.E., Roman troops invaded Judah and destroyed Jerusalem, the land came under Roman control, and they began to call the area Judea. In 135 C.E., the Romans drove the Jews out of Jerusalem, and then renamed the area "Palaestina," or Palestine.

Most of the Jews who continued to practice Judaism fled or were forcibly exiled from Palestine. In time, Christianity spread to most of Palestine, with the exception of its northernmost part, Galilee, where Jewish communities continued to carve out an existence for themselves. The rest of Palestine was now settled, according to Isseroff, by Jewish converts to Christianity and paganism, peoples imported by the Romans, and others who had probably been long-time inhabitants of Palestine.

Reliable Resources

In Jerusalem today, about 450,000 Jews live with 200,000 Palestinians.

Enter the Muslims

Muslim Arab armies moved north from Arabia around 600 C.E. and conquered most of the Middle East, including Palestine. Muslim rule and influence continued thereafter, almost uninterrupted, until the early 1900s.

It is, therefore, important to understand a few things:

◆ Muslims allowed Christians and Jews to practice their religions, although most of the local population gradually converted to Islam.

◆ Both Jews and Palestinians can state that they have occupied the area for thousands of years based on their histories of settlement.

◆ Jews, Christians, and Muslims mostly lived in peace in the Middle East for more than a thousand years.

◆ Jerusalem became holy to Muslims as the site where Muhammad ascended to heaven. The al-Aqsa mosque was built on the site generally regarded as the area of the Jewish temples.

By 1880, according to Isseroff, "only" about 24,000 Jews were living in Palestine, out of a population of about 400,000. However, because of increasing oppression of Jews in Eastern Europe, by the late 1800s, emigration of Jews to Palestine began to increase dramatically due to a fast-growing movement known as Zionism.

Zionism

Zionism is the national movement that calls for the return of the Jewish people to, and the resumption of Jewish sovereignty in, the Land of Israel. The term *Zionism* was coined in 1893 by Nathan Birnbaum. While a student at the University of Vienna in 1893, Birnbaum published a brochure titled "The National Rebirth of the Jewish People in Its Homeland as a Means of Solving the Jewish Problem." As a result, Jews of all persuasions, left and right, religious and secular, joined to form the Zionist movement.

Following the first Zionist congress organized by Theodore Herzl in 1897, the Zionist movement gained momentum as a formal organization. The Zionists' goal was to establish a "Jewish homeland" in Palestine, and to that end Herzl and his followers began to help millions of European Jews immigrate to Palestine, which was not an independent country at the time. First establishing farms, and later, the new city of Tel Aviv, the Jews began to till the soil.

As more and more Jews embarked on a journey home, Palestine's Arab population grew rapidly, too. By 1914, Palestine was home to about 700,000 people, of which about 600,000 were Arabs and 100,000 were Jews.

Birth of a Nation

In 1917, at the end of World War I, Britain issued the Balfour Declaration. In it, the British government proclaimed its support for the creation of a Jewish homeland in Palestine, without violating the rights of the existing communities.

Following World War I, the newly created League of Nations (precursor of the United Nations) divided much of the defeated Ottoman Empire into mandated territories, and in 1920, Britain received a mandate over Palestine—to help the Jews build a country.

British officials hoped to establish self-government in Palestine, but their proposals for such institutions fell on deaf ears because the Arabs wanted nothing to do with the Jews; thus they would not participate in municipal councils. Lord David Ormsby-Gore, undersecretary of state for the colonies, stated that "Palestine is largely inhabited by unreasonable people" (Isseroff, 2001).

The Arabs hotly opposed the idea of a Jewish national home because they considered Palestine to be their land; thus they formed a national movement to combat the terms of the British Mandate. Tellingly, at hearings to determine how the Mandate was proceeding, Palestinian leader Aref Pasha Dajani said of the Jews, "Their history and their past proves that it is impossible to live with them. In all the countries where they are at present, they are not wanted … because they always arrive to suck the blood of everybody …" (Isseroff, 2001). Nevertheless, because of persecution in Eastern Europe and Nazi Germany, Jewish immigration in Palestine swelled in the 1930s. After World War II, the United Nations Special Commission on Palestine recommended that Palestine be divided into an Arab state and a Jewish state. Jerusalem was to be put under international control.

Landmine!

German concentration camps were responsible for the systematic deaths of more than six million Jews during World War II.

The Jews accepted the U.N. decision. The Arabs rejected it. On May 14, 1948, following an international legal mandate, the Jews proclaimed the independent state of Israel, and the British withdrew from Palestine. The next day, neighboring Arab nations attacked Israel. At the same time, about 700,000 Arabs voluntarily fled or were driven out of Israel, becoming refugees in neighboring Arab countries.

The United Nations created a series of cease-fires between the Arabs and the Jews in 1948 and into 1949. In the meantime, Palestinian attempts to set up a state were blocked by Egypt and Jordan. Finally, U.N. Resolution 194 called for a cessation of hostilities and a return of refugees who wanted to live in peace.

When the fighting ended, Israel held territories beyond the boundaries called for by the United Nations. Egypt owned the Gaza Strip, and Jordan held the West Bank. Because the Arab countries refused to sign a permanent peace treaty with Israel, the borders of Israel established by the United Nations never received legal international recognition, and the refugee problem was never resolved.

Peacekeepers

I am saying these words for history: Nasser was born in a poor family, and I promise that he will live and die a poor man.

—Gamel Nasser, Egyptian President

The Suez War

Not only was Israel a new country, but so were many of the Arab states, having gained independence from the colonial powers of Great Britain and France. So in 1956, as part of Egyptian President Gamel Nasser's new nationalist agenda, he seized control of the Suez Canal from the British and French companies that owned it.

According to historian Roger Lee, Nasser ordered his forces to block the Straits of Tiran, the thin strip of water that was Israel's only outlet to the Red Sea. Britain and France, in an effort to reassert control over this vital waterway, decided upon a joint invasion and occupation of the Suez Canal zone, and coordinated their invasion with Israel.

As Lee notes, on October 29, 1956, Israeli troops attacked and invaded the Sinai Peninsula in Egypt, overcame the opposition, and moved on toward the Suez Canal. The next day, France and Britain stated that they would agree to create a buffer zone between Egypt and Israel at the canal, but Egypt refused this premeditated offer. So on October 31, Egypt was attacked by Britain and France.

As with all things that happened in the world politically in the 1950s, the Cold War then intervened. The Soviet Union, which was having its own problems with Hungary at this time, nevertheless offered to help Egypt. A nervous President Eisenhower then successfully pressured Britain, France, and Israel into agreeing to a cease-fire and an eventual withdrawal from Egypt. Israel obtained guarantees from the United States that international waterways would remain open to Israeli shipping, and a U.N. force was stationed in Sinai.

The war lasted but a week, but the results were clear. Egypt was now part of the Soviet's sphere of influence, and would arm Arab nations for years to come.

The Six-Day War

Over the ensuing years, doves in the region consistently expressed a desire to negotiate a peace, but hard-line elements across the board refused. Thus, for example, in an address to the United Nations General Assembly in 1960, Israeli Foreign Minister Golda Meir unsuccessfully challenged Arab leaders to negotiate a peace settlement.

The Arabs were adamant in their refusal to negotiate either a peace with Israel or a settlement for the Palestinian refugees. As Nasser told the United Arab Republic National Assembly on March 26, 1964, "The danger of Israel lies in the very existence of Israel as it is in the present and in what she represents."

In essence, the Arab states adopted a "kill two birds with one stone" policy. If they could rid the world of Israel, the Palestinian refugee problem would also be resolved in the process. So it was that in 1964 The Palestine Liberation Organization (PLO) was formed. Its charter stated that its aim was to destroy Israel and allow Palestinians back into historical Palestine.

In the spring of 1967, the battle between Egypt and Israel erupted again when Nasser once again closed the Straits of Tiran to Israel, and then sent U.N. peacekeepers packing. The United States, which had pledged to keep the waterway open, failed to live up to its promises. And so, on June 5, 1967, Israel attacked the Egyptians. The Syrians and Jordanians then attacked Israel.

Six days later, the war was over. Israel had pummeled its enemies and now occupied the Gaza Strip, the West Bank, the Sinai Peninsula, and the Golan Heights.

Clearly the most enduring and disastrous result of the 1967 war for all concerned was that roughly one million Palestinians fell under Israeli rule as a result of Israel taking over the West Bank (of the Jordan River), as well as the Gaza Strip. So whereas the

Landmine!

According to Ami Isseroff, "As of 2001, about 200,000 Israelis had settled in areas of the West Bank and Gaza, and an additional 200,000 were settled in areas of Jerusalem and the environs conquered in 1967. About 15,000 Jews were settled in the Golan Heights taken from Syria."

conflict had mostly been about animus between Arab and Jew, after 1967, it took on the additional, and far more complex, issue of the fate of the Palestinians.

Problematically, although the Israeli government had declared that it was ready to return all the territories except Jerusalem in return for peace treaties with its Arab neighbors, religious and nationalist groups within Israel wanted to annex and settle the West Bank and Golan Heights. An increasing number of Jewish settlements began to sprout up, and settlement expansion became official Israeli policy after the opposition revisionist Likud party came to power in 1977.

The Yom Kippur War

Yom Kippur is the holiest day of the year for Jews. Called the day of Atonement, it is the day that people of that faith ask God for forgiveness for their sins and pray to be a better person in the upcoming year.

In October 1973, on Yom Kippur, while the people of Israel were in synagogue, Egypt and Syria launched another war against the tiny Jewish state, catching the Israelis by surprise. Their goal was to regain control over Arab territory lost in preceding wars, which have left the entire Arab world frustrated and turned large groups of Palestinians into refugees. Although the war was technically fought between Israel on one side and Egypt and Syria on the other, Iraq, Jordan, and Saudi Arabia all supported their Arab brothers economically and militarily.

Syria made serious inroads in the Golan Heights, and Egyptians crossed the Suez Canal and retook a strip of the Sinai Peninsula. Israel then reconquered the Golan and advanced into Syria. In the Sinai, Israeli forces crossed the canal and cut off the entire Egyptian third army. The war was over in three weeks.

Peace in Our Time

Egyptian President Anwar Sadat had seen enough—enough war, enough bloodshed, enough hate. Something had to change, so, in 1977, he decided that he was the one who would have to change it.

Realizing that his path of action (as well as that of his predecessors) had brought neither peace nor prosperity, and realizing that his country would likely never defeat Israel, Sadat concluded that something new had to be done. So instead of listening to the worn-out tapes of advice he had received from Egyptian advisors, from other Arab leaders, from Washington, and from Moscow, he decided to do something altogether different—something that no one had ever dreamed of. He would go to Israel.

He did, and it was historic, but it did not bring about peace between the two countries. Would another war result? Not wanting to let this unique opportunity slip away, President Jimmy Carter summoned Sadat and Israeli Prime Minister Menachem Begin to the presidential retreat, Camp David.

After almost two weeks of intense, secret negotiations at Camp David, the Israeli-Egyptian negotiations resulted in two historic agreements. For the first time ever, Israel and one of her neighbors had agreed to live in peace.

The first agreement addressed the future of the Sinai and peace between Israel and Egypt. The second agreement provided a framework for the conduct of negotiations for the future of the West Bank and Gaza.

Reliable Resources

Camp David is located 70 miles from the White House in the Catoctin Mountains of Maryland. It was established in 1942 when President Franklin Delano Roosevelt needed to escape the summer heat of Washington, D.C., and the higher latitude of the camp provided cool breezes and good security. Named Shangri-La by Roosevelt, it was renamed Camp David in 1953 by President Eisenhower in honor of his grandson David Eisenhower. Guests at Camp David can enjoy a pool, putting green, driving range, tennis courts, and a gymnasium.

The Camp David Accords called for Israel to withdraw from the Sinai Peninsula and return it to Egypt. Egypt would agree to break with its Arab brothers and live in peace with its sworn enemy.

Since the signing of the Camp David Accords on September 17, 1978, Egypt and Israel have not gone to war against each other again. For their heroic efforts, Sadat and Begin were awarded the Nobel Peace Prize in 1978.

Landmine!

In 1983, terrorists killed 241 American Marines when a car bomb blew up next to the base where the Marines were stationed. Under pressure from Congress, President Reagan "redeployed" the marine contingent to the safety of ships off the coast.

The Campaign in Lebanon

Yet, while one border was finally secured, the same could not be said for Israel's other borders. In March 1978, PLO terrorists killed an American tourist walking near an Israeli beach and hijacked a civilian bus; 34 hostages died in the attack.

In response, Israeli forces invaded Lebanon and attacked terrorist bases, in order to move the terrorists away from the border. Two months later, the Israeli forces withdrew and U.N. forces entered the region. By 1981, some 18,000 PLO members were encamped in scores of locations in Lebanon, and another 5,000 to 6,000 foreign mercenaries had joined them. Israeli strikes and commando raids were unable to stem the growth of this burgeoning army, and attacks by the PLO against Israel from Lebanon forced thousands of Israelis to flee their homes or to spend large amounts of time in bomb shelters.

Israel then invaded Lebanon again. The success of this second invasion forced Lebanon's President, Amin Gemayel, to sign a peace treaty with Israel, but only one year later, Gemayel reneged on the agreement under Syrian pressure.

The Lebanon war was very controversial in Israel. Prime Minister Begin eventually was forced to resign as demands to end the fighting intensified. By 1984, Israel withdrew from Lebanon.

Though Israel's primary mission—driving the PLO out of Lebanon—was successful, terrorist threats from Lebanon persisted. In all, 1,216 Israeli soldiers died in the campaign.

The Intifada

The intifada ("insurrection" in Arabic) erupted in the Gaza Strip in 1987. It began as a general strike and grew rapidly thereafter. The intifada was a watershed event that would transform Palestinian society and politics.

One of the essential elements was that the spontaneous revolt was led by Palestinian youths who had never known anything except the occupation and who took, at least during the first few years of the insurrection, leadership of the uprising. Moreover, the images of Palestinian youth fighting Israeli tanks with little more than rocks proved to be a powerful image, strengthening their cause all the more. Indeed, the intifada brought about an awareness of the Palestinian problem both by the Israeli people themselves and by the rest of the world.

Reliable Resources

Seeds of Peace is a group that tries to create friendships among children growing up in war zones. It is a nonprofit, nonpolitical organization that brings together young people from the Middle East as well as kids from other areas, such as Bosnia, Serbia, and U.S. inner cities. From May 1 to May 7, 1998, Seeds of Peace hosted the first 75 youths from Israel, Palestine, Jordan, Egypt, and the United States. Then, they drafted an Israeli-Palestinian peace treaty that was later presented to their leaders and U.N. Secretary, General Kofi Annan.

Israel tried many things to suppress the uprising, including killing and injuring thousands of people, closing down the educational system, prohibiting alternative forms of teaching for two years, invading Palestinian towns, extending curfews, and imposing administrative detentions. Despite all that, the intifada continued. It was becoming increasingly obvious to all concerned that a solution for the Palestinian refugee problem was now a necessity.

On to Oslo

It is encouraging that although one constant in the Middle East has been incessant fighting, there has also been a constant search for answers. For every intifada, there is an attempt at peace. So it was that in the early 1990s, Israeli and Palestinian negotiators met in secret in Oslo, Norway, in another attempt to bridge the gap.

These talks proved fruitful when, on September 19, 1993, Yasser Arafat, chairman of the PLO, and Israeli Prime Minister Yitzhak Rabin signed the Declaration of Principles, also known as the Oslo Accords, on the White House lawn under the endorsement of former President Bill Clinton. The Oslo agenda divided the peace process into an interim phase to establish limited Palestinian autonomy and a final status phase to discuss more explosive issues, including the Palestinian refugee problem.

As summarized by Global Exchange, the provisions of the Oslo Memorandum included the following:

- The creation of the Palestinian National Authority and future PNA democratic elections

- Newly recognized Palestinian entities—that is, the West Bank and Gaza Strip

- A gradual withdrawal of Israeli troops from the Occupied Territories (OCT)

- The transfer of authority of the OCT from Israel to the PNA during a five-year period

On September 28, 1995, the Israeli-Palestinian Interim Agreement on the West Bank and Gaza Strip was ratified. In addition to other provisions, including those outlined in the Oslo Accords, this document, commonly known as Oslo II, detailed the implementation of the second phase of Palestinian self-rule in the Occupied Territories, including …

- ◆ Elections for the Council of the Palestinian National Authority.

- ◆ A gradual withdrawal of Israeli forces from the centers of Palestinian populated areas.

- ◆ The establishment of Palestinian self-rule in the OCT.

- ◆ The transfer of planning and zoning authority in the West Bank and Gaza Strip from the Israeli Military Authorities to the PNA.

Landmine!

Fifty percent of the population of the Gaza Strip is younger than 16 years old.

In return, the Palestinians agreed to abandon the armed struggle against Israel and recognize the Jewish state. In exchange, they expected that Israel would recognize a Palestinian state in the Gaza Strip and the West Bank, including East Jerusalem, and acknowledge some measure of responsibility for the Palestinian refugees.

Although Oslo was good as far as it went, it is where it did not go that became the problem. Neither of the Oslo treaties satisfactorily addressed the most important issues of the region—the status of Jerusalem, the future of Palestinian refugees, and the right to and boundaries of a future Palestinian state. With enmity as high as it is in this part of the world, security always a concern, and attacks and counterattacks a way of life, it is not surprising that the parties had a difficult time implementing both the spirit and the letter of the Oslo Accords. Extremists on both sides tried to derail the process.

Death of a Statesman

On November 3, 1995, Israeli Prime Minister Yitzhak Rabin, a genuine war hero turned peacemaker, was assassinated by a right-wing Israeli opponent of the peace process, Yigal Amir. Rabin was then succeeded by his Foreign Minister, Shimon Peres, another proponent of the peace process. But in a subsequent election in May 1996, Peres was beaten by Benjamin Netanyahu of the opposition party, which pledged to slow the peace process.

The Song That Never Ends

Yet the Israeli people longed for peace, and the Palestinians longed for a home. Neither side was yet ready to toss aside Oslo, despite the violence perpetrated by the extreme elements on both sides.

At the urging of new Israeli Prime Minister Ehud Barak, President Clinton invited Barak and Palestinian Authority Chairman Yasser Arafat to Camp David to continue their negotiations on the Middle East peace process.

On July 11, the Camp David 2000 Summit convened. The parties negotiated intensely for 15 days. Clinton tried to use his legendary personal charms and negotiation skills to cajole the parties into a final settlement, one that would address all the unresolved issues left for later by Oslo I and II. "A later day" had finally arrived.

Israeli Prime Minister Barak pushed the limits of the possible, offering the Palestinians more than had ever been offered. Barak gambled that he could reverse his sagging political fortunes at home by bringing back a comprehensive peace deal, and then winning convincing endorsement for it in a popular referendum.

Specifically, Barak was prepared to make unprecedented concessions at Camp David. According to Stanford historian Joel Beinin, Barak was willing to recognize a Palestinian state on roughly 94 percent of the West Bank. Barak was also willing to trade land near the Gaza Strip for three Jewish settlements in the West Bank.

It may be that Barak's boldest move was to finally negotiate over Jerusalem, heretofore a taboo subject in Israeli politics. Barak offered Palestinians administrative autonomy over Arab East Jerusalem, as well as control over the Temple Mount. Under Barak's plan, Israel would retain actual sovereignty over the city. Finally, Barak agreed to the resettlement of about 100,000 Palestinian refugees inside Israel, as well as agreeing to participate in an international compensation fund for the 4 to 5 million other Palestinian refugees.

But in the end, as usual in this part of the world, old grievances triumphed over new solutions. The main sticking points were Jerusalem and the refugee question. Sharing Jerusalem was not good enough for the Palestinians, and Israel refused to address the refugee problem in a way that was acceptable to Arafat. The talks collapsed.

Israeli Prime Minister Barak and President Bill Clinton both blamed the Palestinian President Yasser Arafat for missing a historic opportunity to resolve the Arab-Israeli dispute. Barak was praised by Clinton for his courage for offering the Palestinians the

best deal ever proposed by an Israeli leader. It seems
that Arafat wanted 100 percent or nothing, and the
Israelis refused to budge on ultimate control of
Jerusalem.

It was a tragic result, one that led to much ensuing
bloodshed. It is also a result that could have been
avoided. One thing you will see consistently throughout this book is that peace usually only occurs when a
leader emerges who is willing to buck conventional
wisdom, take a big risk, and who is prepared to teach
his or her people a new way. Although Barak seemed
willing, Arafat was not, and, as they say, it takes two
to tango.

After the collapse of the talks at Camp David, whatever power Oslo had left vanished.
A new Palestinian intifada erupted, the peace process died, Israeli hawk Ariel Sharon
was swept into power, and the Middle East mess continued.

The Least You Need to Know

- Israelis and Palestinians have both lived in the Middle East for centuries.

- After years away, the Zionist movement brought Jews back.

- Wars have erupted every few years between Israel and her neighbors.

- The Oslo Accords put off the hard questions.

- The cycle of violence continues.

Chapter 5

Israel and Palestine Struggle for Peace

In This Chapter

- ◆ The issues
- ◆ Ariel Sharon and Yasser Arafat
- ◆ Other players
- ◆ What peace may look like

The issues that continue to divide the Israelis and Palestinians are not insignificant; if they were, peace would have been far easier to achieve. But the fact is, each group is trying to share a very small plot of land with people who are dissimilar in religion, history, values, and beliefs and who dislike one another. It is no small task.

Yet even so, there have been many attempts to create a workable solution by various factions at different times. Sometimes the *hawks* are ascendant, sometimes it's the *doves*. Hopes are raised and dashed. Solutions come and go. The only constant is that peace remains elusive.

def•i•ni•tion

A **hawk** is a person who is pro-military and believes that military solutions often work best. A **dove** is someone who believes that negotiations and peaceful solutions are the way to go.

However, if there is any good news, it is that peace in the Holy Land seems to be getting closer. As the issues become clearer, so too do the solutions. Not long ago, the idea of a "two-state" solution (i.e., one Israel, the other Palestine) was unthinkable in many Jewish and Palestinian quarters. Now it is a given. Accordingly, because the parties now know what the issues are, the only question is, how to resolve them?

Major Issues

There are five main issues forming a wedge between the Palestinians and the Israelis. Three are geographical and two are not:

- The Gaza Strip
- The West Bank
- East Jerusalem
- The "right of return"
- Security

Gaza

As you will recall from the Chapter 4, the Gaza Strip fell under Jewish control after the Israelis decisively won the Six-Day War in 1967. But it proved to be a Pyrrhic victory because the problems the Israelis had occupying Palestinian land have been enormous.

The Gaza Strip is home to some 1.4 million Palestinians. Over the years, some hearty (some would say foolhardy) Israelis moved into the occupied Gaza territory to build Jewish "settlements" (towns).

But 8,000 Jews were no match for 1.4 million Arabs, and the situation in Gaza grew increasingly untenable for both sides:

- The Israeli settlements and Jewish occupation were extremely hard on the residents of Gaza. Twenty percent of all Gaza land was devoted to Israeli roads, settlements, and military bases. Israeli soldiers were everywhere, as were checkpoints and watchtowers. Curfews were common. Poverty, unemployment, and helplessness ran rampant.

♦ Amazingly, things may even have been worse for the Jews. The hatred of the Israelis by young Palestinians especially resulted in hundreds of Gaza-born suicide bombers blowing up thousands of innocent Israeli men, women, and children.

So it is not hard to understand why the Israelis wanted out of Gaza and why the Palestinians wanted them out. It was thought for many years that a Gaza pullout by the Israelis would be part of an overall peace settlement, so it came as a great surprise when, in 2004, Israeli Prime Minister Ariel Sharon declared that Israel would unilaterally pull out of the Gaza Strip in 2005.

> Ironically, many members of Sharon's right-wing Likud party opposed his plan, while many members of Israel's more dovish Labor party supported it. The right-wingers believed that leaving Gaza meant that terrorists would be able to establish a beach-head on Israel's border.

Landmine!

Sixty-eight percent of all suicide bombers in Israel were from the Gaza strip. Twenty-nine percent of the suicide bombers graduated high school. Eighty-three were single, and 64 percent were between the ages 18 and 23 years old.

Source: IsreaInsider.com, June 4, 2001

There is a saying in politics: "Only Nixon could go to China." It means that only the virulent anticommunist Richard Nixon had the standing and background to visit Communist China without people questioning his motives. He had the stature to pull it off. In the same vein, it may be that only the well-known hawk Sharon had the stature to unilaterally pull out of Gaza without being considered weak.

And so it was that on August 17, 2005, 14,000 Israeli soldiers began to evict Jewish settlers from Gaza. Whereas some settlers left voluntarily, albeit reluctantly, others were physically expelled against their will from their homes and synagogues. But within a week, all Israeli settlers had been evicted from Gaza, and the Jewish compounds were being bull-dozed.

With that, Israel ended its 38-year occupation of Gaza.

> **Reliable Resources**
>
> Israel has demonstrated that it has the requisite maturity to do what would be required to achieve lasting peace, and the Israeli Defense Forces have demonstrated their ability to discharge their mission with carefully calibrated restraint. Prime Minister Sharon should be commended for his determination and courage to carry out the disengagement in the face of forceful and strident internal opposition.
>
> —Ibrahim Gambari, United Nations under-secretary-general for political affairs, August 24, 2005

The West Bank

The West Bank is a plot of land, significantly bigger than Gaza, which Israel captured from Jordan during the Six-Day War. It is populated by 2.4 million Palestinians and 400,000 Jewish settlers. Far more than Gaza, religious Jews consider the West Bank to be part of biblical Israel (specifically, Judea and Samaria). For the Palestinians, the West Bank is considered the heart of their future homeland, Palestine.

As in Gaza, Jewish settlers have built compounds throughout the West Bank. It was long thought that the status of this area too would be part of a negotiated settlement between the Israelis and Palestinians, but once again, Ariel Sharon had a different plan.

After the failure to achieve peace at Camp David in 2000, many Israelis became convinced that there could never be a negotiated settlement with the Palestinians, especially as long as Yasser Arafat was in charge (see Chapter 4). Apparently, Sharon thought so, too, especially as he never trusted his old nemesis Arafat.

The failure at Camp David gave rise of the second intifada, and suicide bombers from Gaza and the West Bank poured into Israel, causing havoc and death in their wake. Desperate to stem the tide of such bombings, Prime Minister Sharon decided that the best way to stop such fanatics was to build a wall.

The wall around the West Bank is a 440-mile concrete barrier with electronic sensors and watchtowers, topped by razor wire, and surrounded by a ditch of fine sand so as to capture footprints.

The wall is controversial for a host of reasons. The most obvious is that it is not being built around the pre-1967 borders but instead encroaches on Palestinian land. As such, it seems to be unilaterally setting the border for the two future states without negotiation.

In 2004, the International Court of Justice in the Hague ruled that the wall violates international law and is essentially a forced annexation of Palestinian land. The Israelis rejected that ruling, firm in their belief that the wall is a security measure. This conviction is bolstered by the fact that there has been a drastic reduction in suicide bombers emanating from the West Bank since the wall has gone up.

But although the International Court of Justice ruling carries no legal weight in Israel, an Israeli Supreme Court ruling does, and that court held in 2004 that while building the wall, Israel had to endeavor to limit damage to the Palestinians; one section of the wall was to be rerouted for this reason.

> **Peacekeepers**
>
> The International Court of Justice is the judicial arm of the United Nations. Its role is to resolve disputes of international law submitted by member states and to give advisory opinions on various legal issues. The court is made up of 15 judges, each of whom serves a 9-year term. Only one judge of any nationality can serve on the court at any given time.

Although international condemnation of the wall has been fairly universal, Israel has moved forward with its construction. This much is clear: Whatever peace settlement eventually results between the Israelis and Palestinians, the West Bank wall will have to be taken into account.

East Jerusalem

Jerusalem may be the most holy city on the planet, vital as it is to Christians, Jews, and Muslims. It is the capital of Israel and home to some of the world's most revered religious sites. In 1967, the Israelis captured East Jerusalem from the Jordanians as part of the West Bank. Resolving the issue of East Jerusalem is fundamental to the resolution of this conflict as a whole.

The essence of the issue is that both Jews and Muslims lay claim to the same holy sites, and how to share these sites has yet to be figured out. They are ...

- ◆ **The Temple Mount/Haram al-Sharif.** How intractable is this issue? The same exact site is given different names by the two sides yet is considered vital to each. For the Israelis, the 35-acre Temple Mount is the home of the Western Wall, also known as the Wailing Wall. It is the site of the biblical first and second temples and is the most holy place in Judaism. Haram al-Sharif is almost, but not quite, as important to Muslims the world over.

♦ **Dome of the Rock.** Also part of the Temple Mount complex, the Dome of the Rock is said to be the spot where the Prophet Muhammad ascended to heaven. For Jews, it is the spot where Abraham offered to sacrifice his son Isaac as well as the spot of the innermost room of the Old Temple.

♦ **Al-Aqsa Mosque.** This is the third most holy site in Islam, aside from Mecca and Medina.

Needless to say, East Jerusalem is also the place where the Palestinians want to establish their capital, an idea resisted by Israel as Jerusalem is already the Israeli capital. Here is a novel plan: share.

The "Right of Return"

When hundreds of thousands of Palestinians either voluntarily left or were otherwise displaced from their homes during the Jewish War of Independence in 1948, as well as the Six-Day War of 1967, they were told by Arab leaders that they would have the right to return to their homes and homeland one day.

Accordingly, Palestinians have long asserted the right to return their people to these places, despite the fact that much of this land is now legally part of Israel as part of a U.N. mandate and that most of the Palestinian refugees left voluntarily.

Most problematically, allowing them back would be tantamount to surrendering Israel to the Arabs. Israel is a land of 6.6 million people, 5.4 million of whom are Jewish. There are 4 million Palestinians scattered across the globe. If you do the math you will see why Israelis claim that allowing Palestinians back demographically threatens the Jewish state. But the Palestinians argue that U.N. Resolution 194, passed in 1948, states that Palestinian "refugees wishing to return to their homes and live at peace with their neighbors should be permitted to do so at the earliest practical date."

It is Israel's position that the Palestinians should either live in a future Palestinian homeland in the West Bank and Gaza, or should be absorbed by other Arab countries where they now live. Arab nations have refused.

This seems to be one of the most intractable issues facing the two parties. Israel can't very well let 4 million Palestinians back into the country without losing the country. Similarly, the Palestinians can't easily give up such a long-held demand, although it is hard to see how they will be able to continue to cling to this notion when the time for a final resolution is at hand.

A Homeland and Security

The final issues facing the two sides when all of the above are resolved are bigger and broader. Where will the Palestinian homeland be, and if it is going to be Gaza and the West Bank, how will the two separated lands be connected? Will a people who are taught to hate Jews be able to live in peace with their Jewish neighbor next door? Will democracy thrive?

For Israel, the questions are no less perplexing and profound: If a Palestinian homeland is created, how will Israel's security be protected? Will the terrorist elements that make up some of the Palestinian population turn their swords into ploughshares after they have their own country?

> **Peacekeepers**
>
> GAZA CITY, Gaza Strip (CNN)—The Palestinian National Council has declared it no longer seeks the destruction of Israel through an armed struggle.
>
> Members voted 504–54 with 14 abstentions Wednesday to eliminate all such references in the 1964 charter. The council also vowed to begin writing a new charter.
>
> April 25, 1996

Who's Who?

The main players who will make these momentous decisions, as well as those who got us to this point, are an interesting cast of characters.

Ariel Sharon

Ariel Sharon is a big, gruff, ox of a military man who is determined to provide for Israel's security and who, as a result, is despised by many a Palestinian. Yet his life and that of the Jewish state are inextricably linked, for good or ill.

def•i•ni•tion

The **Knesset** is the Israeli parliament, akin to Congress.

Sharon was born in 1928, long before Israel was a state, in what was then British Palestine. He fought in the War of Independence and eventually became a general in the Israeli army. He was elected to the *Knesset* in 1973, later resigned, and was elected again in 1977.

In 1982, Sharon led an ill-fated invasion of Lebanon which expelled the Palestine Liberation Organization (PLO) from Beirut, but which also resulted in the massacre of hundreds of innocent Palestinians at the Sabra and Shatila refugee camps. The world was outraged at this unprovoked attack, and in 1983 Sharon was found indirectly responsible for the killings and removed from office. Although he remained a popular figure among the right wing in Israel, many thought that Sharon had just had his Waterloo.

But more than a decade later, in 1996, Benjamin Netanyahu's right-wing Likud party came to power and he appointed Ariel Sharon to be his foreign minister, rehabilitating the general in the process.

Sharon had his eyes set on becoming prime minister. How would he get there? As he always had—by confrontation, force of personality, and a willingness to offend for the sake of doing what he thought was right.

In 2000, after the collapse of the Camp David talks, Sharon famously visited the holy Muslim al-Aqsa mosque in East Jerusalem. This visit was an affront to Muslims and sparked the second Palestinian intifada. That Sharon knew his visit would incite violence, and that such violence might turn the Israeli electorate to a right-wing military man, is not an illogical conclusion.

In 2001, Ariel Sharon, the once-deposed and -disgraced general, won a landslide victory, becoming Israel's next prime minister. He was finally in a position to impose his security ideas upon the Middle East.

Yasser Arafat

Although Yasser Arafat died in 2004, he will be long remembered as the father of the Palestinian liberation movement. And like his nemesis Ariel Sharon, Yasser Arafat will also long be considered a controversial figure—one who put the idea of a Palestinian homeland on the map, but also one who did not have the ability to get his people to the promised land.

He was born Muhammad Abdul Rahman Abdul Raouf Arafat al-Qudwa al-Husseini on August 24, 1929, in Cairo, Egypt. His father was Palestinian, and the 1948 creation of Israel, on what was Palestinian land, was the turning point in young Arafat's life; he went on to create Fatah, the Movement for the Liberation of Palestine. He fought as an Egyptian in the 1956 Arab-Israeli War and gained an expertise in explosives. After 1967, his star began to rise as his Fatah organization became the main opposition force to Israel's power.

In 1969, Arafat was elected chairman of the PLO, a group that had been created a few years earlier by the Arab League. He would remain the chairman of the PLO until his death. The PLO was first based in Jordan, but King Hussein did not want them there and threw the organization out in 1970. Thereafter, the PLO was based in Beirut, Lebanon.

The PLO was also a terrorist organization, engaging in airplane hijackings, assassinations, and bombings. In 1974, Arafat addressed the U.N. General Assembly with a gun holstered on his waist. "I have come bearing an olive branch and a freedom fighter's gun," he said. "Do not let the olive branch fall from my hands."

Landmine!

Maybe the most barbaric terrorist attack prior to September 11 was the murder of the 11 members of the Israeli Olympic team by Palestinian gunmen in 1972. At the Munich Olympics that year, eight members of Black September, a subset of Yasser Arafat's Fatah organization, scaled a chain link fence at the Olympic village and attempted to kidnap the 11-member Israeli Olympic team. Two Israelis died in the initial attack.

The world watched, horrified, as the spectacle unfolded on television. The Palestinian terrorists demanded the release of more than 200 Palestinians in Israeli jails, as well as 2 German terrorists. A day of negotiations failed, and the terrorists transported themselves and the hostages to the Munich airport. German sharpshooters at the airport were ready and opened fire. All remaining hostages died, along with five of the eight Palestinians and one German policeman.

In 1982, Ariel Sharon's controversial invasion of Lebanon resulted in the expulsion of Arafat to Tunis, Tunisia, in north Africa. Not only was Sharon thought to be washed up after the ill-fated Lebanese invasion, but so, too, was Arafat. Like Sharon, the Palestinian leader proved to be a cunning survivor.

In 1987, the first Palestinian intifada began as stone-throwing youth attacked the Israeli military in the West Bank and Gaza. Somehow, though he really had nothing to do with spontaneous uprising, Arafat became identified with the intifada and began a long political comeback.

Yet Arafat, though a survivor, was not the wisest of politicians. In 1990, he supported Saddam Hussein during the first Gulf War, and as a result, support for the PLO withered.

Weakened, adrift, and lacking options, Arafat had little choice but to engage in peace negotiations when the subject was secretly broached by Israel's then-prime minister, Yitzhak Rabin, in 1993. The product was the Oslo Peace Accords, resulting in, among other things, the return of Yasser Arafat to Gaza in 1994.

But, as explained in the last chapter, Oslo eventually led nowhere, Rabin was assassinated in 1995, and Arafat did not have the courage to make peace at Camp David in 2000.

A second intifada erupted, the suicide bombers re-emerged, and the Israeli military responded by attacking Arafat's Palestinian Authority complex in Ramallah. Arafat the survivor survived, but his compound lay in ruins, and there he stayed, in the rubble of his bombed-out West Bank headquarters, in effect, under house arrest.

Arafat died on November 11, 2004, in Paris after undergoing treatment for a mysterious illness (some say he died of AIDS) without ever getting to see the Palestinian homeland he dedicated his life to creating.

Mahmoud Abbas

After the death of Yasser Arafat, Mahmoud Abbas, also known as Abu Mazen, was named chairman of the Palestine Liberation Organization. In January 2005, Abbas was elected president of the Palestinian Authority.

Born in British Palestine in 1935, Abbas is one of the founding members of Fatah and was with Arafat in Jordan, Lebanon, and Tunisia. He is widely credited with being the architect of Oslo and was with Arafat at the White House in 1993 to sign the Oslo Accords.

Yet unlike Arafat, Abbas is considered a moderate, someone with whom the West can work. It is hoped that he will be able to deliver on the promises that Yasser Arafat could not.

Roadmap to Peace

So is peace possible? Is there any choice? These two peoples have to learn how to share a common land, despite the fact that many loathe one another.

In 2003, the European Union, the United States, the United Nations, and Russia proposed a "roadmap" for peace. It is the closest framework available for what an eventual peace deal may look like.

The preamble of the roadmap envisions "a two-state solution to the Israeli-Palestinian conflict." It calls for an end to Palestinian "violence and terrorism," the creation of a democratic Palestinian state, Israel's willingness to assist in that, "and a clear, unambiguous acceptance by both parties of the goal of a negotiated settlement."

The essence of that settlement would be as follows:

- In Phase I, the Palestinians would undertake an unconditional cessation of violence. This would include the Palestinian leadership issuing an "unequivocal statement reiterating Israel's right to exist" and Israel issuing an "unequivocal statement affirming its commitment to the two-state vision of an independent, viable, sovereign Palestinian state living in peace and security alongside Israel."

- All settlements erected since March 2001 would be dismantled and all future settlements frozen.

- In Phase II, an international conference would be held "to support Palestinian economic recovery" and to start the process of creating an independent Palestinian state with provisional borders. Arab states would restore links to Israel.

- In Phase III, Palestinian institutions and security forces would be fortified, and Israeli-Palestinian negotiations would take place in order to forge a permanent agreement.

- Another international conference would be held at this stage to come up with an "agreed, just, fair, and realistic solution to the refugee issue, and a negotiated resolution on the status of Jerusalem."

- The final negotiated settlement would "fulfill the vision of two states, Israel and sovereign, independent, democratic and viable Palestine, living side by side in peace and security."

- Finally, the conference would call for "Arab state acceptance of full normal relations with Israel and security for all the states of the region in the context of a comprehensive Arab-Israeli peace."

An undertaking to be sure, but no one ever said peace is easy.

Not Easy Indeed

If the turbulent seas of the Middle East tell us anything, it is that as soon as peace seems to be on the horizon, a new swell usually arises to block its view. In 2006, there were actually two waves which, when combined, seemed to crash on the shore of two peaceful states living side-by-side.

The first was the stroke and subsequent coma of Ariel Sharon. Sharon had just left the far-right Likud party and had started a more moderate party with the intent of forging a two-state solution. His stroke threw that into doubt.

The second event was the parliamentary election of the Islamic militant group Hamas in the Palestinian territories. Sweeping the ruling Fatah party from power, Hamas' victory signaled a sea-change in Israeli-Palestinian politics, fully committed, as it is, of destroying the State of Israel. How peace could ever be achieved between Hamas and Israel is one for King Solomon.

The Least You Need to Know

- Geographic, historical, religious, and security issues stand between Israel, Palestine, and peace.
- Ariel Sharon is imposing his security vision on the situation via the Gaza pullout and the West Bank wall.
- Although Yasser Arafat could not get his people to the promised land, it is hoped that his successor can.
- The "roadmap" for peace envisions two democratic states living side by side in peace, in a region finally accepting of Israel.

Chapter 6

Iraq I: The Rise of Saddam Hussein

In This Chapter

- ◆ Iraq: An ancient civilization
- ◆ The rise of Islam
- ◆ Saddam Hussein takes control
- ◆ The Iran-Iraq War
- ◆ The Gulf War

Home to humanity's first civilization, Sumer, the area around Iraq has been the backdrop to thousands of years of momentous human events.

In recent years, no country has been more in the crossfire of human conflict than Iraq. In this chapter, I look at its war with Iran, the invasion of Kuwait, the subsequent Gulf War, and the resulting intransigence of Saddam Hussein, all of which led up to the American-led invasion of Iraq in 2003 and the fall of Saddam (discussed in the next chapter).

Iraq: In the crossfire.

Don't Know Much About History

The Old Testament refers to modern Iraq as Mesopotamia—a land of lush vegetation, abundant wildlife, and copious, unpredictable water resources. By 6000 B.C.E., Mesopotamia had been settled, chiefly by migrants from the Turkish and Iranian highlands.

Reliable Resources

The Epic of Gilgamesh is, perhaps, the oldest written story on Earth. It was originally written on 12 clay tablets in cuneiform script.

Sumer is the ancient name for southern Mesopotamia, and the people who populated it were known as Sumerians. Sumerian culture marks a watershed in human history.

To begin with, the Sumerians were the first people known to have devised a system of writing, called pictograms. Pictograms were created by drawing pictures, using reeds as writing instruments, on wet clay. The clay would then dry into hard tablets. Through this method the Sumerians passed on agricultural techniques to later generations.

Sumerians also recorded and preserved one of the oldest known pieces of literature, the story of Gilgamesh. Dated approximately 2700 B.C.E., it is the story of the king of the city-state of Uruk.

The Sumerians are also responsible for creating one of the world's first systems of monarchy. According to historian Richard Hooker, "the very first states in human history, the states of Sumer, were likely ruled by a type of priest-king whose duties included leading the military, administering trade, judging disputes, and engaging the most important religious ceremonies."

The most important and far-reaching of all Sumerian inventions, however, was their invention of law. Although little is known about Sumerian law, scholars agree that the Code of Hammurabi, written by a Babylonian monarch, reproduces Sumerian law almost exactly. (If you are ever in Paris, you can see the giant Code of Hammurabi tablet on display at the Louvre.)

And so it is that modern Iraq has a rich history to live up to.

The Rise of Islam

The prophet Muhammad created Islam late in the sixth century, and as with much of the rest of the Arabian Peninsula, the religion was quickly adopted by ancient Iraq, although a schism that soon developed in Islam would affect Iraqi politics to this very day.

Sunni Versus Shiite

The most critical problem that faced the young Islamic community revolved around finding the rightful successor to the office of *caliph*, or successor to Muhammad, following the assassination of the second caliph of Islam, Umar of Arabia. The two contenders vying for the power and the glory were Uthman and Ali ibn Abu Talib (Ali), the prophet Muhammad's cousin and son-in-law. In the end, Uthman's conservatism, which promised continuity with the goals of the previous leadership, convinced the electorate to choose him over Ali as caliph—much to the disappointment of Ali's supporters, who opposed and never acknowledged Uthman's appointment.

def•i•ni•tion

The person acting in Muhammad's place after his death, that is the leader of Islam, is called the **caliph**. Through history, there have been many caliphs; the last one, however, was removed by the Mongols when they conquered Baghdad in 1258. The term is seldom used for anything other than the leader of the entire Muslim community.

Ultimately, this historical split between contenders and their supporters led to a division in Islam:

♦ Shia, or Shiites, are the party of Ali. Shiite Muslims are the smaller of the two parts of Islam. The Shiites supported the claims of Ali and his line to presumptive right to the caliphate and to leadership of the Muslim community.

♦ Sunnis (from *sunna*, "orthodox") are members of the larger of the two great divisions of Islam. The Sunnis supported the traditional method of election to the caliphate, and they accepted the Umayyad line that began with caliph Muawiyah in 661.

The politics and conflicts of Iraq are dominated by this split to this day. Saddam Hussein was a Sunni Muslim and the Sunnis controlled the "old" Iraq, but 80 percent of Iraq is not. Rather, it is made up of either Shiites or Kurds, and these days the majority Shiites are ascendant.

The British Mandate

What is now known as the modern state of Iraq resulted from the breakup of the Ottoman Empire after World War I. At the 1919 Paris Peace Conference, under Article 22 of the League of Nations, Britain was given a mandate over the so-called "Fertile Crescent," which included the areas known today as Iraq, Palestine, Kuwait, Jordan, and Egypt. Syria was placed under the French mandate.

Some of these territories had never been considered independent nations before; instead, previous conquerors had merely absorbed the lands and people of the Middle East into their own empires. Indeed, the borders of many modern Arab countries have no roots in history whatsoever.

This time, however, the victors decided to carve the area into new nation-states. The vast majority of nations that now occupy the Middle East were simply created out of whole cloth by France and Britain. And problematically, and not surprisingly, a basic lack of understanding of the history, geography, and religion of the area by these colonial powers would cause problems and conflicts for years to come.

The Creation of Modern Iraq

At the Cairo Conference of 1921, the British set the parameters for Iraqi political life that were to continue until 1958, choosing Faisal ibn Hussein, a member of the same family that continues to rule neighboring Jordan, as Iraq's first king. However, this

British-created monarchy suffered from a legitimacy crisis, not only because the concept of a monarchy was foreign to Iraq, but also because Faisal wasn't even Iraqi! What's more, Iraq was almost too complex and too diverse a society to have any sort of peace for long. The country was beset by conflict from the moment the British set it free. Sunnis and Shiites, cities and tribes, sheiks and tribesmen, Assyrians and Kurds, all fought for places in the emerging state structure.

The longstanding Sunni-Shiite conflict in particular continued to cause a rift in the country: Shiites feared Sunni domination. Ultimately, lacking legitimacy and unable to establish deep roots, the British-imposed political system would be overwhelmed by these conflicts.

Faisal I died in 1933 and was succeeded by his 21-year-old son, Ghazi. King Ghazi then died in an automobile accident six years later when he drove his car into a lamppost. He left the crown to his only son, the 3-year-old Faisal II, who would "govern" for only a short while himself.

The lack of respect for the crown, combined with the quick lackluster succession of kings, fostered ferment among the masses. So it was that by 1958, Iraq was ready to rid itself of the British-imposed monarchy. Modern politics and the birth of modern Iraqi conflict occurred that year when the army murdered the young King in a bloody coup d'état, also killing the crown prince, several princesses, their relatives and servants, as well as the prime minister and most of the cabinet.

Reliable Resources

The Middle East is a land of deep interpersonal connections. One place that helps forge these connections is Victoria College in Alexandria, Egypt. Not only was this school attended by the bin Laden brothers, but their schoolmates also included the likes of King Hussein of Jordan and actor Omar Sharif.

The Times, They Are A-Changin'

The Republic of Iraq was then formed on July 14, 1958, with coup leader Abdul-Karim Qassem being the first prime minister of the newly formed government. The presidency of the country was entrusted to a three-member Sovereignty Council comprising a Sunni, a Shiite, and a Kurdish leader.

However, like the kings who preceded him, Qassem was to rule Iraq for only a short time. Five years after he took the reins of power, he was murdered by members of the pan-Arab Baath (Renaissance) party in a successful coup against him and his government.

> **Landmine!**
>
> Qassem's executioners used television to prove to the country that he was dead. They strapped his corpse into a chair, and one of his executioners occasionally moved the head back and forth to convince viewers this was no mannequin, but Qassem himself.

A succession of even more coups during the next few years left the country in disarray, and, as such, the time was ripe for the emergence of a strongman who could control the ever-fluctuating, volatile political situation. That man was Saddam Hussein.

Saddam Hussein Emerges

Saddam Hussein joined the Arab Baath Socialist Party in 1957. Two years later, he was involved in an unsuccessful attempt to assassinate Prime Minister Qassem and was forced into exile. When Saddam returned, he was imprisoned; however, he escaped from jail, and in 1968, he helped lead the successful Baathist coup. As a result, control of the country landed in the hands of Saddam Hussein and General Ahmad Hassan al-Bakr, who became president and vice-president, respectively. From his new position of power, Saddam Hussein would build an elaborate network of secret police to root out dissidents.

Bakr, who had been a long-time defender of Arab nationalist causes, brought the party legitimacy and support from both Baathist and non-Baathist army officers. Saddam Hussein, by contrast, was the politician of the pair, adept at "outmaneuvering" political opponents. Although Bakr started out as the more legitimate leader of the two, by 1969 Saddam Hussein clearly had become the major player in the Baath party.

This trend accelerated throughout the 1970s, especially because Bakr was beset by illness and a series of family tragedies. Disinclined in any case to share power, Saddam Hussein consolidated his base and began to view the Revolutionary Command Council (Iraq's highest executive body) as well as the cabinet as rubber stamps. On July 16, 1979, Saddam Hussein deposed Bakr and plastered the streets with portraits of himself.

Saddam Hussein came to full power. His titles included the following:

- President of the republic
- Secretary general of the Baath party regional command

◆ Chairman of the Revolutionary Command Council

◆ Commander in chief of the armed forces

So Just Who Is Saddam Hussein?

Summarily despised as the enemy of the Western world, Saddam Hussein was a ruthless dictator. The son of poor farmers, he grew up in Auja, a tiny village northwest of Baghdad. Inspired by his nationalistic uncle, an Iraqi army officer, Hussein gravitated to politics as a young man, immersing himself in the anti-British and anti-Western sentiments of the day.

His treatment of the Shiite majority in the south of his country was repressive and violent. Shiites make up 60 percent of Iraq, and Iraq's fundamentalist neighbor Iran is a Shiite Muslim country. As such, the Sunni Saddam had reason to worry. It was his policy therefore to keep the Shiite population under tight control and scrutiny.

But maybe surprisingly, on the streets of other Arab cities, Saddam Hussein was an admired figure for his ability to (for a while) defy the United States and challenge Israel and the West. For many in the Middle East, he was a symbol of Arab steadfastness in the face of Western influence.

That he was also a bold, possibly reckless, risk taker is similarly beyond doubt. Saddam Hussein endeavored to be more than a thug. Since the death of the greatest *pan-Arab* leader of the twentieth century, Gamal Abdul Nasser, in 1970, the Arab nationalist movement has been looking for a new leader, and Saddam Hussein always longed to be that person. As Saddam Hussein saw it, when he took power in 1979, the time to fulfill that ambition had arrived, for several reasons.

def•i•ni•tion

Because the Ottoman Turks rose to power and conquered the Middle East in the fourteenth century, there have been stirrings among Arabs for reunification as a means of reestablishing Arab political power. **Pan-Arabism** is the modern movement calling for political unification among Arab states.

First of all, Saddam Hussein was a leader of a large industrious country that was benefiting from the 1970s oil boom. His country is situated on the edge of the Persian Gulf, one of the most strategically important regions in the world. And just when the Arab nationalist movement was looking for a new champion after the Camp David accords, Iraq found itself with the upper hand as the 1979 Iranian revolution weakened Iran, and made it an enemy of the United States. Finally, Saddam Hussein wielded a powerful army and large financial reserves.

So as the 1980s dawned, Saddam Hussein was poised and ready to make a name for himself. The question was—how? Unfortunately for his ambitions, Saddam Hussein was not the greatest strategist around. Rather than wait to exercise his power with some savvy, the void left by Nasser was too great a temptation for him. He crassly concluded that if he could quickly defeat his neighbor Iran in war, he would emerge as the undisputed king of the Arab world.

That he had an ostensible reason to do so made the idea that much more palatable. Saddam Hussein feared that Iran's new Shiite leadership would threaten Iraq's delicate Sunni-Shiite balance. He was also concerned about a longstanding territorial dispute regarding access to the Persian Gulf. In this respect, Hussein's decision to invade Iran had historical precedent; the ancient rulers of Mesopotamia, fearing internal strife and foreign conquest, also engaged in frequent battles with the peoples of what is now Iran.

With both a political and a personal reason to attack, Hussein calculated that a war against Iran would be both quick and fruitful. So on September 22, 1980, Iraq launched a land and air invasion against Iran.

The Iran-Iraq War

Saddam Hussein has always held that his attack on Iran was the result of a dispute over the Shatt al Arab, a waterway in the Persian Gulf that forms the boundary between Iran and Iraq. But his reasons were not so pure because there was no legitimate dispute at all: The fact is that in 1975, Iraq had signed over to Iran partial control of that waterway. But sensing weakness in Iran after the fall of the shah, Hussein concluded that the time was ripe to wipe out the treaty. That he thought he could also capture the western Iranian region of Khuzestan, an area with extensive oil fields, was further reason fueling the Iraqi invasion.

Although initially successful, the Iraqi invasion bogged down in 1982. Iranian resistance was stronger than Iraq had anticipated. Iran was backed by Syria, Libya, North Korea, and China. Iraq had much more support that included many Western nations (including the United States!). What had begun as Saddam's attempt to quickly grab some oil fields and power had instead turned into a grudge match in which neither side could win, yet neither was willing to lose.

As the war dragged on into its seventh year, the United States and several Western European nations intervened after Iran started to attack oil tankers. These attacks greatly harmed Iran's reputation, making it difficult for Khomeini to obtain arms.

As this war of attrition dragged on into its eighth year, Iran was finally forced to accept a U.N.-mandated cease-fire. It is estimated that some 1.5 million died in the Iran-Iraq War. Amazingly, when it was all over, the conditions that existed at the beginning of the war remained virtually unchanged.

The Iran-Iraq War strained the Iraqi economy, as well as its political and social life. Hussein knew that he needed to do something to revive his, as well as his country's, sagging fortunes, but what? Just as he had a decade earlier, he concluded that war was his salvation. Again he would attack a neighbor—this time, Kuwait.

> **Landmine!**
>
> An important part of the energy resources of the free world are under Iran's control. The free world cannot tolerate the loss of Iran, and there is no power in the world which can impose the smallest thing against Iran's national interests.
>
> —Mohammad Reza Pahlavi, shah of Iran, 1976, three years before he was ousted by Ayatollah Khomeini's revolution

The Mother of All Battles

Iraqis had always believed that Kuwait was part of Iraq and long had plans to invade the tiny country. In 1939, for example, King Ghazi of Iraq mobilized his army to conquer Kuwait, which was then still a colony of Britain. Just before the army was ready to strike, however, King Ghazi died in a car crash, and the invasion was called off.

In 1961, when Kuwait finally gained its independence from Great Britain, Iraq again began preparations for an invasion of the tiny land and only backed down when Britain sent troops back into the region.

Countdown to War

Tensions between the two Muslim countries began to rise, however, at the end of the Iran-Iraq War. Because that war had been partially financed by Kuwait, after the war was over, Kuwait began to demand that its loans be paid back. At the same time, the price of oil, which had provided Iraq with most of its income, had dropped sharply at the dawn of the 1990s.

On July 17, 1990, Saddam alleged that Kuwait was flooding the world oil market and stealing oil from the disputed Rumailia oil field. Then, fatefully, a week later, the U.S. ambassador to Iraq, April Galespie, told the Iraqi president that his dispute with Kuwait did not affect the United States.

Apparently Hussein thought this meant that he was free to do as he liked, and on August 2, he invaded Kuwait. His troops easily overran the little country. The Kuwaiti emir and his cabinet fled to Saudi Arabia, and on August 8, 1990, Iraq annexed Kuwait.

In response, the United Nations passed various resolutions demanding that Iraq withdraw from Kuwait. Iraq resisted, claiming it had been "invited" by rebels who had overthrown the emir.

> ### Peacekeepers
>
> It is not easy to vote in Kuwait. In fact, only 10 percent of all citizens are eligible to vote. Only adult males, who have been naturalized for 30 years or more or have resided in Kuwait since before 1920, and their male descendants can vote at age 21 or older.

As he did in the war with Iran, once again Saddam Hussein miscalculated the opponent. What he failed to realize was that by invading Kuwait, he seemed to be threatening the stability (such as it is) of the entire region. Whether Saddam Hussein had greater aims beyond Kuwait is another topic altogether, and it actually matters little. In politics, perception is reality, and the perception was that Saddam was in fact threatening the entire Persian Gulf region.

Oil fuels the American economy. The possibility that someone like Saddam Hussein could control much of the world's oil supply was seen as a direct threat to the interests of the United States, as well as other industrialized nations. Accordingly, President Bush (the first) began to forge a broad, international coalition to force Iraq out of Kuwait.

The first order of business was to get the United Nations to permit an embargo on trade with Iraq. It did, and the world waited to see whether the embargo would work. At the end of November, the United States and Britain secured another U.N. resolution authorizing the use of force to drive Iraq out of Kuwait if the Iraqis did not leave voluntarily before January 15, 1991.

The United States took it from there. The Bush administration helped foster a multinational force composed of several NATO countries as well as neighboring Arab states. Even former Warsaw Pact countries sent in units to join this colorful international alliance.

Operation Desert Storm

The deadline passed, the Iraqis didn't budge, and soon waves of Allied aircraft began a five-week bombing campaign of Iraq and Kuwait that marked the beginning of Operation Desert Storm. The American air forces employed their most advanced technologies, quickly destroyed Iraq's air defense network, and from then on owned the skies.

Compared to its airborne cousin, the ensuing ground offensive was anticlimactic— Iraq's army disintegrated in a mere 100 hours. At the end of February, Allied forces arrived at the gates of Kuwait City, which had been shrouded by clouds of acrid black smoke from the hundreds of oil wells the Iraqis had set afire during their hasty retreat.

Because the U.N. mandate was to excise Iraq from Kuwait, President George Bush decided not to invade Baghdad, nor to go after Saddam Hussein directly. The decision not to oust Saddam was augmented by a fear that Iran might overtake Iraq should Saddam fall, and that in any case, Saddam Hussein might be overthrown by his own people.

> **Landmine!**
>
> In 1994, Kuwait convicted several Iraqis on charges of attempting to assassinate former President George Bush when he visited the emirate the previous year. The plot, according to the Kuwaitis, was uncovered and foiled at the last minute.

Postscript

After the war, the United States and United Kingdom were determined to clip Iraq's wings: They created two "no-fly" zones in the country, one north of the thirty-sixth parallel to protect the Kurds, and another below the thirty-third parallel to protect the Shiites.

In addition, Saddam Hussein was ordered to destroy all his weapons of mass destruction (WMDs). After years of noncompliance and a cat-and-mouse inspection game with U.N. inspectors, Saddam finally kicked them out of Iraq in 1998.

Of course (as will be explained in Chapter 7) it turned out that Hussein had no WMDs at all, so why he kicked out the inspectors remains a perplexing mystery. Yet even so, it is a decision that would have enormous ramifications for the entire world: Kicking out the inspectors lent credence to the theory that Hussein had something to hide, and after September 11, that alone seemed to be enough (for some people) to invade the country again.

Needless to say, the result of that second Iraq war is far different from the result of the first. Saddam Hussein was ousted from power, the United States became an occupying force, and a nascent Islamic republic began to form in the once-secular Iraq.

The Least You Need to Know

- Iraq is an ancient culture with a rich history.
- The Sunni-Shiite rift in Islam affects Iraq to this day.
- Saddam Hussein was a ruthless dictator who suppressed the majority of his country.
- The Iran-Iraq War was a miscalculation on Saddam's part.
- The Gulf War was another miscalculation.

Iraq II: Ground Zero for the War on Terror

In This Chapter

- ◆ Preparing the country for war
- ◆ Shock and awe
- ◆ The fall of Saddam
- ◆ Aftermath

As you know, after September 11, the United States, with ample reason and proof, attacked al-Qaeda and its state sponsor, Afghanistan. In the War on Terror, that was, as they say, the low-lying fruit. The real question was: What to do after that?

The decision of the Bush administration was to invade Iraq. The idea was to "attack the terrorists there so they couldn't attack us here." It seemed to be a dubious theory. But if Saddam Hussein did indeed have weapons of mass destruction (WMDs), the West would be hard put to do nothing. Was it the right decision? Let's see.

Drumbeat for War

In his State of the Union address in January 2002, President George W. Bush named three countries he declared were state sponsors of terrorism, thereby making them an "axis of evil": Iran, Iraq, and North Korea.

These three countries were among the most repressive regimes on the planet, seemingly capable of creating WMDs (if they had not done so already), and certainly siding with terrorist organizations if not outright supporting them. Of the three, North Korea had the greatest likelihood of possessing nuclear weapons, making the decision to attack Iraq one that many would question. Why did the United States choose to invade Iraq, rather than Iran or North Korea?

> **Reliable Resources** _____
>
> The term *axis of evil* was used for three reasons. First, it harkened back to World War II, where Germany, Italy, and Japan were the "Axis powers." Second, the phrase was reminiscent of Bush's political hero Ronald Reagan calling the Soviet Union the "evil empire." Finally, the phrase certainly had a ring to it.

Iraq and September 11

The first reason is that the president and his team seemed convinced that Iraq had played some part in the 9/11 attacks. Former counterterrorism czar Richard Clarke says that the day after the attacks, on September 12, the president told Clarke that he wanted a memo about Iraq's connection to the attacks. Clarke, however, was convinced that 9/11 was the work of al-Qaeda and not Iraq. In point of fact, the president had been specifically warned that al-Qaeda was planning an attack on the United States.

Every day, the president is given a foreign affairs briefing, outlining the previous day's events and upcoming issues he might face. This is called the "Presidential Daily Briefing," or PDB.

On August 6, 2001, a little more than a month before the September 11 attacks, the PDB given to President Bush was titled "Bin Laden Determined to Strike in U.S." The PDB explained that Osama bin Laden was determined to bring his fight to American soil. The PDB even said that there was an increasing likelihood that al-Qaeda was going to hijack planes.

Yet even so, there is no doubt that the Bush administration tried to link Iraq to the 9/11 attacks in the minds of the American people. In his State of the Union address on January 28, 2003, the President said, "Evidence from intelligence sources, secret communications and statements by people now in custody reveals that Saddam Hussein aids and protects terrorists, including members of al-Qaeda."

Similarly, Vice President Dick Cheney repeatedly went on television discussing the two, implying that Saddam Hussein had longstanding ties to Osama bin Laden and that Iraq had something to do with September 11.

The Bush administration was so effective in this campaign that by the time of the invasion of Iraq, 44 percent of all Americans believed that at least some of the hijackers had been Iraqi (19 of 20 were Saudis, none were Iraqi), and fully 45 percent erroneously believed Iraq was behind the attacks.

> **Reliable Resources**
>
> Mr. Cheney's "longstanding ties" [between Iraq and al Qaeda] amount to one confirmed meeting, after which the Iraq government did not help Al Qaeda. By those standards, the United States has longstanding ties to North Korea.
>
> —*New York Times* editorial, June 19, 2004

But as numerous investigations have since made clear, including that in the 9/11 Commission Report, Iraq in fact had nothing to do with either al-Qaeda or the September 11 attacks.

WMDs

But September 11 was not the only reason the Bush administration wanted to confront Saddam Hussein, or even the most important one. Of more importance was its belief that Iraq had or was creating WMDs that it was preparing to use against the United States and its allies.

In February 2003, Secretary of State Colin Powell went before the United Nations Security Council and made a dramatic, forceful case for war, offering satellite photographs and reports that seemed to prove that Saddam Hussein was in the process of creating WMDs.

Secretary Powell had spent several days previously at CIA headquarters looking at the evidence he would present, almost all of which turned out to be incorrect.

Landmine!

Colin Powell would come to regret the speech before the United Nations. On September 8, 2005, Powell (who had since retired) told ABC News that the speech was a "blot" on his record. Said Powell, "I'm the one who presented it on behalf of the United States to the world, and (it) will always be a part of my record. It was painful. It is painful now."

If the allegations were true, if Saddam Hussein had in fact reconstituted his WMD programs in violation of U.N. resolutions, then it would have been grossly negligent not to take action against Iraq.

So the Bush administration began a two-pronged effort: First it went to the Security Council asking for resolutions (which it got) demanding that Iraq comply with previous U.N. resolutions and allow weapons inspectors back into the country; second, it began to cobble together a coalition of countries willing to take a stand should Iraq not comply.

Iraq didn't comply, and in October 2002, the U.S. Congress authorized the president to wage war against Iraq if necessary, citing, among other reasons, Iraq's WMDs, its "threat to the national security of the United States," its assassination attempt on George W. Bush's father, and its connection to al-Qaeda.

War!

On March 18, 2003, President Bush gave Saddam Hussein and his sons 48 hours to leave Iraq or face the consequences. They did not, and 49½ hours later, the second U.S.-Iraq war began.

Utilizing a military theory called "shock and awe," the United States military endeavored to not only win the war quickly, but do so in such an overwhelming, spectacular fashion that the enemy would lose its will to fight. The firepower utilized was no doubt impressive:

- 1,700 "sorties" were launched.

- 504 sorties were cruise missiles.

- British marines, the British Royal Navy, the Royal Australian Navy, and many others joined U.S. forces to launch a massive air, sea, and land campaign.

The Fall of Baghdad

Three weeks later, Baghdad, the capital of Iraq, and the Iraqi government, fell. Although Iraq's elite Republican Guard was expected to provide stiff resistance to the advancing coalition army, it never materialized. U.S. forces easily moved into the Iraqi capital, capturing Saddam's palaces in the process and using them as staging areas.

On April 9, 2003, the sadistic, despotic rule of Saddam Hussein had come to an end. The dictator vanished into thin air and ordinary Iraqis celebrated wildly in the streets of Baghdad. For a short while, the United States was in fact greeted as a liberator.

Reliable Resources _____

Transcript, *Meet the Press*, March 16, 2003:

VICE PRES. CHENEY: I think things have gotten so bad inside Iraq from the standpoint of the Iraqi people, my belief is we will, in fact, be greeted as liberators.

MR. RUSSERT: If your analysis is not correct and we're not treated as liberators but as conquerors and the Iraqis begin to resist particularly in Baghdad, do you think the American people are prepared for a long, costly and bloody battle with significant American casualties?

VICE PRES. CHENEY: Well, I don't think it's unlikely to unfold that way, Tim, because I really do believe we will be greeted as liberators.

Coalition forces tried in vain to control the ensuing chaos, but their inability to do so foreshadowed the fact that, although the war had been planned meticulously, the peace had not.

When looters started ransacking buildings and running off with priceless artifacts from Iraqi museums and such, Secretary of Defense Donald Rumsfeld said:

> The task we've got ahead of us now is an awkward one … It's untidy. And freedom's untidy. And free people are free to make mistakes and commit crimes and do bad things. They're also free to live their lives and do wonderful things. And that's what's going to happen here. [F]or suddenly the biggest problem in the world to be looting is really notable … Stuff happens.

Meanwhile, in Other Parts of the Country

As the battle for Baghdad concluded, coalition forces began to occupy key cities, roads, and facilities throughout Iraq.

It turns out that years of sanctions against Hussein's government had taken their toll. The Iraqi army proved to be ill-equipped, lacking morale, poorly trained, and none-too-loyal. As coalition forces marched through the country, much of Saddam's army, including the so-called elite Republican Guard, simply disappeared into the crowds.

This was also true in the northern, Kurdish, part of the country. The Kurds have long been a people without a homeland, much like the Palestinians. Historic Kurdistan is made up of parts of Iraq, Iran, and Turkey, but historic Kurdistan is long gone.

However, after the Gulf War in 1991, the northern part of Iraq, a traditional enclave of the Kurds, was given protection by coalition forces. A sort of mini-Kurdistan was carved out. After the U.S.-led invasion of Iraq began in 2003, Kurdish forces quickly and easily routed the Iraqi army there too, further securing the nascent Kurdish homeland.

Mission Accomplished?

A mere two weeks after the fall of Baghdad, the president, landing on an aircraft carrier in full Air Force togs, in front of a banner proclaiming "Mission Accomplished," declared that major combat operations in the war were over. The president had no way of knowing that the intransigent, small rebellion facing coalition forces would soon turn into a full-fledged resistance. Even so, if the mission was to bring peace, stability, and democracy to Iraq, the mission most certainly had not been accomplished.

 Landmine!

Iraq fact sheet:
- ◆ Weapons of mass destruction found: 0
- ◆ Average number of U.S. troop deaths, per day: 2
- ◆ Civilian deaths: More than 100,000
- ◆ Cost of the war, per week: $1 billion
- ◆ Number of new U.S. military bases planned: 6–14

Source: Institute for Policy Studies

The Day After

The fall of Saddam Hussein's regime led to an outbreak of violence throughout the country because there were no police to stop the hoodlums and, in what can only be seen as a major oversight, the Iraqi army was disbanded, exacerbating the situation.

In December, post-war events took a turn for the better when Saddam Hussein was found, hiding in an underground cellar of a farmhouse near his hometown of Tikrit. He was jailed and as of this writing is standing trial for crimes against his people.

The capture of Saddam was supposed to be a turning point in the violent and ugly aftermath of a very successful war, but it was not. Several other events also came and went that were supposed to signal better days ahead:

- In June 2004, "sovereignty" of the country was transferred back to the Iraqis, but what had now become a guerilla war only gained strength.

- In January 2005, Iraq held its first election. The insurgency continued.

- In October 2005, Iraqis ratified a new constitution (which states that Islam will be "a main source" of law). The guerilla war, which was now almost a full-fledged civil war, was in full swing.

The Islamic Republic of Iraq?

To complicate matters even more, whereas Saddam Hussein's Iraq might have been a rogue state, by most accounts terrorists had little sway there. This was especially true of Islamic terrorists, who loathed the secular Hussein (and vice versa). But the new Iraq appears well on its way to becoming a home for Islamic terrorism. Did George Bush create the opposite of what he intended?

No less an authority than Donald Rumsfeld has wondered the same thing. In a memo to his staff, three years after the September 11 attacks, while the Iraq imbroglio was in full swing, Rumsfeld wondered whether the United States was winning or losing the War on Terror:

> Today, we lack metrics to know if we are winning or losing the global war on terror. Are we capturing, killing or deterring and dissuading more terrorists every day than … the radical clerics are recruiting, training and deploying against us?

It is no wonder then that by the end of 2005, the American public began to question whether the war, and the deaths of its young men and women in support of the war, were worth it. Whereas 63 percent of all respondents to the CBS/*New York Times* poll in December 2003 thought the United States did the right thing by invading Iraq, only 44 percent thought so by September 2005.

The Problem

Several things combined to create the unstable situation that is post-Saddam Iraq. First, Saddam Hussein's regime was in fact so rigid that the ethnic and religious differences we see today were held in check. The war unleashed internal strife, power, and feelings that had been quashed for years.

Second, recall that Iraq is not a natural nation state. Carved, as it was, out of the old Ottoman Empire by Britain after World War I, the country should rightly be three countries: one Kurdish, one Shiite, and one Sunni.

Finally, imposing the idea of democracy on a region and a people with no history or feel for such a political system is idealistic and brave, but also naive. If it works, it might be a monumental achievement. If the democratic country that is created decides to become a fundamental Islamic state, it might be a disaster.

The Least You Need to Know

♦ Although it seems clear that Iraq had nothing to do with 9/11, that it possibly had WMDs was reason enough for most in the United States to want to go to war.

♦ Overwhelming firepower enabled the United States to easily topple Saddam.

♦ A persistent insurgency unexpectedly sprang up after the war.

♦ Iraqis may yet form a stable, democratic government, or they might form an Islamic republic.

Chapter 8

Sudan: A Land Divided

In This Chapter

- Sudan's history
- Sudanese civil war
- Peace at last
- Darfur in conflict

Sudan is a land with a tragically troubled history of conflict and strife. A country that has been run by extremists and military dictatorships, Sudan has also been ravaged by civil war. Millions of refugees have resulted, millions have been murdered, and millions more have been starved to death. It is an unbelievably sad story of ideology, corruption, and power winning out over humanity and decency.

A Sudan Divided Against Itself Cannot Stand

Military dictatorships promoting an extreme Islamic government have mostly run Sudan since independence from Great Britain in 1956. Over the past two decades, at least 1.5 million lives were lost in a vicious civil war pitting black Christians and animists in the South against Arab Muslims in the North.

Sudan should probably be divided in half.

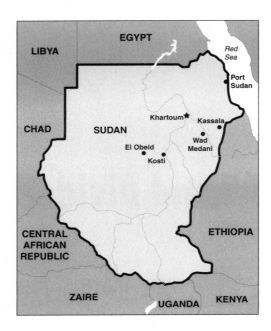

Sudan Backgrounder

Sudan is the largest country in Africa. It has been populated for more than 9 million years, and the ox-driven water wheel, introduced to the region some 2,500 years ago, still plays a vital role in the economy today.

For as long as Sudan has been around, Egypt has seemed to control it. Egyptian dominance in this region probably began in 2500 B.C.E., when Sudan was known as Nubia, with ruined temples and monuments a sure sign of ancient Egyptian influence.

> **Reliable Resources**
>
> The modern inhabitants of southern Egypt and Sudan still refer to themselves as Nubians. They speak the Nubian language and Arabic.

A succession of foreign invaders followed the independence that Nubia had attained in the eighth century B.C.E. The Romans invaded Nubia around the time of Christ, and Christian Ethiopia overtook the country 300 years later, resulting in the conversion of most of the population to Christianity.

Sudan Piques Their Interest

In 1854, by a French initiative, the viceroy of Egypt decided that it was technically feasible to build a canal that would connect the Mediterranean to the Red Sea. In 1858, a company was formed to construct and administer the Suez Canal. Both French and Egyptian interests owned the company, and it was decided that they would administer the canal for 99 years.

The canal project proved to be a very expensive proposition, and as a result, Egypt found itself heavily in debt to foreign powers. As such, in 1873, the British were able to get one of their own, General Charles George Gordon, appointed governor of Egyptian Sudan.

And that is how it came to be that Sudan would be governed by Egypt through Egypt's British colonial master. It was this dichotomy—Egyptian Muslims and British Christians controlling the Sudanese populace in a joint, and often-conflicting, manner—that would eventually shape all contours of Sudan.

The Dichotomy Emerges

Because of their differences, and because they mutually needed each other if they were to control the vast Sudan, British and Egyptian forces made the fateful decision to jointly administer Sudan as two regions. In the North, the Egyptians would run the country and Islam became the main religion. In the British-controlled South, Christianity became the dominant religious and moral influence.

By the turn of the twentieth century, the British colonies were growing restless. In 1924, the British governor-general of Sudan was assassinated in Cairo. In retaliation, Britain expelled all Egyptian officials from Sudan. Sudan was their puppet.

By 1936, Britain and Egypt had ended hostilities, but the signing of their 1936 peace agreement only served to stimulate Sudanese nationalists who were clamoring for independence.

> **Reliable Resources**
>
> Bartleby.com describes Sudan as an overwhelmingly agricultural country. However, although agriculture in the late 1990s occupied some 80 percent of the workforce, it contributed only 33 percent of the GDP. In general, agricultural production varies from year to year because of intermittent droughts that cause widespread famine.

Independence Day

Finally, on February 2, 1953, Britain and Egypt agreed to grant Sudan self-government within three years, and also provided for a Senate, a Council of Ministers, and a House of Representatives. Elections were to be supervised by an international commission.

The elections were held during November and December 1953, and Ismail al-Aihari became Sudan's first prime minister in January 1954.

Despite this rosy beginning, the problems caused by jointly administering Sudan and essentially running it for years as two very different countries soon came home to roost. The Muslim-Christian division was just too much for the country to understand, absorb, and deal with.

In 1955, fighting broke out between the northern Islamic Arabs and the southern Christian and animist blacks. In 1957, all Christian schools in the south were closed and Christian missionaries were kicked out of the country. Things worsened when, on November 17, 1958, General Ibrahim Abboud took power via a coup. General Abboud explained to the population that he would rule through an army junta and that democracy had to be suspended in Sudan.

Southern Christians and animists, alarmed by the coup, began a rebellion, demanding more and more autonomy from their Muslim brothers in the north. Although successive prime ministers visited the south, nothing stopped the rebels. Civil war was on, and would continue for 17 years, misusing national resources by diverting them from development and services to the purchase of war machinery.

The Civil War Era

Another coup, in 1969, led this time by Colonel Jafaar Mohammed al-Nimeiry, set up government under another revolutionary council. But in 1972, having consolidated his hold on power, Nimeiry held elections and became the Sudan's first elected president. Wanting to end the strife between north and south, Nimeiry worked with combatants in the south to forge some sort of peace for the impoverished, war-torn country.

The Addis Ababa Agreement finally brought the war to a halt in 1972. An uneasy peace was maintained for almost a decade, and in 1983 Nimeiry was reelected for a third term of office.

Reliable Resources

Nimeiry was temporarily expelled from high school in 1948 after leading a student strike against British rule.

Emboldened by his success, Nimeiry decided to make Sudan into an Islamic fundamentalist country. Coming on the heels of the 1979 Iranian Islamic revolution, this desire to create an Islamic state in Sudan, although not surprising, made much less sense given the demographics of the country. Nevertheless, on September 8, 1983, Nimeiry instituted Islamic law.

The Koran became the rule of law—and, for starters, alcohol and gambling were now prohibited. The southern Christians, already feeling like a minority in their own country, refused to acknowledge the change in the law. A new round of violence began.

Here's a pop quiz! What do people do in Africa when they are unhappy with the government? Altogether now: They stage a coup! Nimeiry was deposed in April 1985. A year of military rule followed before the rise of new leaders and more coups.

The new rulers were neither able to unify the country nor instill Islamic law on the south. Civil war had become a way of life.

Osama bin Laden in Sudan

Osama bin Laden first came to Sudan from Afghanistan in 1991. Although al-Qaeda had been formed three years before, the United States did not yet realize the threat he posed. Yet, by 1998, he was a wanted man. Obviously then, bin Laden's years in Sudan were critical in the development of his terrorist network. So just what was he up to while he was there? Bin Laden seemed like just another businessman. He had recently inherited as much as $300 million (though estimates vary). Accordingly, bin Laden was a most welcome addition to the poor country when he arrived. He started several businesses in Sudan, the biggest being a construction company and a giant farming operation.

Bin Laden opened his first office in Khartoum (the capital), and then moved it to an affluent suburb where he bought a farmhouse. Most often, he could be found at his farm just outside Khartoum. The farmhouse was a single-story building, with no furniture. The floor was the dirt, covered with woolen rugs.

> **Landmine!** _____
>
> Other bin Laden companies included an import-export concern; a currency-trading company; and a farm that grew sesame, peanuts, and corn.

According to a report in the *Guardian* newspaper out of London:

> His men all had nice air-conditioned flats in the city but bin Laden preferred to live simply with his horses and wives. He was just another Saudi investor. Said one associate, "If there is nothing between you, he is very kind. He smiles a lot. I never considered him dangerous."

Meanwhile, according to the *Guardian*, the Sudanese government was augmenting the army with Islamist militias. Bin Laden was rumored to have been assisting the Islamists far more than running his businesses.

This was confirmed by the trial testimony of a former al-Qaeda member, Jamal Ahmed Fadl, a 38-year-old Sudanese man who worked as a general laborer for bin Laden in Khartoum before running off with $100,000 in 1994. He says the businesses were all a front for al-Qaeda. At his trial, Fadl described a web of worldwide Islamist terrorism groups that were supplied by al-Qaeda with guns, money, and expertise.

Fadl said that he smuggled to rebels crates of explosives that he had transported from a stockpile at bin Laden's farm. Fadl also described how he had delivered $100,000 to an opponent of King Hussein of Jordan. He also explained how he had once led a caravan of 50 camels loaded with weapons to Islamic terrorists in Egypt. Fadl concluded his trial testimony describing how, while in Sudan, al-Qaeda supported Islamic terrorists in Saudi Arabia, Algeria, Syria, Chechnya, Turkey, Eritrea, Tajikistan, the Philippines, and Lebanon.

In 1996, the United States government demanded that Sudan expel all its suspected terrorists, including bin Laden.

According to Donald Petterson, the American ambassador to Sudan throughout most of bin Laden's stay, "There was an awareness that he was tagged a dangerous figure, but we didn't have a handle on him as I recall." Sudanese officials actually offered to hand bin Laden over to America, says el-Mahdi, the Sudan's spy chief. "If America had had something against him, we would have looked at extraditing him to America, but they had not."

The Slave Trade

If all this were not enough, consider that in Sudan a massive slave trade has flourished for years, although a recent peace treaty (see below) is expected to diminish the illegal trade. The reasons a slave trade existed are varied, but, in essence, the government's civil war required the assistance of local, unpaid militias. In return, Sudan's Islamic leaders encouraged soldiers to take slaves as reward.

As reported by Associated Press writer Karen Davis, according to Christian Solidarity International (CSI), a humanitarian group that buys slaves and sets them free, young women and children have been the most valuable sorts of slaves in Sudan. Old people are old, and young men cannot be trained into useful, harmless slaves. Says John Eibner of CSI: "According to the Khartoum's regime ideology of jihad, members of the resistant black African community—be they men, women or children—are infidels, and may be arbitrarily killed, enslaved, looted, or otherwise abused."

Interestingly, some groups—including UNICEF—have opposed the work of CSI, believing that by buying slaves, CSI is contributing to the slave trade itself and driving up demand.

Not surprisingly, the Sudanese government denied condoning slavery, and insisted that slavery persisted because holding prisoners for ransom is a tradition rooted in tribal disputes. As Davis reports, however, according to Gaspar Biro, a researcher for the U.N. Commission on Human Rights for Sudan, there has been an "alarming increase in cases of slavery, servitude, slave trade and forced labor" since February 1994. "The total passivity of the government can only be regarded as tacit political approval and support of the institution of slavery," he said. A U.S. State Department report said accounts it received on the taking of slaves in the South "indicates the direct and general involvement" of Sudan's army and militias "backed by the government."

Landmine!

An estimated one million Sudanese died as a result of either war or starvation during the past decade. Three million people have been displaced by the fighting, and the capital, Khartoum, has been inundated with poor, sick, homeless refugees.

An End to the Civil War

Civil war raged in Sudan for most of its history since independence. The latest and longest civil war, from 1983 to 2004, killed nearly two million people. Not surprisingly then, in 2002, the Sudanese government and the southern rebels sat down at the negotiating table. These talks actually bore fruit at the end of 2004 when a peace agreement was reached. The basic terms of the agreement are as follows:

   ◆ The South would be given "autonomy" for six years, after which there would be a vote on actual independence.

   ◆ Islamic law (sharia) would remain in effect in the North.

   ◆ The Sudanese army would be made up equally of combatants from the North and South.

   ◆ A system for sharing the South's oil revenue would be implemented (most of it staying in the South).

   ◆ 70 percent of all civil service jobs would go to the government and not the rebels.

The sad irony of this story: The long-time leader of the southern rebellion was a man named John Garang. As part of the peace deal, Garang was made vice president of a new national unity government. But a mere three weeks after taking his new position, Garang died in a helicopter crash, which, of course, sparked riots in the South.

Crisis in Darfur

As if all of this conflict were not enough, Sudan's western region of Darfur is in the midst of what the United Nations calls the world's worst humanitarian crisis: 2 million people have been made refugees to date and approximately another 250,000 have been killed due to … *ethnic cleansing*.

def•i•ni•tion

Ethnic cleansing is a euphemistic term describing a policy in which a particular ethnic group is targeted and either deported en masse or murdered via genocide.

The crisis began in 2003 when black rebels began attacking government targets, claiming that the Islamist Khartoum government was favoring local Arabs over indigenous black Africans. Because the Arabs in this region are a nomadic people, and the blacks are more established farmers, and because both share a common gene pool, the conflict between the two groups must be seen as more of tribe against tribe than black against Arab.

In response to the black rebel attacks, local Arabs formed their own militia, called Janjaweed. And although both sides are equally guilty of serious human rights abuses, the Janjaweed have been particularly ruthless. Their ethnic cleansing consists of raiding and destroying non-Arab villages, raping, murdering, and hacking the villagers, and causing mass starvation.

In June 2005, the International Criminal Court in the Hague announced that it would, under its own volition, begin investigating war crimes occurring in Darfur. This was the first time that the court was to undertake such an inquiry without a host country bringing charges.

Although the action by the criminal court in the Hague was welcomed by many, and although various countries as well as the United Nations have decried the actions in Darfur, little has actually been done to stop the genocide. It shows no sign of abating any time soon.

The Least You Need to Know

- Sudan is a land divided between the North and South, and between animists, Christians, and Muslims.

- In some parts of Sudan, civil war has become a way of life.

- A peace treaty was signed in 2005, ending the latest civil war.

- Genocide is occurring in Darfur.

Hot Spots in Northern Africa

In This Chapter

- ◆ Egypt at war
- ◆ Egyptian Islamic fundamentalism
- ◆ Democracy, in Egypt?
- ◆ Muslims in Algeria
- ◆ Syria and Lebanon

Egypt's Troubles

Egypt had always been an important route to the East. And so in 1798, the French, led by Napoleon Bonaparte, invaded Egypt in an effort to control trade with the East.

Napoleon had many problems in Egypt. Grain supply was difficult to control, and the British ships occupied ports in the North. So although Napoleon tried to export numerous antiquities back to France, his ships were captured by the British (which is one reason why the British Museum

def•i•ni•tion

A **protectorate** is a relationship in which one state surrenders (or is forced to surrender) much of its sovereignty to a stronger nation.

now has one of the most extraordinary collections of Egyptian antiquities in the world). Napoleon and his French army eventually were forced to evacuate Egypt. The vacuum left by Napoleon was filled by the British, soon declaring that Egypt had become a *protectorate*.

Egypt got the Sinai back in exchange for peace.

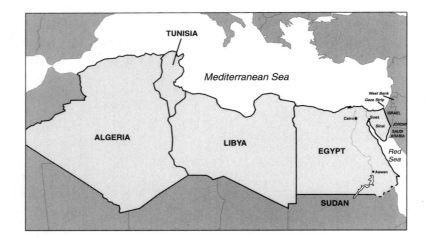

The British were eventually forced to respond to Egypt's desire to become independent and in 1922 gave them sovereignty, but not independence. Faud was made king, and he was replaced by King Faruq in 1936.

Egyptian nationalism continued to grow, and the king and his wealth drew increased criticism. In 1952, mobs rioted in Cairo as the Egyptian army officers seized control. On July 25, King Faruq abdicated the throne and Egypt was under Egyptian control for the first time in more than 2,600 years.

One of the young Egyptians who had fought against British rule for years was Gamal Abdel Nasser. In 1942, Nasser founded the secret Society of Free Officers, a group that fought for independence.

In July 1952, it was Nasser who led the army coup that deposed the king. Although General Muhammad Naguib became the head of the government, in 1954 Nasser arrested Naguib and became premier of Egypt. Nasser would lead Egypt through some of its most bitter conflicts.

The Nasser Years

Nasser would turn out to be one of the most important Arab leaders of the twentieth century. Advocating Arab unity, he undertook a series of actions to increase power to both his country and his cause.

July 26, 1956, was the fourth anniversary of King Faruk's abdication. That day, Nasser appeared in Muhammad Ali Square in Alexandria. With a huge crowd in attendance, Nasser began a three-hour speech. When he said the code word *de Lesseps*, it was the signal for Egyptian engineers and the army to take over the Suez Canal.

At this time, the canal was still owned by the Suez Canal Company, a foreign company with headquarters in Europe. The British prime minister called Nasser's actions theft.

> **Peacekeepers**
>
> Ferdinand de Lesseps came from a family that was long distinguished in the French diplomatic service. In 1832, he moved to Egypt, where he befriended the new Egyptian Viceroy. When the time came to build the Suez Canal, de Lesseps was tapped to oversee its construction. He was, therefore, a symbol of colonial rule in Egypt.

Nasser's nationalization of the canal precipitated a short-lived, abortive invasion by Great Britain, France, and Israel. The Soviet Union, its allies, and many third-world countries supported Egypt. Afraid of further escalating an already cold Cold War, the United States stated that although it opposed the nationalization of the canal, it was against the further use of force. In the end, Nasser kept the canal and promised to guarantee right of access to all ships.

Under Nasser's leadership, Egypt helped ferment pro-Arab, anti-Western feelings throughout the Arab world. For example:

◆ In 1958, Egypt and Syria formed the United Arab Republic, with Nasser as its president. He hoped this would be the first step toward Arab unity. Although the alliance with Syria ended after only three years, Nasser kept the name United Arab Republic. (The name was changed back in 1970.)

◆ In 1967, he precipitated Egypt's third war with Israel by dissolving U.N. peace-keeping forces in the Sinai (see Chapter 3). The quick war, which ended in a massive defeat for Egypt, was nothing short of a personal disaster for Nasser, and, in humiliation, he offered to resign from office.

It says much about what a beloved figure he was that the Egyptian people refused to let him quit. Massive demonstrations of support forced him to stay.

Nasser died on September 28, 1970, of a heart attack while still in office. He is probably best remembered for leading a resurgence in Arab nationalism.

Sadat Takes Over

After Nasser's death, his vice president, Anwar al-Sadat, was elected president. Although he had been one of Nasser's closest associates, Sadat set a new, independent, course. Whereas Nasser had oriented Egypt away from the West and aligned his country with the Soviet Union, Sadat kicked 20,000 Soviet military personnel out of the country 2 years after taking power.

In Egypt, if there had been one constant up until this time, it was a hatred of Israel. Sadat was no different. In 1973, he was one of the instigators of the Yom Kippur War. The war demonstrated Arab military strength, and helped boost Sadat's image in the Arab world.

Reliable Resources

The Begin-Sadat Center for Strategic Studies in Israel is dedicated to the study of Middle East peace and security.

Peacekeepers

The year 1981 was a one for attempted assassinations. Not only was Sadat killed; but also John Hinckley shot President Reagan near the chest outside the Washington Hilton Hotel; and Pope John Paul II was struck by two bullets and wounded in the abdomen, right arm, and left hand by Mehmet Ali Agca. (Both men survived their attacks.)

So it was a huge surprise when Sadat visited Israel in 1977. This visit was motivated by the economic problems Egypt faced after so many wars with Israel. The price of conflict, as Egypt had learned, was a high one. Sadat spoke of peace before the national assembly of Israel, the Knesset. This overture resulted in a peace agreement between the countries—the Camp David Accords (see Chapter 3).

Although he was rewarded with the Nobel Peace Prize in 1978 (together with Menachem Begin), the treaty with Israel isolated Egypt from the rest of the Arab world. Sadat was condemned by the Arabs for making peace with Israel, and Egypt was expelled from the Arab League.

More ominously, the rise of Islamic fundamentalism had begun to take root in Egypt, and the Islamists detested what they considered to be Sadat's capitulation. Aware of this growing threat, in September 1981, Sadat arrested almost 2,000 dissidents, Islamists, and communists. Not coincidentally, a month later he was assassinated at a military parade in Cairo.

The Rise of Islamic Fundamentalism

After Sadat's death, his successor, Hosni Mubarak, was elected president. Under his direction, Egypt endeavored to become a moderate Arab nation. But the rise of Islamic fundamentalism was impossible to root out because its roots run deep.

Islamic fundamentalism began in Egypt in 1928 when the Muslim Brotherhood was formed. Preaching a return to Islamic values, the group developed a huge following in the 1940s when it committed a series of political assassinations. There was a brief respite for the government after the new regime of the charismatic Nasser took power.

But in 1954, Nasser became the next target while speaking to a crowd in the Mediterranean city of Alexandria. The assassination attempt failed, Nasser had hundreds of Muslim Brothers arrested, and the movement was crushed for another 20 years. After Nasser's death, Sadat decided to let the leaders out of prison in an amnesty effort. But he had opened Pandora's box; it was an Islamic fundamentalist who plotted Sadat's killing.

Islamic groups were then repressed again by Mubarak. But in the 1980s, they slowly regained strength. They took control of many powerful unions and professional associations, set up numerous charities, enjoyed growing support, and established a network of schools and hospitals in an effort to gain legitimacy.

But the government fought back. New laws were introduced to reverse their power in the unions, and the government began to keep a tight watch on all charitable institutions. Nevertheless, by the early 1990s, two organizations, Islamic Jihad and the Islamic Group, continued to flourish. How serious is this threat? Consider that Egypt's Islamic Jihad is headed by Ayman al-Zawahiri, Osama bin Laden's right-hand man.

The problem for modern Egypt is that corruption and poverty help foster huge slums around the country, and that in turn fosters the desire for something different, something better. As in other countries in this region, Islamic fundamentalism offers that something. Until those problems are addressed, Islamic fundamentalists are likely to remain a fact of life in Egypt.

Egyptians Go to the Polls

As has been examined throughout this section of this book, the Middle East is a land basically bereft of democracy and western values such as a free press, an independent judiciary, free speech, and a respect for pluralism. That is why President George W. Bush's attempt to plant a democracy in Iraq, in the heart of the Middle East, is both controversial and bold. The odds are long, but if it succeeds, all bets are off. It radically changes the Middle East equation, which begs the question: Will it succeed?

Maybe. As explained in this chapter and others, democracy does seem to be taking hold, albeit gingerly, in various parts of the Middle East. The Palestinian Authority has held elections, as has Lebanon. Now even Egypt has ostensibly hopped on the Middle East democracy bandwagon.

In early September 2005, Egyptians went to the polls in what was being billed as the country's first-ever contested presidential election. Ten candidates, including incumbent president Hosni Mubarak, vied for the presidency, although because no one really knew any candidate except Mubarak, the outcome seemed to be a formality. And it was. President Mubarak "won" with 88 percent of the vote, although only 23 percent of the electorate bothered to vote, and opposition candidates alleged that the election was a fraud.

Still, it is a start.

Algeria Has Its Own Problems

The rise of Islam has also affected that other large country in northern Africa, Algeria. And Algeria, with its strong French influence, has endeavored to remain a secular country, even if that requires implementing martial law.

The French conquered Algeria in 1830 and ruled it for more than 100 years. Pressure for independence began in the early 1950s with the formation of the *Front de Liberation Nationale* (FLN). The Algerian war for independence resulted from French resistance to Algerian desires for freedom.

The Algerian war for independence was more brutal than most; it is estimated to have led to one million casualties. Independence was finally achieved in 1962, bringing to power an FLN-controlled government under Ahmed Ben Bella. Ben Bella was subsequently deposed by Houari Boumedienne, who ruled until his death in December 1978.

In 1990, local elections were held. Although the FLN secured another majority, Islamic parties made a surprisingly strong showing, frightening the ruling FLN party officials. The most prominent of these new Islamic parties was the Islamic Salvation Front (FIS). So strong were they, and so strong was the growing Islamist movement, that in January 1992, FIS won a resounding victory in national elections.

The Algerian government proved itself to be a repressive regime when it immediately annulled the election results and declared a state of emergency. The military took over complete control of the country, with the support and collaboration of civil servants and intelligence officials.

A brutal civil war was the inevitable result. In 1994, the government distributed arms to villagers. This was necessary because 400 villagers had just been killed by machete-wielding Islamic rebels.

So far, since the outbreak of violence, some 80,000 people have been killed in Algeria. The police arrest leaders of the Islamic movement one day, and the next day they kill others. Islamists then retaliate. The cycle of violence continues, and war goes on.

Syria Leave Lebanon

Long ago, Beirut, Lebanon, was considered the "Paris of the Middle East" because of its big, broad streets, beautiful architecture, and peaceful way of life. But that indeed was long ago—pre-1975. In the early 1970s an influx of Palestinians, including the PLO and Yasser Arafat, began to change this cosmopolitan capital.

In 1975, a bloody civil war broke out between the ruling Christian Maronites on one side and the interloping Palestinians and other Muslims on the other, leaving the country in tatters and without a strong central government. The next year, Lebanon's neighbor Syria sent 40,000 troops into the country, ostensibly to protect the Maronites.

Syria had no intention of leaving, and it stayed in Lebanon, controlling the state apparatus and effectively running the country as its surrogate for the next few decades. At the same time, southern Lebanon continued to be used as a staging ground for PLO attacks on Israel, causing Israel to invade for a short time in 1978.

In 1982, two events of note occurred in Lebanon. First, Israel invaded southern Lebanon again, this time with the intent of forcing out the PLO and creating a buffer zone. Second, an international peacekeeping force led by the United States landed in the country to help facilitate a PLO withdrawal as well as a Syrian withdrawal from Beirut. Although the PLO did in fact leave Lebanon, Syria continued to run the war-torn country, and Israel continued to occupy southern Lebanon.

The Lebanese civil war lasted for 15 years, until 1990. In a peace deal negotiated by the Arab League, political power was eventually transferred away from the Christian Maronite minority and given to the Muslim majority (The Maronites had gained

Landmine!

On October 23, 1983, a truck loaded with explosives crashed through a barbed wire fence at the Beirut airport and barreled through several military checkpoints. The truck crashed into the barracks where U.S. Marines were stationed, and the suicide bomber driving the truck detonated 120,000 pounds of TNT. A total of 241 Marines were killed.

power during French colonial rule.) Yet despite the peace agreement, Syria still stayed. (In 2000, Israel withdrew from southern Lebanon.)

For 15 years, from the end of the war until early 2005, Lebanon lived in relative peace and recovered from its war years (estimated dead: 100,000). Then, on February 12, 2005, popular former Prime Minister Rafik Hariri was assassinated in a car-bomb attack. It was widely believed that Syria was responsible for this attack because Hariri had been publicly defying Syria's ruler Bashar al-Assad.

Spontaneous mass anti-Syrian demonstrations then erupted in Beirut, calling for the ouster of the Syrian-led government. Although pro-Syrian demonstrations were organized, they had little impact. On March 14, 2005, a month after the demonstrations had begun, almost one million Lebanese protestors demanded an investigation into Hariri's murder and the ouster of Syria from their country. The writing was on the wall.

By the end of the next month, Syria had in fact withdrawn the last of its troops from Lebanon, due to international pressure, as well as strong Lebanese anti-Syrian sentiment. In May, elections were held in Lebanon, and the son of the assassinated leader, Saad Hariri, won a majority and became the country's new political leader.

The Least You Need to Know

- Egyptian Islamic Fundamentalism is on the rise.
- Egypt had its first contested election in 2005.
- Algeria's military government is at odds with its Muslim population.
- Syria left Lebanon after 29 years in 2005.

Part 3

Central and Southern Africa

In terms of conflict, Africa can be proud that the most intransigent of conflicts—the one between Africans and Afrikaners in South Africa—was peacefully resolved.

But on the rest of the continent, the brutality and mayhem that are part of everyday life are almost too horrific to believe.

10

Death Around the Horn

In This Chapter

- ◆ Ethiopian civil war
- ◆ Ethiopian famine
- ◆ Eritrea wants independence
- ◆ Somalia falls to pieces

No continent on Earth is more wracked with mindless violence, conflict, and bloodshed than Africa. Military dictators readily steal money and goods intended for their country, callous to the desperate blight that daily surrounds them. This senseless greed and need for power, when combined with famine and poverty, has become a recipe for unimaginable disaster.

Ethiopia

Ethiopia is a country that prides itself on its independence. In 1896, Italy attempted to invade Ethiopia, but was rebuffed. However, in 1935, Italy was finally able to invade the country, and Ethiopian King Haile Selassie was forced to flee to British protection. However, in 1940, Italy entered World War II and was occupied with other matters, so Selassie was able to return to Africa, and in 1941, he re-entered Ethiopia and regained his throne.

The Horn of Africa is a dangerous place.

Reliable Resources

Jamaican Black Nationalist Marcus Garvey said in 1920, "Look to Africa, for when a black king shall be crowned, the day of deliverance is at hand." The prophesy was to be fulfilled in 1930 when Ras Tafari, who claimed to be a direct descendant of King David, was crowned emperor Haile Selassie 1 of Ethiopia.

Despite financial support from the United States, Ethiopia remained an underdeveloped, undemocratic country. In 1960, although Selassie was able to crush a revolt by a group of young army officers who were demanding an end to oppression and poverty, dissatisfaction with the Ethiopian monarchy grew.

By 1974, the desire for reform had hit a crescendo, and the army was able to seize more and more control from the king. Haile Selassie was slowly stripped of his powers and finally, on September 12, 1974, deposed in a palace coup. He was murdered in prison at the orders of the coup leaders in 1975.

Is This Place Coup Coup or What?

In Africa, it seems, the only thing worse than your present leader is the next one. The Ethiopian coup leaders suspended the constitution, parliament was dissolved, a Marxist-Leninist course was plotted, and Colonel Haile Mengistu became head of the government. Under his regime, thousands of political opponents were crushed, property was confiscated, and defense spending was greatly increased. Soon enough, Mengistu wielded absolute power.

In 1976, Mengistu began a campaign that he officially dubbed the "Red Terror." At a rally in the capital of Addis Ababa, he threw to the ground before a huge crowd bottles filled with a red substance representing the blood of enemies of the revolution. The time was now, he told his audience, to root them out. In particular, the campaign targeted students and young people suspected of membership in the Ethiopian People's Revolutionary Party, a group opposed to the petit dictator.

Thousands of young men and women turned up dead in the streets of Ethiopia in the next two years. Not only were they murdered by roaming militias, but what's worse is that these students were fingered by local neighborhood watch committees who served during this period as security surveillance units for the militias.

Landmine!

When victims' families attempted to reclaim their loved ones' bodies for burial, the watch committees required the families to reimburse the committee for the price of the bullets used to kill the victims.

The process of elimination was well organized. Neighborhood committees met and discussed potential suspects. After a decision had been made, each member of the committee would then sign documents to confirm the decision that had been reached at the meeting. These decisions were then sent on to the party, which would in turn condemn the suspected counterrevolutionaries to death, thus leaving a huge paper trail of murder. The Mengistu regime was able to pay for its mass murder with help from the Soviet Union. The USSR, caught up as it was in its own Cold War, saw Mengistu as a potential ally. Because the Horn of Africa borders the Red Sea, and because Ethiopia had been an American puppet during the Selassie years, the strategic importance of the country was obvious. Pouring weapons and money into the corrupt Mengistu regime, as well as Cuban troops and "special advisers," Moscow gained itself a puppet and helped fuel the fire that would engulf the region for decades.

However, even as he was murdering his own people, Mengistu faced two other problems. On one hand, a longstanding dispute with Somalia regarding the border erupted anew. Similarly, another longstanding dispute with Eritrea was revived when the Ethiopian province began its war of liberation. With the Eritreans attacking in the North, Somalis in the South, and counter-revolutionaries to kill in the middle, the Mengistu regime diverted all monies to the army to fight its many enemies, both real and perceived.

War and Famine

As a result of all this incessant warfare, the Ethiopian people had one of the lowest standards of living in the world. Then, in 1984, things got worse. A famine hit; the Ethiopian harvest looked likely to be very poor that year.

In March, according to BBC Online's Kate Milner, the Ethiopian government stated that five million people were at risk of starvation. Aid agencies put the number at six million.

Despite the very real threat of mass starvation, Western governments were hesitant to get involved. As the BBC has noted, the West feared the military government of Mengistu might steal and spend the incoming aid money. And yet, the specter of starvation forced their hand; food and aid began to pour into the country.

The fears turned out to be prophetic:

- Delivery by the Mengistu government of incoming aid to the needy was sporadic at best.
- Food for civilian famine victims was diverted to feed troops.

With the situation as dire as it was, relief organizations appealed for more help anyway, but Western governments balked. Aid agencies were forced to buy grain on the open market. By October 1984, eight million people were in danger of starvation.

What fended off this potential disaster was a wave of increased television and newspaper coverage throughout Western Europe and the United States. Public donations flooded in; the U.K. public alone gave $8 million in one three-day period. With Western awareness now high, people wanted to help, including musicians. Two Live Aid concerts and the hit single "Do They Know It's Christmas?" alone provided millions of dollars for relief efforts.

The worst was over. Unfortunately, drought and famine are recurrent problems in Ethiopia.

Is This the End of Mengistu?

The end of the Cold War meant that Ethiopia would have to face its wars, insurgents, and drought by itself without Soviet aid. That it could not do. After the 17 years of Mengistu's dictatorship, the economy was in shambles, and civil unrest had grown beyond the control of the military.

In May 1991, two secessionist forces closed in on Addis Ababa, and Mengistu fled the country. He was eventually granted asylum in Zimbabwe. A transitional government consisting of a coalition of 27 political organizations came to power, and set out to transform Ethiopia into a free and democratic nation.

The new government inherited six million people facing famine, a shattered economy, and no funds. Despite all the problems, the new government steered the country toward democracy, giving Eritrea its freedom and establishing a commission to prosecute war crimes. May 1995 saw the first parliamentary elections, and Meles Zenawi was confirmed as prime minister.

In 1995, Mengistu was tried *in absentia* and found guilty on charges of mass murder, relating to the assassination of Emperor Selassie and the deaths of thousands of his political opponents during the Red Terror period.

Reliable Resources

Threatened by the turmoil surrounding the famine and the impending collapse of the Mengistu regime were some 14,000 Ethiopian Jews. Rather than let them die, Israel sent in relief planes, airlifted them out of chaos, and brought them to Israel to be resettled.

def•i•ni•tion

When a person who is on trial is not present for the proceedings, he is **in absentia;** literally, he is absent.

Eritrea Fights for Freedom

Eritrea lies next door to Ethiopia, separating that country from the Red Sea. Like so many other African countries, Eritreans, long part of other countries and empires, also wanted their freedom.

Italy ruled Eritrea from the end of the nineteenth century, but in 1941, Allied forces forced Italy out of the country. Thereafter, it was administered by the British military. Set to divide the country along religious lines, Britain decided to give the coast and highland areas to Eritrea's neighbor Ethiopia, and the Muslim-inhabited northern and western lowlands to British-ruled Sudan.

But the Eritreans wanted independence, and so, in 1952, the United Nations created the Eritrean-Ethiopian federation. In 1962, Haile Selassie ended the federation. A civil war ensued and lasted for the better part of 30 years. Finally, with the overthrow of the Mengistu regime, Eritrea was finally given its independence.

For a while, Ethiopia and Eritrea got along well. Ethiopia no longer had a border along the Red Sea; and therefore, had to go through Eritrea to ship and trade goods. Eritrea introduced its own currency in 1997, which destabilized the Ethiopian economy, such as it was. As a result, tensions rose. In 1998, of course, these two neighbors, who had once been part of the same country, decided war was the way to resolve their differences.

The war between Eritrea and Ethiopia has been brutal. More than 100,000 people have been killed, probably 1 million have been displaced, and hundreds of millions of dollars has been diverted into war instead of development.

Both Ethiopia and Eritrea have since been accused of gross human rights violations. Amnesty International reports that the Ethiopian authorities detain a large number of Eritreans simply because of their Eritrean heritage, while also recruiting child soldiers for the front lines.

As if this were not enough turmoil, severe drought threatens both Eritrea and Ethiopia. On the Horn of Africa, some places have gone without enough rain for up to two or three years.

On December 12, 2000, the two countries ended hostilities (for now) by signing an internationally brokered peace agreement. Whether it will hold is only as predictable as the rains.

> **Peacekeepers**
>
> U.N. Secretary General Kofi Annan said the agreement represents "victory for the voice of reason, for power of diplomacy and for the recognition that neither one of these countries—nor the continent as a whole—can afford another decade, another year, another day of conflict."

Somalia

Americans know of Somalia because of a failed rescue mission in 1993. But that is only a small slice of the sorrow that is Somalia. Like so many countries in Africa, Somalia was devastated by colonial rule and has yet to resolve the conflicts that resulted.

During the colonial era, the British were able to control the northern part of Somalia. In southern Somalia, Italy was the main colonizer, acquiring its first possession in 1888 when the sultan of Hobyo agreed to Italian "protection."

Following Italy's defeat in World War II, the British established military administrations in what had been Italian Somaliland; almost all Somali-inhabited territories were now under British rule.

Political protests and a desire for independence in 1956 forced Britain to introduce representative government in its Somali protectorate. Accordingly, in 1957, the Legislative Council was established, composed of six members appointed by the governor to represent the principal clan-families that make up Somalia.

Although unified as a single nation at independence, the South and the North were, in actuality, two separate countries. Italian and British rule had left the country divided, with separate administrative, legal, and education systems in which affairs were conducted in different languages. Police, taxes, and even the currencies differed. Educated elites had different interests, and economic contacts between the two regions were virtually nonexistent. Somalia was one country in name only.

Nevertheless, in 1960 the first elections were held. Muhammad Igaal was chosen as prime minister. During the nine-year period of parliamentary democracy and stability that followed Somali independence, politics was a rambunctious, open, heated affair, and freedom of expression was widely accepted.

Peacekeepers

Women have long had political rights in Somalia. They have voted in Italian Somaliland elections since 1958, and suffrage was extended to women in former British Somaliland as well in 1963.

All Good Things Must Come to an End

As it is throughout the African continent, paramilitary groups run roughshod over civilians when they don't like what is happening in the country. On October 15, 1969, a bodyguard killed the Somali president while Prime Minister Igaal was out of the country. Igaal returned to the capital of Mogadishu to arrange for the selection of a new president. His choice was a member of the Daarood clan-family, even though Igaal was of the Isaaq clan.

Army officers, unhappy with the choice, decided to take matters into their own hands. Capturing strategic points around Mogadishu and rounding up government officials and other prominent political figures, the military staged a coup. With the help of local police, who supported the coup, army commander Major General Muhammad Siad Barre assumed leadership of Somalia.

Of course, one of Siad Barre's first acts was to prohibit the existence of any political association. He then plotted a socialist course for the country, despite the fact that

Somalia had no history of class conflict. To be more precise, Siad Barre explained that his official ideology consisted of three elements, which he called "scientific socialism":

◆ Community development based on self-reliance

◆ Marxist socialism

◆ Islam

Siad Barre was a dictator, like so many dictators who ran rampant through the world in the 1960s and 1970s. Clearly enamored of the cult of personality that Mao Tse Tung had fostered in China, Siad Barre soon began to call himself Somalia's "Victorious Leader." Portraits of him in the company of Marx and Lenin littered the streets. Advice from this paternalistic leader, who claimed he had found a uniquely Somali path to socialist revolution, were widely distributed in Siad Barre's little blue-and-white book.

> **Landmine!**
>
> The arsenal in the streets is awesome. I went to the main arms market—the baqara market. Everything is on sale here including anti-aircraft missiles. The only restriction to the sale is that you must belong to the Hawiye clan.
>
> —Hussein Ali Soke, correspondent for *Africa Conflict Journal*

But power corrupts, and absolute power corrupts absolutely. Siad Barre became a tyrant, and by the early 1980s, his grip on power was slipping as criticism of his repressive regime came from both inside and outside the country. Faced with shrinking popularity and an armed and organized domestic resistance, Siad Barre did what all dictators do—he unleashed his private army on his enemies, mainly the three clans who opposed him: the Majeerteen, the Hawiye, and the Isaaq.

Things Get Worse

In November 1986, Siad Barre's elite and dreaded Red Berets began to terrorize Somalia's citizens. While the people were distracted, government ministers and bureaucrats plundered what was left of the national treasury. Chaos reigned.

Clans were systematically targeted and murdered. These genocidal actions were waged first against the Majeerteen clan, then against the Isaaq clans of the North, and finally against the Hawiye, who occupied the strategic central area of the country, including the capital of Mogadishu.

The powerful Hawiye clan organized an armed resistance. Faced with increasing opposition, Siad Barre finally ordered his Red Berets to kill ordinary civilians who seemed to oppose him, regardless of their clan affiliation. By 1989, torture and murder had become commonplace in Mogadishu.

On July 9, 1989, Somalia's Italian-born Roman Catholic bishop was gunned down by an unknown assassin in his church in Mogadishu. It was a widely held belief that Siad Barre ordered the hit.

Soon thereafter, the Red Berets killed 450 Muslims who were demonstrating against the treatment of the leaders. Then, on July 15, 47 more people were executed.

The regime grew desperate. At an anti–Siad Barre demonstration, people began to riot, causing army officials to panic and open fire on the demonstrators, killing almost 100 people. A week later came the Stadia Corna Affair, when Siad Barre sentenced to death 46 prominent intellectuals who had been calling for elections and improved human rights.

Things came to a head when, on July 13, a besieged Siad Barre dropped the charges. As the city celebrated, the president was forced to retreat into his bunker in his military barracks to save himself.

After Siad Barre was deposed in January 1991, anarchy ensued. The people of the northern regions declared the independent state of Somaliland. Political leaders in the southern regions refused to acknowledge this. Power throughout the land was contested by heavily armed guerrilla movements based on clan loyalties. Savage struggles for economic assets by the various factions led to anarchy and famine.

Black Hawk Down

Somalia was now without a central government. As warlords gained hold, stealing food and money wherever they went, famine and poverty spread rapidly. The subsequent fighting among rival faction leaders resulted in the killing, dislocation, and starvation of thousands of Somalis.

In 1992, the United Nations decided to intervene militarily. As part of this effort, the United States created Operation Restore Hope. Eighteen hundred American Marines landed in Mogadishu on December 9, 1992: The first of nearly 30,000 troops to arrive with the mission of restoring some semblance of order.

Over the next 2 years, about 50,000 Somalis were killed in factional fighting, and an estimated 200,000 died of starvation. It became impossible to transport relief supplies through the war-torn country without rebels killing the messenger and stealing food intended for the starving. Mogadishu had become the most dangerous city in the world, and 14 armed factions, each led by its own warlord, were fighting to dominate Somalia.

Peacekeepers

Every American has seen the shocking images from Somalia. The scope of suffering there is hard to imagine. Only the United States has the global reach to place a large security force on the ground in such a distant place quickly and efficiently, and thus save thousands of innocents from death.

—President George Bush, Oval Office address, December 1992

On August 26, 1993, a U.S. Army task force flew into Mogadishu. The Rangers' mission was to capture a local warlord named Mohammed Aidid, a man thought to be the most successful of the many warlords vying for power. Aidid's authority was absolute and feudal within his main power base in south Mogadishu.

October 3, 1993, was a Sunday. Seventeen helicopters took off from their base at the airport. This raid would take the Rangers into the heart of Aidid's territory. Intelligence had it that Aidid was meeting with his associates. According to Ranger Jason Moore, as the helicopters came in to where Aidid was supposed to be, "We heard a loud explosion, and the whole helicopter shook. And the two door gunners just started screaming, 'Go! Go! Go! We're taking fire! Get out of the bird.'"

The next morning, Somalis celebrated the downing of not one but two American helicopters. Eighteen Americans were dead. More than 80 were wounded. One was being held prisoner. U.S. troops had come to help feed a starving Somalia. Now Somalis dragged an American soldier's body through the streets.

Terrorists in Somalia

It shouldn't be surprising that, given the lawlessness that is Somalia, as well as it being a Muslim country, Osama bin Laden's al-Qaeda terrorists have found it to be both a perfect breeding ground and a great hiding place. "Somalia has been a place that has harbored al-Qaeda and, to my knowledge, still is," said U.S. Defense Secretary Donald Rumsfeld in 2002.

Since 1995, the United States had gathered intelligence about terrorist cells in Somalia through its embassies in Nairobi and Addis Ababa. Renewed U.S. interest in Somalia began within days after the September 11 attacks, when a Somali group, Al Ittihaad Al Islamiya (Islamic Unity), appeared on the U.S. hit list of foreign terrorist organizations. The United States claimed that Islamic Unity had links with Osama bin Laden. It also believed that al-Qaeda fighters helped in the 1993 killings of those 18 American servicemen, and that Somalia subsequently hosted terrorist training camps.

After the American War on Terror began, the United States also decided to freeze the assets of al-Barakaat, a money-transfer company based in Somalia, saying it had evidence that Barakaat funneled millions of dollars to al-Qaeda.

As the American hunt for bin Laden escalated, some speculated that the terrorist might have been hiding in Somalia. But by and large, Somalis thought that bin Laden would be stupid to hide out there: The $25 million on his head would be too great a temptation.

"We would hand him over to the international court and claim the money," said Mogadishu Police Chief Hassan Awaale. "We have enough problems of our own without more from this man."

The Least You Need to Know

- The Ethiopian civil war has killed or displaced millions.

- Relief efforts to help the Ethiopian famine were thwarted by the government and the military.

- Eritrea fought for independence for 30 years, and then went to war against Ethiopia.

- Somalia is a ruined country.

Chapter 11

Insanity in West Africa

In This Chapter

- ◆ European domination
- ◆ Sierra Leone scrapes the bottom of the barrel
- ◆ Liberia's wacky dictator
- ◆ Senegal's secession
- ◆ Nigeria: Oil and politics don't mix

Although nomadic tribes have lived in West Africa for thousands of years, the first permanent settlements did not exist until about 800 B.C.E. These tribes settled in the rain forests along the coast and in the river basins to the North. They were hunters and gatherers, thriving on the plentiful animal and vegetable populations in the area. The religion of these early tribes was based on mythology and magic and often involved sun worship.

Although several empires rose and fell, none of these centers of influence was prepared for what came next: the power of Allah in the seventh century. Many tribes throughout West Africa converted to Islam. In the sixteenth century, European explorers arrived, and it was this clash of values and power—European versus Islamic—that would affect West Africa for the next 400 years.

West Africa is awash in blood.

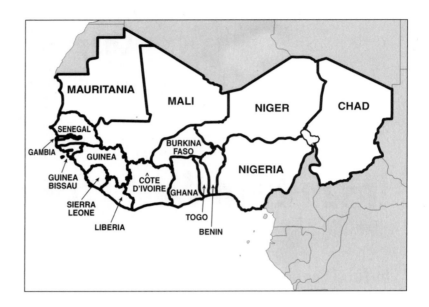

Take, Rattle, and Roll

Led by promises of the untold wealth that lay in the inner kingdoms of West Africa, several European nations soon had outposts in the area. Before long, the regions of the continent were renamed to reflect the products that were being taken: Ivory Coast, Gold Coast, Slave Coast.

> ### Reliable Resources
> How big was the slave trade? Between 11 and 20 million people were stolen and sent across the Atlantic Ocean.

Colonialism in this part of Africa reached its peak in 1895 with the establishment of French West Africa. Thereafter, the French dominated the region for several decades. England dominated along the Gambia River, and down the coast in Ghana, Portugal kept its colony in present-day Guinea-Bissau until the 1970s.

> ### Reliable Resources
> The European colonial empires are said to have held sway over more than 85 percent of the rest of the globe by the advent of World War I.

After World War II, European colonists began to lose influence as a pan-African movement toward independence emerged. For most countries, this culminated with independence around 1960. But because the goal of colonialism was to plunder the natural resources of a country for the good of the empire, and keeping people poor and uneducated supported that goal, the newly freed countries of Africa had a difficult time making the transition from feudal colony to free society.

Underdeveloped, stricken by poverty, torn between Western ways and Muslim values, uneducated for the most part, with few resources to export and little industry, these countries started down the road to freedom with more than their share of problems. The brutal conflicts that followed were ample evidence of this.

Sierra Leone: Making Kosovo Look Good

How bad have things been in Sierra Leone? According to Amnesty International, civilians continued to be deliberately and arbitrarily killed, mutilated, raped, and abducted a year after the peace agreement between the government of Sierra Leone and the Revolutionary United Front (RUF) was signed.

In 1991, a little-known corporal, Foday Sankoh, declared to the one-party government of then-President Joseph Saidu Momoh that unless multiparty elections were held within 90 days, the RUF would launch an armed campaign to overthrow the government. The rebels were embittered over what they saw as a corrupt elite that took over following the end of British rule in 1961. Poor rural people increasingly resented the richer ruling class of Freetown (the capital) while battles to control the wealth of the country's lucrative diamond mines further fanned the flames of conflict.

> **Peacekeepers**
>
> Sierra Leone was founded by repatriated slaves. In 1789, the first freed slaves arrived from Great Britain. In 1792, more came from Nova Scotia, and in 1800, even more came from Jamaica. In 1808, Sierra Leone became a British colony.

Unwilling to cede power, President Momoh was ready to fight. The rebels in turn knew that alone their forces would have a hard time displacing the powers that be, so they formed an alliance with Liberian rebel leader Charles Taylor. Together, they launched a war against the Sierra Leone government.

It first seemed that the rebels were nothing but a puppet movement—an offshoot of Liberian fighting factions. But the Sierra Leone rebellion soon took on a life of its own, attracting disaffected young men from the country's impoverished countryside. A gun gave these fighters power and the chance to avenge themselves on a society that often offered them little.

Reliable Resources

When the rebels reached the city, in a matter of days they are said to have amputated the limbs of around 1,500 people.

As the rebellion got underway, a group of army soldiers arrived in the capital of Freetown in 1992, ostensibly to demand better pay and conditions. In actuality, their mission was to overthrow the government. Due to rapidly deteriorating social conditions, the coup was extremely popular.

The RUF, struggling as it was to make headway, decided to attack economic targets, focusing on the diamond-rich Kono district. It worked, and by 1994, the military situation had tilted in their direction, depriving the government of its major source of revenue, the diamond trade. Bolstered by its success, the RUF overran titanium and bauxite mines in 1995, two of the biggest employers in the country and major sources of state income.

Landmine!

An often-cited U.N. report describes an incident in which a rebel commander ordered that all virgin girls report for a physical examination. Those who passed a virginity test were dispersed among the RUF soldiers. Most of the girls were younger than 15. The United Nations says it presumes that every abducted girl was sexually assaulted.

A Campaign of Systematic Torture

Although the rebel RUF has called the various governments corrupt and accused them of mismanagement of diamond and mineral resources, which might well be true, the fact is, the rebels are a heartless, ruthless band of animals.

Unlike most wars—where civilian causalities are an unfortunate by-product of the fighting between the combatants—the RUF stands out for its policy of deliberately targeting civilians. Human Rights Watch took testimony from dozens of survivors and witnesses of gross violations of human rights committed by the RUF on Sierra Leonean civilians. They included the following:

- Machete lacerations to the head, neck, arms, legs, feet, and torso
- The gouging out of one or both eyes
- Rape
- Gunshot wounds to the head, torso, and limbs

- Burns from explosives and other devices
- Injections with acid
- Genital mutilation

The RUF also introduced a particularly new phenomenon to civil conflicts: the amputation of limbs as a tool of terror. The RUF uses two types of amputation: the "short sleeve," where the arm is amputated close to the shoulder; and the "long sleeve," where the arm is amputated at the wrist. Human Rights Watch found ample machete amputation evidence among civilians of one or both hands, arms, feet, legs, ears, and buttocks as well as one or more fingers.

Sending Children to War

Both sides have also used a large number of child soldiers. The United Nations estimates that of those that fought with Sierra Leone government forces, a quarter are teenagers below the age of 18.

Children have told Human Rights Watch they were forced to kill and commit atrocities. A teenager described removing the heart and liver from his victims for food. He decided to join the rebels only after discovering that his pregnant mother had been murdered. He wanted revenge.

According to Human Rights Watch, children have been forced to witness the murder of their own parents, and the organization also has described how RUF rebels would inscribe "AFRC" (for Armed Forces Revolutionary Council) on children's chests with a razor blade after kidnapping them.

UNICEF says that many of the children who have been released are "malnourished, haggard, and in tattered clothing." Many of the girls were pregnant, and most of the children suffered from various ailments.

> **Landmine!**
>
> A young girl's report: "We went to find wood in a village, and one of the rebels grabbed me. He made me pound rice and wash his clothes, and he was the one who had sex with me. I begged him to let me go, but he said, 'I'm going to have sex with you until they disarm us.' I wanted so much to escape, but he kept saying he'd kill me if I ever tried to get away. Some days I complained to his wife. She was so nice. She sympathized and said she too had been abducted. I'm only 11 years old."

Is Peace Possible?

Practically half the country's 4.5 million inhabitants were displaced by the war. Another half million became refugees in neighboring countries, and at least 50,000 died in the fighting, and there are an estimated 100,000 mutilation victims. The economy is in ruins, and the national infrastructure needed to run the country has effectively collapsed.

The cost of conflict is higher than the price of peace.

In 1999, the United Nations brokered a peace deal. The so-called Lomé Peace Accord was characterized by a British diplomat as "a very dirty deal, but unfortunately the only one available." It was dirty because, although it did require the rebels to disarm, it also provides amnesty for the rebels. Their years of mayhem would go unpunished, and many believed the agreement therefore tacitly, if unwittingly, condoned their actions. Yet almost as soon as it was signed, the agreement was being violated by the rebels.

The United Nations then sent in peacekeepers to oversee RUF disarmament, troops eventually numbering some 13,000. British military support for the peacekeepers and the Sierra Leone government army finally helped to stabilize the situation. With the help of British troops who were providing security, Sierra Leone was better able to contain the rebels.

The United Nations has especially tried to enforce the disarmament of the rebels near various diamond-rich areas that the rebels controlled. The RUF used the diamonds to fund their atrocities and so the U.N. Security Council imposed an 18-month ban on diamond exports from Sierra Leone.

With the help of the international community, Sierra Leone began to return to a bit of normalcy. The disarmament campaign became a main priority and successfully took weapons out of the hands of perpetrators. In fact, early in 2002, the last remaining 11 rebel commanders handed their guns to United Nations peacekeepers, which it is hoped will end one of Africa's most brutal wars. Peace was finally at hand.

The irony is that Sierra Leone remains one of the poorest countries in the world, despite its vast set of natural resources and minerals, including one of the world's great caches of diamonds.

Peacekeepers

Diamonds were discovered in Sierra Leone in 1930. In 1998, the international diamond industry produced an estimated 115 million carats, which, at the end of the diamond chain, is worth close to $50 billion.

Liberia

Founded in 1822 by freed African American slaves, Liberia became a republic in 1847. After a military coup in 1980, Samuel Doe became Liberia's President in 1986. Doe was pro-Western, but his regime was unstable. The Doe government adopted ever-increasing repressive measures to maintain control, but even so, in 1989, violence erupted after another failed coup. Civil war ensued as three factions fought for power: troops loyal to Doe and two rebel groups. One of them was led by Charles Taylor. The other was led by Prince Yormie Johnson.

In 1990, Doe was deposed and shot. Although Johnson became president, he would last only a short time. The presidency passed through several hands, settling soon with Amos Sawyer, who managed to pacify some parts of the country.

Taylor and his guerrillas nevertheless kept up the fight. To complicate matters further, even more guerrilla groups formed and fought in the war. Two hundred fifty thousand people had died, and more than a million were either internally displaced or had become refugees in other parts of the world.

Yet in August 1995, to the surprise of many, six years of brutal civil war came to an end as the main factions signed a peace agreement. A six-person ruling council took control of the country, and elections were scheduled for 1997. When the elections were finally held, the overwhelming winner was the former warlord, half-American, fugitive from justice, and now politician, Charles Taylor, with 75 percent of the vote.

Although it seemed that Liberia might finally be on the road to peace, it was not. By 2001, rebels now opposing the Taylor government attacked. In May that year, Taylor remobilized the army.

Taylor also called on his old friends, the rebels in neighboring Sierra Leone, for support. Yet he got little help because Taylor has few actual friends in West Africa. In Sierra Leone, for example, they resent his support of the RUF terrorists. In 2003, the United Nations justice tribunal called for the arrest of Charles Taylor, charging him with war crimes, and issued a warrant for his arrest. Among his alleged crimes: crimes

Peacekeepers

The state-owned Liberian Broadcasting System can hardly compete against Charles Taylor–owned Liberian Communication Network (LCN). LCN owns a television station, two radio stations, and two newspapers.

against humanity, and harboring al-Qaeda operatives responsible for the 1998 bombings on U.S. embassies in Tanzania and Kenya.

In August of that year, Taylor resigned and fled to Nigeria. In November, 2003, the U.S. offered a reward of $2 million for the arrest of Taylor and he is now on Interpol's "Most Wanted" list, though he remains free, safe in Nigeria.

Senegal

In Senegal's southern Casamance province, the Movement of Democratic Forces in the Casamance (MFDC) are waging a bloody independence campaign. Due to flaws in recent elections, the government has had much difficulty defusing the MFDC secessionist rebellion.

> **Reliable Resources**
>
> Senegal joined with Gambia to form Senegambia in 1982. It was dissolved in 1989.

In 1997, an escalation of fighting in Casamance between the government and the rebels caused many civilians to flee their villages. Rebel forces reportedly were responsible for, as is their wont in Africa, killings, disappearances, and torture.

MFDC rebels have reportedly used land mines in the Casamance in an effort to terrorize. It is estimated that up to 80 percent of the usable land in some areas has been rendered unusable because of the mines.

The government is no better. In a February 1998 report, Amnesty International alleged that numerous Senegalese civilians have been killed by the government. AI further charges that the victims were buried in secret in hidden mass graves.

Government forces were also suspected of the August 1997 death of a leader of the MFDC who was found murdered. Although no group claimed responsibility for the killing and no direct proof of guilt has emerged, Amnesty International attributed responsibility for the death to the government.

> **Peacekeepers**
>
> Roughly 700 million people live in Africa—about 10 percent of the world's population.

In 1999, the government and the rebels met and began negotiations on the future of the Casamance. An immediate cease-fire was agreed to. Although they also agreed to meet at least once a month, little progress has been made. (Despite the truce, the MFDC's armed wing continues to fight.)

Nigeria

It seems that no matter which country you pick in Africa, the recipe is almost always the same, give or take an ingredient or two:

- A government is elected.

- A rebel group opposes it.

- The government's leader is ousted by a coup.

- Civil war breaks out.

- Atrocities occur.

- The United Nations intervenes.

- Peace is restored (at least until the next coup!).

And so it is in Nigeria. Nigeria is a country that seemingly should have little to fight over. Rich in oil as it is, poverty should be low, education high, and the need to murder nonexistent. But that is not the case. Nigeria is torn by divisions.

Since its independence, Nigerians have experienced more than 25 years of military rule, with only short periods of civilian administration. In the early 1970s, Nigeria became OPEC's fourth largest producer. This oil wealth was both a blessing and a curse—although it was the basis of the country's rapid economic growth, it was also the cause of much corruption and political turmoil.

The unequal distribution of wealth, too, has caused much violence. Very little of the oil wealth has found its way to the poor tribes who work the wells whereas billions of dollars have been paid to the military (dominated by the Hausa tribe).

To make matters worse, according to Human Rights Watch, "multinational oil companies are complicit in abuses committed by the Nigerian military and police." Exploited by international oil corporations, plundered by ruthless dictators, Nigeria has become a country of immense poverty and environmental destruction.

Indeed, the oil companies have been accused of plundering the environment and ignoring the local communities. Oil spills threaten the rich Niger Delta, industrial waste continues to be dumped there, and development projects are never built.

In 1995, eager to keep some of this oil wealth for himself, military leader Sani Abacha seized power. He ruled the country with an iron and corrupt hand.

For example, in 1995, Nigeria's military government hung nine political activists, including the well-known playwright Ken Saro-Wiwa. As a result, the British Commonwealth suspended Nigeria and threatened its military rulers with expulsion unless they restored democracy. The 52-member organization of Britain and its former colonies chose this unprecedented penalty to evidence their deep concern over Nigeria's horrific human rights record.

Abacha's abuses were so obvious that they caught the attention of the U.N. Human Rights Committee. In 1996, the committee stated that it was concerned about the "high number of extra judicial and summary executions, disappearances, cases of torture, ill-treatment, and arbitrary arrest and detention by members of the army and security forces and by the failure of the government to investigate fully these cases, to prosecute alleged offences, to punish those found guilty and provide compensation to the victims or their families."

The expulsion from the Commonwealth and a reprimand from the United Nations forced Abacha to promise that he would hand over power to a civilian government. To that end, he began a circuitous transition process toward elections, forcing each of the country's five political parties (the only ones he would allow) to nominate him for the presidency. But before his plan could work, Abacha died of a heart attack.

Thereafter, Nigeria's new military government said that they intend to release the country's political prisoners, and promised that free elections would be held in 1999. In February of that year, for the first time in many years, Nigerians got to vote for a civilian president.

Postscript: The election was marred by claims of voter fraud and irregularities. Two days later, Nigeria's election commission confirmed the winner: former military ruler Olusegun Obasanjo.

The Least You Need to Know

- Sierra Leone's war atrocities are almost incomprehensible.
- Liberia spreads dissent throughout the region.
- Secessionist forces are still alive in Senegal.
- Nigerian oil makes for a lot of corruption.

Chapter 12

Struggles in Central Africa

In This Chapter

- ◆ The Angolan civil war
- ◆ The Rwandan genocide
- ◆ Hutus and Tutsis in Burundi
- ◆ Catastrophe in the Democratic Republic of Congo

European colonial rule was based on the overwhelming military superiority it held over its subjugated populations. Resistance was futile and dealt with harshly. This was a lesson that subsequent African leaders apparently learned far too well. The modern history of Africa is the history of men blinded by power, succumbing to greed, killing indiscriminately, and caring little for the consequences. This is but one reason why there has been so much bloodshed in the Central African republics of Angola, Rwanda, Burundi, and the Congo.

The Never-Ending Angolan Civil War

The Portuguese arrived in Angola in 1483, establishing colonies and developing a lucrative slave trade. When locals resisted, the Portuguese clamped down by killing, capturing, and exporting even more slaves. Colonial exploitation continued until the mid-twentieth century.

Central Africa used to be a mystery; now it is just a misery.

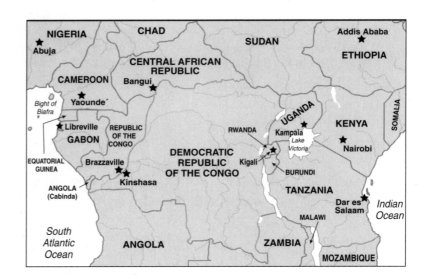

The Portuguese resisted attempts for peaceful decolonization. In 1956, a Marxist group emerged, the Popular Movement for the Liberation of Angola (MPLA), demanding independence.

In the northern part of the country, a rival group also emerged: the National Liberation Front (FNLA), supported by the large Bakongo tribe. In southern Angola, another group became engaged in the effort to oust Portugal. Dr. Jonas Savimbi's National Union for Independence (UNITA) found support among the country's largest tribe, the Ovimbundu.

Each rebel group attracted support from outside Angola, too:

◆ The United States and Zaire supported the FNLA.

◆ South Africa backed UNITA.

◆ Communist nations helped the MPLA, which had the greatest popular support.

def•i•ni•tion

Apartheid was the official state policy of South Africa that forcefully subjugated the African majority to the will of the European minority.

So it came to be that even after the Portuguese were tossed out of the country in 1974, Angola became a Cold War proxy combatant. As a result of meddling by the United States, South Africa, and Cuba, approximately of one million people have been killed in the Angolan civil war.

When the Cold War ended, however, Cuba could no longer afford to make mischief in Africa and disengaged from the continent. Around the same time, South Africa became focused on its transition away from *apartheid* and needed to withdraw from Angola, too. And the United States, no longer concerned about the Soviet menace, also had no reason to stay.

With their state sponsors gone, it became much more difficult for the combatants to continue killing each other. Elections were scheduled.

And so, in 1992, U.N.-monitored elections were held, and the MPLA won 58 percent of the vote. Savimbi, though, refused to accept the results, and his well-equipped guerrillas resumed the civil war.

In 1994, the United Nations decided to send in peacekeeping forces, and another peace deal was struck. Under this agreement, Savimbi was made the vice president of Angola, and his UNITA forces were allowed to join the Angolan army. Despite the concessions to UNITA, divisions remained and trouble festered. Accordingly, the United Nations left in 1997, and Savimbi refused any further participation in negotiations. Angola's civil war had the dubious distinction of being the longest in African history.

Landmine!

Angola is a land replete with landmines. Indeed, it has the greatest concentration of landmines in the world. It is estimated that about 70,000 Angolans have lost limbs because of landmine explosions.

Yes, we said "had." In 2002, Jonas Savimbi died during a military fight. His group (UNITA) and the MPLA thereafter signed a cease-fire, a real cease-fire, that ended the longest civil war in African history. UNITA became a political party, demilitarized, and an uneasy peace has since ensued.

But the results of the war have been horrific. According to CNN (September 25, 1999), 1 in every 356 Angolans is an amputee, and an estimated 2 million Angolans became refugees.

Genocide in Rwanda

The atrocities that occurred in Rwanda in 1994 might be the worst thing you will read in this book. They make Angola look like a vacation spot. To understand what happened and how genocide became public policy, you need to know a bit about the two main tribes in this part of the world—the Hutus and the Tutsis.

History

According to a 1999 report by Human Rights Watch, over the past 2,000 years, the people who are now known as Hutus and Tutsis in Rwanda have created societies that have much in common. They have developed a single language, similar religious beliefs, and a common culture valuing song, dance, and poetry.

How then did the Tutsis and Hutus come to be two separate peoples? When Rwanda emerged as a major state in the 1700s wealth and power were determined by the number of cattle people owned. In fact, the word *Tutsi* first referred to an elite group of people who were rich in cattle. *Hutu* meant a subordinate or follower of a more powerful person.

> **Peacekeepers**
>
> According to the CIA, "Rwanda is a rural country with about 90 percent of the population engaged in agriculture. It is the most densely populated country in Africa, is landlocked, and has few natural resources and minimal industry."

As in most places, members of each group married within their own tribe, creating over generations a shared gene pool. Accordingly, Tutsis came to share several generic characteristics: tall, thin, and narrow-featured. Hutus were shorter, stronger, and with broader features.

At the end of World War I, Rwanda became a colony of Belgium, and as in any colonial situation, the colonist needed assistance from locals. In this case, Belgium chose the wealthier and better-educated Tutsis for the job. As a result, the Tutsis came to have a virtual monopoly on public life. Problematically, however, in Rwanda Hutus far outnumbered Tutsis, which, needless to say, caused strife among the population. Not surprisingly, then, in the 1961 independence election, some 80 percent of Rwandans voted the Hutu-dominated Parmehutu party into power. This became known as the "Hutu Revolution."

The ensuing years brought Rwanda the usual mishmash of success followed by corruption and rebellion. Drought and a sharp decrease in international coffee prices in the late 1980s exacerbated matters, and by the late 1980s, approximately 600,000 people, mostly Tutsis, had left the country.

To compound matters, these economic problems were (as is the norm in this part of the world) made worse by cronyism and corruption. Politicians, journalists, and others throughout the country started to call for economic and political reform, including a return of the refugees. But the Hutu leaders would not permit their return.

But the exiled Tutsis wanted to come home, and so Tutsi opposition forces, called the RPF, decided to head home anyway, whether they were invited home or not, to help create a more democratic government. On October 1, 1990, the RPF entered the country from Uganda and headed for the capital.

In response to this Tutsi "invasion," the majority of Rwandans, both Tutsis and Hutus alike, rallied around their president, Juvenal Habyarimana. But that was not enough for Habyarimana. Worried that the Tutsi attack could embolden the Tutsi opposition within the country, Habyarimana began to hatch the most gruesome of plans.

> **Landmine!**
>
> The male life expectancy in Rwanda is 41. The female life expectancy is 42.

Setting the Stage for Slaughter

As the Human Rights Watch report points out, as the RPF made advances and civil war erupted, the government was forced to make concessions to the rebels.

Unwilling to continue to make further concessions to Tutsi rebels and desperate to stay in power, Habyarimana decided to try to turn the Hutus in the country against the Tutsis, whether the Tutsis in question were part of the rebellion or not, or whether the Tutsis in question were your neighbors or not. All Tutsis became enemies of the state, even Tutsis who were citizens of the state.

On September 21, 1992, Colonel Déogratias Nsabimana, Habyarimana's chief of staff, sent a top-secret memo to his commanders, defining who "the enemy" of the country really was: Tutsis. All Tutsis.

The memo stated that the true enemy of Rwanda were "the Tutsis inside or outside the country, extremist (as they are) and nostalgic for power, who have NEVER recognized and will NEVER recognize the realities of the 1959 social revolution and who wish to reconquer power." The RPF rebels were no longer the country's enemy; rather, its own Tutsi minority had officially become "the enemy."

> **Reliable Resources**
>
> Rwanda is home to some of the world's last remaining mountain gorillas, featured in the movie *Gorillas in the Mist*.

The Stage Is Set

With a plan in place, the president and his closest advisors and associates began portraying Tutsis inside Rwanda as RPF collaborators, even though it was essentially untrue. For almost four years, government propaganda attempted to turn Hutu against Tutsi by redefining the population of Rwanda into "Rwandans" (those who backed the president) and the "accomplices of the enemy" (the Tutsi minority). Habyarimana and his cronies especially worked to remind the Hutus of the Tutsi legacy of control.

But destroying the bonds between Hutus and Tutsis would not prove to be easy. For years, the two people had mostly lived in peace. They shared a common language, history, religion, and cultural practices. They were neighbors and friends, they went to the same schools and churches, and they worked and played with one another. And not a few Rwandans were of mixed parentage.

Nevertheless, utilizing propaganda, the Habyarimana gang was able to increase the divisions between the Tutsi and Hutu. Events began to come to a head in 1993 when the RPF scored a major military victory resulting in a peace agreement favorable to the rebels. The end result was that President Habyarimana and his supporters faced the very real possibility of losing power. Watch out!

It Begins

Their plan? Hutu leaders somehow concluded that the only way to stay in power would be to shatter the peace process by murdering mass numbers of Tutsis. "Hutu Power" became their rallying cry. Hitler would have been proud.

Machetes, guns, rifles, grenades, and other weapons were distributed to the Hutu population, although the genocide would actually occur mostly by machete.

Reliable Resources

BBC News Online pointed out that the Canadian daily, the *National Post,* said it had obtained a confidential U.N. report that provided detailed testimony from Tutsi RPF informants explaining how they shot down the president's plane.

On April 6, the plane carrying President Habyarimana crashed, killing him, and many Hutus believed that it was the work of Tutsi rebels. Said one Hutu who later participated in the genocide (BBC, April 2, 2004), "We thought that if they [the Tutsis] had managed to kill the head of state, how were ordinary people supposed to survive?" The ensuing crisis convinced a small group of Habyarimana's closest associates that the time was right to execute their plan for Tutsi extermination.

Orders from the prime minister began to be handed down, all the way to the local level. The enemies had to be killed, now! Checkpoints were set up throughout the country. If an ID card showed the person to be Tutsi, that person was killed. Neighbor killed neighbor. Wholesale slaughter of men, women, and children occurred throughout the country.

How could such an atrocity happen? Human Rights Watch points out that Rwandan authorities used the media to spread propaganda and lies so as to convince Hutus that their Tutsi neighbors were actually dangerous RPF agents and sympathizers who had to be killed. That the president of the country may have been murdered by Tutsi rebels certainly exacerbated the situation. Meetings were held where community leaders and even the local clergy told the assembled Hutus that they were justified in attacking Tutsis in the name of "self-defense." Hutus believed the claim and so a genocide began.

This was to be genocide in the truest sense of the word, a word that is far too often misused these days. In Rwanda, the Hutus planned a real genocide—the intentional, systematic, premeditated murder of a distinct group (although many moderate Hutus who defied orders to kill were also killed in the process).

Here is an example of just one atrocity: According to a man who participated in the genocide (BBC, April 4, 2004), government officials "said we should surround the church. They said one group would go south and another group would go to the north." He continued:

> People who had grenades detonated them. The Tutsis started screaming for help. As they were screaming, those who had guns started to shoot inside. They screamed saying that we are dying, help us, but the soldiers continued shooting. I entered and when I met a man I hit him with a club and he died.
>
> You would say why not [kill] two, three or four [people]? I couldn't kill two or three because those that entered outnumbered those inside. Some people did not even find someone to kill because there were more killers than victims ....
>
> It was as if we were taken over by Satan. We were taken over by Satan. When Satan is using you, you lose your mind. We were not ourselves. Beginning with me, I don't think I was normal. You wouldn't be normal if you start butchering people for no reason. We had been attacked by the devil.
>
> Even when I dream my body changes in a way I cannot explain. These people were my neighbors. The picture of their deaths may never leave me. Everything else I can get out of my head but that picture never leaves.

Government officials were full accomplices. They drove Tutsis to various places to be murdered. They were in charge of recruiting murderers and giving them the weapons they needed to do their "work." And they helped get rid of the corpses.

Landmine!

On April 17, 1994, thousands of people sought refuge in a convent during the genocide. Sister Gertrude (the Mother Superior of the convent) and Sister Kristo reluctantly put them up in the convent's health-care facility; even though there was no shortage of food, Sister Gertrude refused to feed them.

Two days later, the health-care facility was attacked by Hutu militiamen. Roughly 600 Tutsis then sought refuge in the garage of the health-care facility. The Hutus decided to burn them alive. The two nuns then went themselves and got two cans of gasoline, and Sister Kristo poured it over the garage and set it on fire. Almost 7,000 people died at the convent that day, including everyone in the garage, and Sister Kristo was later sentenced to 12 years in prison.

Mass murder was also fostered by rewarding the participants. The greater the commitment to the genocide, the greater the rewards. Food, drink, liquor, and promotions were given to willing participants.

Authorities encouraged people to steal Tutsi farm animals and crops. Tutsi farms, homes, cars, businesses, and such goods as television sets and computers were given to the murderers. And don't think that not participating was an option. The military, when faced with reluctance to act, forced citizens and local administrators to attack. Chaos reigned supreme.

Reliable Resources

The Rwandan genocide was made into the movie *Hotel Rwanda* starring Don Cheadle in 2004. The movie tells the real-life story of a Hutu hotel manager who opens his resort to more than 1,000 Tutsis during the crisis.

The Rwandan genocide was unique in that rather than hiding their objective, the murderers were open in their goal of exterminating their Tutsi brethren. Using print and electronic media, they encouraged Hutus to join the campaign, insisting that it "concerned everyone." And so, amazingly, the worst massacres often occurred in broad daylight. The dead, too, were usually left out in full view for everyone to see.

When all was said and too much done, roughly 800,000 Rwandans were murdered by their fellow citizens during the course of 100 days.

Aftermath

Years after the events in question, the United Nations set up an international court in the neighboring country of Tanzania to try leaders of the genocide (although millions of Hutus had already fled to other neighboring countries). By 2005, a mere 20 leaders had been convicted.

Local militia leaders down the food chain are being tried in Rwanda. Results here have been better. Mass trials have been held, trying more than 6,000 people to date. But even so, a staggering 120,000 more await trial.

To deal with the backlog, community courts in the villages where particular massacres occurred have been formed and victims who are still alive are confronting their tormentors. Prisoners being tried are required to ask for the victim's forgiveness.

And forgiveness is needed. Ten percent of Rwanda's entire population had been murdered.

Burundi

As indicated, many countries that make up Africa were, by and large, created by European colonialists with often little regard for the people who lived there. As such, for example, the Hutus and Tutsis also make up large portions of Burundi, just as they do in Rwanda.

Belgium took control of Burundi during World War I. After 1948, Belgian officials began to move toward creating a democracy in the country. As that happened, two parties surfaced: the Tutsi party (UPRONA) and the opposition Hutu party (PDC).

In January 1962, in preparation for independence, elections were held between UPRONA and the PDC. The Tutsi-dominated UPRONA party won 58 of the 64 seats in the national assembly, and Luis Rwagasore became prime minister. Thereafter, even through coup after coup, the Tutsis would dominate public life in Burundi.

> **Landmine!** _____
>
> Malaria, tuberculosis, cholera, hepatitis A, meningitis, typhoid fever, yellow fever, and schistosomiasis can be contracted while traveling in Burundi.

Two weeks after being elected, Rwagasore was assassinated by members of the Hutu-dominated PDC. This event was both monumental and detrimental to the future of Burundi, setting the stage as it did for years of civil unrest and instability. Open conflict between the Hutus and Tutsis began.

The subsequent government knew that it had to include Hutus as part of the ruling body or be deemed irrelevant, so a Hutu was named prime minister. In January 1965, he was assassinated. A political crisis was averted, however, when the Hutus procured a majority of the seats in the parliamentary election that May.

Chaos did erupt, though, in October after a Tutsi prince became prime minister and a Hutu group tried to overthrow his government. The Tutsis retaliated, and many Hutu politicians were killed, along with thousands of common Hutus who had supported the attempted coup.

What followed was a series of coups and countercoups. In September 1987, Major Pierre Buyoya seized control of the country. In August 1988, ethnic conflict resulted in 20,000 Hutu deaths and 60,000 refugees escaping to Rwanda. (You know things are bad when you have to escape to Rwanda!)

In an effort of reconciliation, the progressive Buyoya appointed a Hutu as prime minister, and his council of ministers contained equal numbers of Hutus and Tutsis. In 1991, Buyoya called for a new constitution, a new form of government, human rights, and regulations requiring parties to accept a charter on national unity. This new constitution became official on March 13, 1992, and presidential and legislative elections were to follow in June 1993.

Different from past elections, there were few electoral abuses on either side. Although the Tutsi party had ruled for the previous 30 years, it only got 32 percent of the vote. Melchior Ndadaye, a Hutu, won the election with 64 percent. This election made Ndadaye the first civilian and the first Hutu-elected president of Burundi.

Probably the best part of the election was how peacefully it occurred. Ndadaye assumed power, and no shots were fired. Were the days of ethnic violence finally over?

Unfortunately, this being Africa, three months later a coup was led by former president Jean-Baptiste Bagaza. Following the coup, 700,000 refugees fled the country, prompting the new government to call a national emergency and seal off the country's borders.

> **Landmine!** _____
>
> AIDS kills some 6,000 people each day in Africa—more than wars, famines, and floods.

Following the coup, roughly 100,000 people were killed in ethnic fighting, most being Hutus. In response, there was a Hutu-led massacre in which whole families of Tutsis were killed. Thus began a cycle of retaliatory violence because the deaths of people in one tribe led to deaths of people in the other tribe. All-out civil war was on.

In 2000, South African President Nelson Mandela brokered a peace deal that created an interim government in which power would be shared between Hutus and Tutsis. A cease-fire resulted, and South African peacekeepers were sent in during 2001, begging the question—how long would it last?

The Democratic Republic of Congo

Once known as Zaire, the Democratic Republic of Congo (DRC) is the third largest country in Africa, the location for the novella *Heart of Darkness,* and the inspiration for movies such as *Apocalypse Now.* It is composed of four major ethnic groups and more than 200 smaller groups. Many of these tribal groups have home territories that extend beyond the national borders but were divided into separate countries by colonial mapmakers.

Since independence in 1960, the DRC has been ravaged by near continuous inter-ethnic and civil strife, claiming untold lives, plunging the country into chaos and poverty.

Enter the Colonists

Belgium conquered the DRC (soon to be known as the Belgian Congo) in the late eighteenth century and stayed for 150 years. Yet, as suddenly as they arrived, they left, voluntarily relinquishing power in 1960. Elections were held and Patrice Lumumba was made prime minister.

Problematically for Lumumba, the United States was opposed to his nonaligned policies, seeing him as an extension of the Soviet Union. While serving as Lumumba's army chief-of-staff, Mobutu Sese Seko carried out a CIA-backed coup d'état a few weeks after the election, on September 5, 1960. By 1965, Mobutu had consolidated his power, beginning his 30-year reign as one of the most autocratic and corrupt dictators in the world, siphoning literally billions of dollars from the national treasury.

Mobutu the Corrupt

The new president was a repressive despot. He supported rebels in Angola, allied himself with racist South Africa, crushed opposition in his own country, and began amassing personal wealth through his corrupt rule. It was the Mobutu regime that gave rise to the term "kleptocracy"—rule by thieves.

As Mobutu stashed much of the country's economic output in European banks, the newly renamed Zaire became the most notorious example of a country in which state institutions came to be little more than a way of delivering money to the ruling elite.

And there was certainly a lot to steal. The DRC is, in fact, one of the most richly endowed countries in the world in terms of natural resources, including (but not limited to) …

- Water
- Diamonds
- Coltan
- Cassiterite
- Tin
- Copper
- Timber

Reliable Resources

As explained in a 2001 NPR Radio Expeditions episode, Coltan, a contraction of the actual ore name coloumbo-tantalite, is a source of the element tantalum. Tantalum is an essential coating for components found in many modern electronic devices, especially cell phones and computers.

Despite Mobutu's corrupt regime, he continued to receive U.S. and World Bank support because he was aligned with the West during the Cold War. Yet pressure to institute democratic reforms increased through the years as word about Mobutu's theft spread. Finally, in 1991, Mobutu adopted a new constitution and scheduled multiparty elections.

As usually occurs in elections, opposition parties emerged, and they called for Mobutu to resign. He responded by killing 100 student demonstrators at Lubumbashi University. This event provoked international outrage, opposition leaders called for Mobutu's resignation again, and uprisings spread throughout the country.

The election was held anyway, amid this continuing political turmoil. Mobutu was unhappy with the result and fired the new prime minister. Now even the West was outraged, demanding that Mobutu honor the prime minister's election. He refused.

Mobutu had dominated the country for three decades, and he succeeded in staying there by successfully playing rival army factions against one another. He thought he could do it again, but he thought wrong. Events beyond his control would soon bring Mobutu down.

At this time, the Tutsi-led Rwandan government, which took over after the genocide, was concerned that perpetrators and supporters of the mass killing were living with impunity in Zaire. So tiny Rwanda invaded its vast neighbor to try to flush out the Hutu extremists who had committed the genocide.

The corrupt and disorganized Zaire army fled, and the Rwandan army, along with anti-Mobutu rebels, then pushed all the way to the Zairian capital of Kinshasa. Mobutu's army backers had seen enough, and in 1997 removed him from office. At the time of his death, Mobutu was one of the richest men in the world.

The Kabila Era

Lawrence Kabila assumed power after Mobutu left, amid hopes of reform. Kabila changed the name from Zaire to the Democratic Republic of the Congo (DRC) and promised elections.

Soon enough, however, Kabila began to act like every other African dictator. He …

◆ Banned opposition parties.

◆ Arrested the former elected prime minister.

◆ Alienated and angered his allies.

Most tellingly, despite naming the country the Democratic Republic, Kabila never held a single election.

War

Kabila was quickly challenged by a Rwandan and Ugandan-backed rebellion in August 1998. Troops from Zimbabwe, Angola, Namibia, Chad, and Sudan intervened in support of Kabila, and a massive seven-country war was underway in the DRC. The BBC called this the equivalent of "Africa's world war" (August 4, 2005). However, neither World War I nor II has anything on this war: An estimated four million people died during this five-year conflict. (Yes, you read that right.)

> **Reliable Resources**
>
> During the war, there were an estimated 50,000 foreign troops in the DRC.

In July 1999, a cease-fire agreement was signed by all countries involved, but it did not hold. Further complicating the situation, the rebel forces split in 1999 and have at times fought against each other. The struggle eventually degenerated into a series of petty isolated conflicts in which the participants were principally concerned with securing access to the country's still substantial mineral resources.

Then, in January 2001, Kabila was assassinated, allegedly by one of his own bodyguards, although not a few DRC watchers believe that it was his son, Joseph, the new president, who orchestrated the assassination. In February that year, the U.N. Security Council approved a plan for the withdrawal of all fighting factions to be replaced by U.N. peacekeepers throughout the country.

Because of pressure exerted by Britain (it sends a lot of aid to Rwanda and Uganda) and the United States (it sends a lot of aid here too), because a military stalemate was at hand, and because of negotiation efforts on the part of South Africa, all countries involved in this mess finally agreed to a cease-fire.

The fragile peace held—that is, until Rwanda started attacking the DRC in 2004. It seems that Hutu militiamen who had fled Rwanda after the genocide were holed-up in the eastern Congo, and Rwanda wanted to "disarm" them. Presently, the armed incursions into the DRC have been limited and have not caused another all-out war.

Nevertheless, the country is essentially now run by warlords who control their own little fiefdoms. They use violence to grab power and natural resources, and continue to ravage the populace.

Aftermath

Needless to say, the results of such a brutal war on the general population are significant indeed:

- An estimated 1,000 people die in the Congo every day from hunger and disease.

- The child death rate in the country is four times greater than Africa as a whole.

- Because rape became a standard weapon in this ungodly war, a generation of Congolese women have been raped, gang raped, sexually violated with guns and sticks, and worse. As a result, a vast number of them suffer from vaginal fistula. This is a malady in which the lining between the vagina, anus, and bladder is ruptured, causing intense pain and terrible incontinence.

According to *Ms.* magazine (Spring, 2005) "The women [say] they are 'not women anymore.' They are often too physically damaged to farm, or bear children, and there is such stigma associated with rape in Congo—where female virginity is prized and the husband of a rape survivor is considered shamed—that rape survivors are routinely shunned by husbands, parents and communities."

Reliable Resources

Mpala Kikuni bore four children, all now dead. Her year-old daughter was in the hospital with a high fever when rebel attacks forced the doctors and nurses to evacuate. Her 19-year-old son was killed by a grenade as he fled from a soldier. "It's very painful for me," said Kikuni, who did not know her age but appeared to be about 40. "In all my life, I don't have a living child."
—*Washington Post*, February 12, 2005

The Least You Need to Know

- The Angolan civil war was the longest in Africa.
- The Rwandan genocide is unfathomable.
- Burundi Hutus and Tutsis also kill each other.
- The DRC continues to be embroiled in turmoil.

Part 4

Asia and the Pacific

In the coming century, it is not inconceivable to imagine that the largest conflicts will begin in Asia. North and South Korea have been estranged for more than 50 years. China and Taiwan have been at odds for just as long. And of course, we cannot forget India and Pakistan, countries that hate each other and that now have nuclear capabilities.

Yet even beyond these obvious examples, several smaller conflicts also continue to brew just under the radar, any one of which could start a major conflagration.

Chapter 13

All in the Family: North and South Korea

In This Chapter

- ◆ The Korean Peninsula
- ◆ The Korean War
- ◆ Subsequent skirmishes
- ◆ The need for new blood
- ◆ Prospects for unification
- ◆ The nuclear conundrum

No part of the world today is more divided than Korea. Fought over for centuries by China and Japan, its unity and independence have always been fragile. Now the 70 million people of the peninsula, who speak the same language and have the same history, live in two utterly different countries.

The heavily fortified border dividing north from south is one of the last remnants of the Cold War. Tensions between the two countries run the gamut. At times, peace seems imminent; at others, annihilation does.

One thing is certain. Should war ever erupt again, millions of people would die. As related by the U.S. Army Center of Military History, the history of conflict between North and South Korea is frightening indeed.

North and South Korea long for reconciliation.

The Korean Conundrum

The Korean Peninsula resembles Florida in shape, and in total area it is about the size of Tennessee and Kentucky combined, covering about 85,000 square miles. It is a mountainous land where roads and railways climb up vast hillsides only to then wind down through twisting valleys.

China, Japan, and Russia, because of their proximity to Korea, have played important roles in its history. Various invasions by each have made Korea a battleground time and again. Accordingly, Korea rarely has been completely free of conflict with one of its stronger neighbors.

Korea's Conflicted History

China, Korea's huge neighbor to the North, has long influenced Korean thought, customs, and cultures. By the seventh century, Korea had become a virtual Chinese satellite. And, like China, Korea endured the Mongol armies in the thirteenth century. Thereafter, for nearly a hundred years, the Mongols ruled and ravaged Korea.

In the late nineteenth century, China and Japan had designs on Korea. Japan fought the Sino-Japanese War of 1894, in part to prevent Korea from invasion. The Treaty of Shimonoseki terminated the war in Japan's favor. Thereafter, the Japanese integrated Korea's industry into its own economy and Korea became dependent, economically and otherwise, upon Japan.

As the U.S. Center for Military History points out, the Japanese came to control key governmental and economic functions by banning Koreans from responsible positions and from educational opportunities. Comprising only 3 percent of the population of Korea, the 750,000 Japanese residents ran the country. Nearly 80 percent of the Korean people were illiterate.

Despite the heavy-handed Japanese rule, the spirit of independence remained strong in Korea. When World War II broke out, Korea was regarded by the Allies as a victim of, and not a party to, Japanese aggression.

Korea Is Divided

As the war wound down and it became apparent that the Allies would win, plans were being made for how and where the Japanese surrender would be accepted, detailed in what was known as General Order No. 1. In mid-August 1945, copies of the draft order were sent to the White House. President Truman gave his approval to the plan, and General Order No. 1 became official U.S. policy.

The essence of the order was that Japanese forces north of the 38th Parallel in Korea would surrender to the Russians and those south of that line would surrender to U.S. forces. That dividing line, the 38th Parallel, was an arbitrarily chosen line, which sliced across Korea.

At the time, North and South Korea were two parts of the same country, economically, agriculturally, and industrially interdependent. For instance, North Korea furnished the fertilizer for the South, from whom it got many of its crops.

Landmine!

According to the U.S. Army Center of Military History: "The 38th Parallel cut through more than 75 streams and 12 rivers, intersected many high ridges at variant angles, and at that time, divided 181 small cart roads, 104 country roads, 15 all-weather roads, 8 highways, and 6 north-south rail lines."

Now, it is true that differences between north and south had always been part of the Korean scene. While South Koreans considered their Northern neighbors backward, North Koreans dismissed their Southern cousins as lazy. Yet they also knew they were one people.

Even so, the country was divided at the end of the war, and the Russians moved into the North to take the Japanese surrender and the Americans moved into the South. Afterward, neither was willing to move out. South of the 38th Parallel, the American zone held an estimated 21 million people. North of the line, the Soviet zone contained about 9 million people. Of the 20 largest Korean cities, 12 were inside the American zone, including Seoul, with a population of nearly 2 million. The American zone included 6 of Korea's 13 provinces in their entirety, the major part of 2 more, and a small part of another one.

By 1948, the emerging split in the country, exacerbated by the arbitrariness of the 38th Parallel and the heat of the Cold War, led both areas to adopt different forms of government as the time for actual liberation drew near.

On August 15, 1948, the Republic of Korea was established south of the 38th Parallel; and on September 9, 1948, the inappropriately named Democratic People's Republic of Korea was established in the North. From this moment on, the one people were divided into two countries, with two different agendas, two different value systems, two different economies, and two different paths. Like any bad divorce, anger and tensions ran high.

The two governments could not have been more different. North Korea became a Communist state in the Soviet mold. There were no free elections, no privately owned land, and few consumer goods. South Korea became a capitalist country and soon would have one of the strongest economies in the world.

The Korean War

After partition, North Korea was determined to conquer South Korea and make it a Communist state. In the 1950s, communism was on the rise, and the North Koreans saw it as their historical duty to indoctrinate their one-time countrymen. To this end, agents and terrorists from North Korea began to infiltrate the South and carry out subversive actions. Border incidents occurred time and again. By 1950, the North Korean military machine was ready, and the people had been psychologically prepared for war.

Invasion

According to the war history provided by the U.S. Army Center of Military History, North Korea invaded South Korea at 4 A.M. on June 25, 1950. Striking without warning, northern units "gained complete tactical surprise as they swiftly burst across the 38th Parallel in numbers. Coordinated columns of Soviet-made tanks and Soviet-trained infantry followed."

Whole units of South Korean defenders were destroyed as the North Koreans invaded in a well-conceived and carefully prepared all-out assault. North Korean planes, giving tactical support, went virtually unchallenged.

What North Korea did not anticipate was the swift decision by the United States to commit forces in support of South Korea. The United States, worried about the *domino theory*, and fearing that inaction in Korea might be interpreted as appeasement of Communist aggression elsewhere, was determined that South Korea would not fall. Truman ordered the use of U.S. planes, naval vessels, and ground troops in support of the South Koreans.

def•i•ni•tion

During the Cold War, it was the conventional wisdom that if one democratic state in a region fell to communism, all other democracies might fall, too, like so many dominos; hence the name **domino theory**.

The United States also asked the United Nations to intervene. When the Soviets made the mistake of walking out of the Security Council emergency session, that body decided that the United Nations would send troops to South Korea. This was the first collective action for the newly formed United Nations, and 16 member nations sent troops and assistance to South Korea. The major advances by the U.N. forces marked the second phase of the war, in which the North Koreans suffered a complete reversal of fortune.

China then got involved. Mao Tse Tung feared that the West might not stop in Korea, but would continue across the Yalu River into China and attempt to overthrow his Communist regime on the mainland. He therefore dispatched some 850,000 troops to China's Korean border in the third phase of the war.

The last phase was a stalemate, during which neither side would risk vast casualties in an attempt to gain a complete victory. By the end of May 1951, the battle lines had been established and set. Fighting continued, but there would be no more large advances and withdrawals up and down the peninsula.

Truce talks began in 1951, but the fighting continued until 1953, when the conflict ended with a cease-fire agreement.

Aftermath

The war left long-term marks on the Korean Peninsula and the world. The Korean Peninsula was ruined, and roughly 180,000 South Korean and United Nations troops died. The number of Communist soldiers estimated killed range as high as 500,000 North Koreans and 900,000 Chinese.

> **Peacekeepers**
>
> It is a landscape of nightmare, this wasteland of the demilitarized zone: artillery craters, barbed wire, minefields, graveyards, the skeletons of villages, and the remains of rice paddies. The earth has been shelled, mined, overgrown, booby-trapped, burned, and abandoned to grow wild yet another time.
>
> —William Holinger in *The Fence Walker*

Fifty years later, in June 2000, the U.S. Department of Defense said that it was revising the number of Americans killed in the Korean conflict. Dramatically dropping the number of dead from 54,246 to 36,940, the DoD declared that it had mistakenly included 20,617 nonbattlefield U.S. military deaths that had occurred worldwide during the 3 years of the conflict as part of the Korean dead number.

The cease-fire took effect on July 27, 1953, but no peace treaty was ever signed. Technically, the two countries are still at war. The dividing line now is the demilitarized zone (DMZ), today the most heavily fortified border on the planet, with more than a million soldiers on both sides.

Subsequent Skirmishes

The end of the war did not end the conflict. Through the years, countless small battles and several large ones have erupted between the now virulent enemies.

The Blue House Incident

On January 21, 1968, 31 commandos from a North Korean special forces unit made a bold incursion across the border and into Seoul. Their destination: the presidential residence, also known as the Blue House. Their aim: to kill key government officials, including the South Korean president.

The commandos, outfitted in South Korean military uniform, were armed with submachine guns and hand grenades. They got within 1,500 feet of the Blue House before being detected. South Korean military units killed them all.

The Pueblo Incident

Two days later, on January 23, 1968, North Korean patrol boats seized the USS *Pueblo*, a Navy intelligence-gathering vessel that was sailing in international waters. One USS *Pueblo* crewmember died during the siege, and 82 others were taken hostage. This was the first U.S. Navy ship to be hijacked on the high seas by a foreign military force in more than 150 years.

The *Pueblo* crew was taken to North Korea and held in two different compounds, one in Pyongyang, the other in the nearby countryside. The North Koreans pressured the crew to write letters home telling of the humane treatment they were receiving and asking that the United States apologize for spying and for its intrusions into Korea's waters. The crewmembers were also forced to give rehearsed presentations at two different press conferences.

The crewmembers were held by North Korea for 11 months while negotiations continued. Upon the United States admitting to espionage in the coastal waters of the Sea of Japan, the 82 prisoners were freed. The crewmembers were released on December 28, 1968. The ship remains in Wonson Harbor, North Korea, to this day.

> **Reliable Resources**
>
> The crew tried to signal to the people at home that their "confessions" were in fact false by using innuendo, lacing their letters with obviously false information, and displaying obscene gestures in photographs and movies. During the press conferences, they also used slang and corny and archaic language.

The Tunnels Incident

On November 15, 1974, a joint Korea/U.S. military team in South Korea discovered an underground tunnel that seemed to extend into North Korea. Upon further examination, the team found several Soviet-made items and a North Korean–made telephone, as well as traces indicating that the tunnel had been dug by the North Korean army.

Apparently, North Korea had built the tunnel to infiltrate, and invade, South Korea. According to South Korean armed services, the tunnel was wide enough to handle the passage of 15,000 soldiers per hour. On March 19, 1975, a second tunnel was discovered. North Korea denied involvement.

Based on information revealed by defector Kim Bu-song, the Korean army was then able to detect the presence of a third tunnel on October 17, 1978. This tunnel's exit was discovered to be but a few miles from the South Korean capital of Seoul.

Kim Bu-song testified that the orders to build the tunnels came from North Korean dictator Kim Il-sung, who is alleged to have said at the time, "Blitz tactics are the only means to enable North Korea to liberate South Korea, and 1 tunnel must be regarded as effective as 10 nuclear weapons."

On March 3, 1990, a fourth tunnel was discovered. It is estimated that there might be more than 20 such tunnels and that North Korea is still digging tunnels under the DMZ.

> ## Landmine!
>
> WASHINGTON—North Korea has built a network of tunnels in several countries in the Middle East designed to conceal weapons of mass destruction and ballistic missiles. One unnamed U.S. official said that North Korea is regarded as a leader in the construction of tunnels, adding that Pyongyang has equipment and know-how to quickly build tunnels.
>
> —*World Tribune*, Monday, October 16, 2001

The Tree Incident

Near the Bridge of No Return in the DMZ sits a row of poplar trees, one of which would always grow and block a line of sight at Checkpoint 3. The trimming of the poplar tree each summer had become a routine procedure. However, in early August 1976, a South Korean work force was threatened with death by North Korean troops if they tried to trim the tree.

The work force returned later with American troops at their side. The North Koreans, true to their word, attacked. Among the victims were two American officers beaten to death with the blunt end of axes after they ignored the North Koreans' order to halt.

After a mobilization on both sides, President Ford decided the appropriate response would be to chop down the tree. On the morning of August 31, 1976, a joint mission involving South Korean and U.N.-supported American troops began Operation Paul Bunyan. Supported by an armed platoon, 27 helicopters, and B-52 bombers, the troops chopped down the tree, proving that conflict can take you from the sublime to the ridiculous in short order.

Are Things Getting Warmer or Colder?

As the Cold War was ending with the demise of the Soviet Union, the client states of that superpower were being squeezed. Money was drying up. In January 1991, the Soviet Union demanded that North Korea begin to pay for its goods with hard currency. This only exacerbated the worsening economic conditions that were occurring throughout the communist regime, including food and power shortages.

Although peace is sometimes the result of brave men taking bold action, just as often, it is the result of calculating men deciding that it is the lesser of two evils. So, with the Cold War ending, times being tough, and maybe a realization that overthrowing the South was not going to happen, North Korea's leadership decided that the time for rapprochement was at hand.

This was even truer given that, despite their many differences and conflicts, North and South Koreans were one people, sharing a common ancestry, gene pool, and history, if not ideology. The arbitrary split at the 38th Parallel, exacerbated by the Cold War, did not change the fact that South Koreans had family members they hadn't seen in 40 years living in North Korea, and vice versa. If peace didn't happen soon, generations would die without ever seeing their loved ones again.

The Reconciliation Agreement

Negotiations had been an on-again, off-again affair for some time, but in the early 1990s they were on again. In late 1991, North and South Korea signed an "Agreement on Reconciliation, Non-aggression, Exchanges and Cooperation and the Joint Declaration on the Denuclearization of the Korean Peninsula."

The declaration, which came into force on February 19, 1992, stated that the two sides "shall not test, manufacture, produce, receive, possess, store, deployed use nuclear weapons," and that they "shall not possess nuclear reprocessing and uranium enrichment facilities." This was important because the international community feared that North Korea had in fact begun a nuclear weapons program, and the West was demanding access to various sites within North Korea, who had so far refused.

In recognition of the reconciliation agreement, and as a gesture of goodwill, President George Herbert Walker Bush pulled all American tactical nuclear weapons off the Korean Peninsula, hoping to get North Korea to open up its nuclear program for inspection. But it didn't work.

The implementation of the reconciliation accords ground to a halt almost immediately after they were signed because of the nuclear issue. The United States and South Korea insisted that North Korea live up to the joint declaration and open a suspected nuclear plant to inspections.

On February 10, 1993, North Korea refused to permit the International Atomic Energy Agency (IAEA) to conduct inspections as permitted under the terms of the Treaty on the Non-Proliferation of Nuclear Weapons (NPT). In March 1993, unable to shake off a persistent IAEA insisting on exercising inspection rights under the NPT, North Korea announced its intention to withdraw from the NPT.

The West threatened sanctions against North Korea if they wouldn't comply, and North Korea threatened to go to war if sanctions were imposed. A nuclear crisis had begun.

After a period of high tension brought on by failure to resolve the nuclear issue, the Clinton administration decided to send former-President Jimmy Carter to Pyongyang in June 1994 to see whether he could help defuse tensions. Just days later, Carter successfully obtained Kim Il-sung's pledge to freeze North Korea's nuclear program. Kim also said that he would allow nuclear inspectors into his country and would agree to high-level talks with the United States for the first time in 40 years. This apparent willingness of Kim to even discuss such matters foreshadowed that the time was coming for reconciliation discussions. Leaders on both sides of the DMZ seemed ready for change.

New Blood in the South

Kim Dae-jung began experimenting with anti-establishment politics in South Korea while working in the shipping industry. In 1961, after his fifth run for office, Kim was elected to the National Assembly. One month after Kim's election, General Park Chung-hee organized a military coup and seized control of the government, forcing Kim to step down. The authoritarian Park, however, became the perfect foil for the charismatic Kim.

The more Park persecuted Kim, the more Kim grew in popularity. In 1971, when Kim called for the reunification of North and South Korea, Park branded him a Communist. He ran for president and won 46 percent of the vote against Park. Kim was headed to a rally in Seoul a month after the election when a truck forced him off the road, an event widely believed to have been an assassination attempt.

Park tightened his hold on the country in 1972 when he scrapped the constitution. In 1979, with people angry over his autocratic rule, Park was assassinated by the head of the Korean Central Intelligence Agency. Another general imposed martial law as Kim and other leading opposition figures were arrested when tens of thousands of South Koreans protested.

After two more failed attempts for the presidency, in 1987 and 1992, Kim decided to retire his political aspirations. His retirement did not last long though. In 1997, he joined forces with another opposition leader and was finally elected president on his fourth try.

According to CNN News, shortly after winning the presidency Kim told *Time* magazine, "Throughout my life I have faced death five times. For six years I was in prisons, and for 10 years I was in exile or under house arrest … I never lost hope that someday there would be something like this."

Kim's election set in motion a major thaw in relations between Seoul and Pyongyang, culminating in a historic North Korean–South Korean Summit in 2000, an unprecedented achievement that brought Kim accolades from around the world and won him the label "visionary."

While Up North ...

At the same time, new blood was also emerging in North Korea. Kim Il-sung had run North Korea since its inception in 1948. He had taken the country down a Soviet-style path, complete with Soviet-style purges, Soviet-style gulags, and even a Soviet-style Kim personality cult. But Kim knew as he got older that he would need a successor. And who better than his own son?

Kim Jong-il is that son, and after a period of grooming for leadership, was officially designated successor to his father in 1980, power in title only. The South Korea media portrayed Kim as a playboy, with permed hair, lifts in his shoes, and a penchant for foreign liquor. In addition, journalists reported rumors of young women being kidnapped to be his courtesans in a string of luxury villas.

> **Reliable Resources**
>
> In 1998, North Korea called Kim Il-sung (dead, at this point, for more than four years) their "eternal president."

Kim didn't hold any positions of real power until 1991, when he took control of the armed forces despite his lack of military experience. Some analysts also believe the younger Kim was responsible for developing North Korea's suspected nuclear weapons program. He finally took over the country upon his father's death in 1994.

Before his death in 1994, Kim Il-sung surprised everyone by announcing that he would meet with South Korea's President Kim for a summit. The summit never happened because Kim Il-sung died on July 8 of that year.

Summit

Things brightened, though, in 1997 with the election of opposition leader Kim in South Korea. At the same time, Kim Jong-il in the North seemed ready to shed his secretive ways. For years, North Korea had been one of the world's most enigmatic, secretive societies, but there were clear signs that decades of rigid isolation might be coming to an end.

Once suspicious of all contact with the outside world, Pyongyang went on the diplomatic offensive, meeting with leaders in the United States, China, and Japan. Most important, Kim was ready to meet his counterpart in the south.

In June 2000, a joint summit between the two Kims was held in North Korea. By all accounts, it was a jubilant affair, and the once-reclusive North Korean leader turned out to be an affable host. It was, for most, their first glimpse inside North Korea in more than half a century.

The summit ended with the two Koreas signing a five-point accord that was to open up the insular Stalinist state to capitalist development. In the months since, the ice continued to melt between the two sides:

- Following the summit, North Korea stopped propaganda radio broadcasts against the South.

- In July, high-level officials from the two sides met in Seoul to find ways to implement agreements made in the June summit, including improving economic and military ties. They also agreed to reopen border liaison offices.

- In August came the most dramatic action: 100 North Koreans met their relatives in the South in a highly charged, emotional reunion. The meeting was followed by a group of 100 South Koreans visiting relatives in the North.

On October 13, 2000, the once-ostracized South Korean President Kim Dae-jung won the Nobel Peace Prize for his efforts toward reconciliation with North Korea.

Said Kim, "I thank all the citizens who love democracy and human rights, who have supported these efforts with our people. I will keep up my efforts for human rights, democracy, and peace on the Korean peninsula, Asia, and the world."

Of course, like everywhere else, September 11 changed the course of events on the Korean peninsula, too.

An Axis of Evil

The positive direction that emanated from the historic Korean summit in June 2000 quickly dissipated after September 11, 2001. The year between the summit and the terrorist attacks on America was too short a time for any substantial unification efforts to take place, and the attacks were a wedge that North and South Korea could not ignore. The long-standing concerns the West had about North Korea's nuclear ambitions and terrorist ties came to the fore.

On January 29, 2002, President George W. Bush gave his famous "axis of evil" speech, in which he stated that

> North Korea is a regime arming with missiles and weapons of mass destruction, while starving its citizens. Iran aggressively pursues these weapons and exports terror, while an unelected few repress the Iranian people's hope for freedom. Iraq continues to flaunt its hostility toward America and to support terror….

> States like these, and their terrorist allies, constitute an axis of evil, arming to threaten the peace of the world.

South Korea, unwilling and afraid to offend its American protectors, did not publicly dispute the characterization of North Korea as an evil nation. North Korea in turn was offended that its newfound "friends" in the South did not speak up on its behalf. Whatever warming had occurred over the previous few years was suddenly gone.

Nuclear Nightmare

In December 2002, North Korea restarted the nuclear reactor it had shut down in 1994, threw out two U.N. nuclear inspectors, turned off monitoring cameras, and dropped out of the nuclear nonproliferation treaty. By June 2003, North Korea had apparently extracted somewhere between 55 and 70 pounds (25–30 kilograms) of plutonium from the 8,000 spent fuel rods at its nuclear power plant.

By February 2005, North Korea announced that it had in fact created nuclear weapons, but analysts say that it is difficult to discern the truth of such assertions. If North Korea's nuclear reactor did in fact become fully operational, analysts believe it could have produced enough enriched uranium to create a few nuclear weapons a year. Again, however, without IAEA inspectors on hand to verify the veracity of such claims, it is impossible to ascertain the actual facts.

Aside from the very real threat that North Korea might grow desperate enough, or Kim kooky enough, to use such weapons on South Korea (or some other Asian neighbor), the other real fear the United States has is that Pyongyang might offer its weapons of mass destruction to other rogue states or terrorist organizations.

Six-Party Talks

Whereas everyone from the United States to China to Japan and Russia want North Korea to abandon its nuclear weapons program, it is not difficult to understand either Pyongyang's desire for such weapons or its reluctance to get rid of them.

- ◆ **Nuclear weapons level the playing field.** The fact is, possession of such weapons means that North Korea is much less likely to be attacked by either of its perceived enemies—the United States or South Korea. Any such attack would result in a nuclear exchange, and rational countries are loathe to instigate such an exchange.

- ◆ **Nuclear weapons are a substantial bargaining chip.** North Korea's weapons put the country in a far stronger negotiating position. It could, if it so chooses (and if other countries believe it is telling the truth), agree to give up the weapons for almost whatever it wants (food, energy, and so forth), so nervous are other countries about Pyongyang's nuclear ambitions.

So, not surprisingly, as of 2005, six-party talks were underway between both Koreas, the United States, Russia, China, and Japan in an effort to rid the Korean Peninsula of nuclear weapons. Will the talks be successful? We can only hope so. A Korean nuclear exchange can only mean one thing: the loss of millions of lives.

And so it goes.

The Least You Need to Know

- ◆ The Korean Peninsula was divided after World War II.
- ◆ The Korean War ended in a stalemate.
- ◆ Subsequent skirmishes erupted over the years.
- ◆ New leaders brought in new ideas.
- ◆ A nuclear North Korea complicates matters even more.

Chapter 14

Enter the Dragon: China

In This Chapter

- ◆ The Communist revolution
- ◆ Taiwan
- ◆ Tibet
- ◆ Xinjiang
- ◆ Russia
- ◆ The United States

The twentieth century has often been called the American century. It is not inconceivable that the twenty-first century will come to be known as the Chinese century. Although China has long been considered a third-world country, the economic boom unleashed by the relaxing of Communist ideology in the 1980s, combined with a population of more than one billion and a resurgent military, might well propel the country into the forefront of nations.

Certainly the economic changes wrought by abandoning orthodox communism raised the country's standard of living, but it also has created a potentially troubling resurgence in Chinese nationalism. The question now is whether the powers that be—the controlling, rigid, Communist party—will be able to retain control in light of the country's economic liberalization and newfound prosperity.

China may yet need more room.

Who Lost China?

Chinese society has developed out of some 5,000 years of recorded history. The so-called Middle Kingdom was marked by the cyclical rise and fall of imperial dynasties. An ethical system of relations also developed during this time, governed by rules of propriety (known as the Confucian school), which defined each person's place in society. In this system, harmony of social relations, much more than the rights of the individual, was the ideal.

You Say You Want a Revolution?

Despite its ancient creed of harmony, China has long been a target of foreign interest and invaders. The Middle Kingdom, so secret and intriguing, made for many alien incursions. First from Mongolia, then from Japan, and later from Great Britain, these invasions often found China being dominated by stronger countries. In 1895, for example, the Chinese lost another war, the first of two Sino (Chinese)-Japanese wars.

Burdened with the legacy of thousands of years of imperial rule and nearly a century of humiliations at foreign hands, China was ready for a revolution as the twentieth century dawned. The imperial dynasty system was overthrown in favor of a republic in 1911, but civil war continued for nearly 40 more years, accompanied by war with Japan (again) between 1937 and 1945.

The real revolution came with the Chinese Civil War of 1945, which was won by the Chinese Communist Party in 1949. Except for the island of Taiwan (which became the home of those who lost the civil war—see the section "China and Taiwan," below), the new government unified the nation and achieved a stability China had not experienced for generations. However, eagerness on the part of its new leader, Mao Tse Tung, resulted in some horrific social and public policy blunders, including …

◆ **The Great Leap Forward (1958–60).** A program that attempted rapid economic modernization but proved disastrous.

◆ **The Cultural Revolution (1966–76).** An amazing time of upheaval, whereby Mao attempted to keep the revolution "alive" via radical experimentation and political chaos that brought the educational system to a halt and severely disrupted attempts at rational economic planning. When Mao Tse Tung died in 1976, the Cultural Revolution era came to an end.

On his deathbed, Mao anointed Hua Guofeng, a former party secretary, as his successor. Hua survived Mao, but National Defense Minister Ye Jianying led a coup that eventually put the country in the hands of Mao's one-time foe, the diminutive (five-foot-tall) Deng Xiaoping.

The Capitalist Revolution

Deng created a second revolution, one possibly more powerful than the first. When he became head of the Chinese state in 1978, Deng realized that China's economic problems stemmed from state control of the economy. He decided to challenge the very precepts of *Karl Marx* and communism itself by adopting a hybrid system not quite like anything seen before. Outside analysts often call it "market socialism"; Deng called it "socialism with Chinese characteristics." Whatever you call it, the fact is that it was capitalism.

Deng decided to liberate the energies of the individual, a daring concept not just for a Marxist but for a Chinese. (The concept of individualism can have a negative connotation in Chinese society.) He began with agriculture, which had been collectivized by Mao. The land

def•i•ni•tion

Karl Marx was a German social philosopher and the chief theorist of modern socialism and communism. His book, *Das Capital*, laid out his ideas for a world controlled by the working class in which people worked not for the good of themselves, but for the good of the whole community.

was worked by communes that grew what the state directed and turned over all food produced to the state for distribution.

Deng's reforms slowly abolished the communes and replaced them with a contract system. Although the state continued to own the land, families were allowed to grow anything they wanted and sell it for profit. Farmers were encouraged to build privately owned houses. The results were phenomenal. Chinese farmers increased food production around 8 percent beginning in 1978, about 2½ times the rate over the preceding 26 years.

The success of the agricultural reforms expanded into all kinds of businesses—small businesses like hotels, restaurants, stores, tailor shops, and beauty parlors—as well as larger businesses such as manufacturing, oil exploration, and technology companies. All were all given the right to compete.

def•i•ni•tion

A country's **gross domestic product** is the value of all goods and services provided within the borders of a nation.

Output quadrupled over the ensuing 20 years, and China now has the world's second largest *gross domestic product* in the world.

This unprecedented growth has made China a much stronger country, and now a much more formidable foe. In 2000, China stood as the second largest economy in the world after the United States.

No longer forced to be anyone's whipping boy, China has emerged as one of the strongest countries in the world, buoyed by its 1.2 billion people. To wit ...

- ◆ China's People's Liberation Army is the largest in the world, with 3 million soldiers.

- ◆ China's soldiers directly supervise and control more than 15,000 business enterprises and 50,000 factories. They operate shipping companies, airlines, arms exporters, factories, telephone companies, and toy companies. The military reinvests its profits back into feeding troops and modernizing its military capabilities.

With this newfound economic prosperity and military might has come a greater willingness to deal with several conflicts that have been on the backburner for years.

China and Taiwan

In 1895, China lost the first Sino-Japanese War. In article 2 of the Treaty of Shimonoseki, which ended that war, China ceded Taiwan (then called Formosa) to

Japan in "perpetuity and full sovereignty." Japan's sovereignty over the island would not be disputed by China or any other state for the next 50 years.

During World War II, in paragraph 3 of the Cairo Declaration (1943), the United States, Great Britain, and China declared that Japan would be stripped of all the islands in the Pacific the country had seized or occupied since the beginning of World War I in 1914. In the same vein, the declaration demanded that all the territories Japan has taken from the Chinese, such as Manchuria, Formosa, and the Pescadores, would be restored to the Republic of China.

In accordance with this sentiment, Taiwan was returned to China as a province after the war. But after the war, in 1945, the Chinese were in the middle of their own civil war. There really was no one to give Taiwan back to because no one controlled the country.

As the civil war wound down in 1949, Nationalist leader Chiang Kai-shek and his forces withdrew to Taiwan, vowing to reclaim the mainland. Since then, China has considered Taiwan to be a renegade, runaway province that must someday be reunited with the mainland.

The Renegade Province

Following the outbreak of the Korean War in 1950, U.S. President Harry S. Truman hoped to prevent a possible Chinese attack on the island by sending the 7th Fleet into the Taiwan Strait. For Truman, Taiwan came to represent a buffer against Communist expansion in Asia, and to guarantee its safety, he sent money and military supplies to the island. Although this was the first time the United States had intervened in the conflict between Taiwan and China, it would not be the last.

During the following 20 years, from 1952 to 1972, Taiwan grew economically. But on the diplomatic front, they lost ground. As China also grew, it became more and more difficult for countries to choose Taiwan over the mainland. The Chinese market, with its one billion people, was simply irresistible.

> **Peacekeepers**
>
> Richard Nixon was the most intense, feared anti-Communist of his day. In fact, he made his name by trying to root out "Red" spies in the government. Thus, when he went to China, no one could accuse him of being soft on communism. That is why people now say, when a politician does something unexpectedly against the grain, that "only Nixon could go to China."

In 1972, President Richard Nixon made a historic trip to Beijing, opening up China to the West. China and the United States then signed the Shanghai Communiqué, which "acknowledged" the Chinese position that there is but one China and that Taiwan is part of China.

Nixon's trip, and the Shanghai Communiqué, reinforced a growing belief in the international community that, 20 years after the Chinese Civil War, there was one China and that the Communists ruled it, despite Taiwan's protestations to the contrary. The United Nations expelled Taiwan in favor of the Communist China.

Eight years later, the United States formally recognized the People's Republic of China, severing official diplomatic relations with Taiwan. The U.S. move meant that America accepted Beijing's "one China" claim (stating that there is but one China, and Communist China is it). Within months, though, the United States Congress reinstated unofficial economic ties with Taiwan, including the sale of arms.

Taiwan Becomes a Democracy

Although international relations were not going Taiwan's way, it still was not part of the mainland and was still a thorn in China's side. But, like China, it, too, was a dictatorship.

That began to change in 1979 when police crushed a rally in the southern city of Kaoh-siung that had turned violent. The leaders were jailed and later defended by a then little known, yet successful, maritime commerce lawyer named Chen Shui-bian. Twenty years later, Chen would become the first non-Nationalist party president elected into office.

In 1996, contemporaneous with the first ever direct presidential election in Taiwan, China decided to conduct missile tests and concurrent joint military exercises close to Taiwan. China admitted the drills were meant to intimidate Taipei into dropping any pretensions toward full independence.

The United States responded by sending warships to the Straits of Taiwan, the tiny slip of water that separates China from Taiwan. This became the largest show of naval force for America since the Vietnam War. President Clinton ordered two aircraft carrier battle groups to the straits.

The elections went forward as planned, and Lee Teng-hui was elected president. It was the first time voters had elected their own president in 5,000 years of Chinese history.

Tensions increased dramatically during the 2000 election when, for the first time, the opposition party called for full independence from China. According to a *PBS Online News Hour* report, "Chinese Premier Zhu Rongji threatened 'bloodshed' if the Taiwanese voters 'acted on impulse.' The statement was pointed at supporters of Chen."

Despite the veiled threats, for the first time in 50 years, a non-Nationalist party leader took control in Taiwan. The former defense attorney, Chen Shui-bi, was elected president. During his inaugural speech, Chen backed off a bit, saying that as long as China refrained from using military means to take control of Taiwan, he would not push for independence from Beijing.

Given that China could overrun Taiwan in a matter of hours and has remained steadfast in its insistence that the province return to the fold, the likelihood of this conflict turning violent is not remote by any means.

How the United States Fits In

Any war between China and Taiwan could easily involve the United States. Under the 1979 Taiwan Relations Act, American law says that the United States would view any conflict over Taiwan with "grave concern."

The United States takes this matter very seriously. Aside from the naval showing in 1996, a similar show of force occurred in 1995. That year, Taiwanese President Lee went to visit his alma mater, Cornell University. China responded by conducting military exercises near Taiwan, leading the United States to send an aircraft carrier through the straits for the first time in 17 years.

If China ever did invade, the United States might be forced to intervene. And if that were to happen, all bets would be off.

> **Peacekeepers**
>
> Although it may be difficult to understand China's position, consider the following analogy presented by the Cox News Service: "Imagine how Americans might feel if the Civil War had ended just 50 years ago and the Confederates escaped to Florida. Americans might demand that Florida be repatriated." Many Chinese, for the same reason, want Taiwan back.

China and Tibet

Tibet lies at the center of Asia. The earth's highest mountains, as well as a vast arid plateau and great river valleys, make up the physical homeland of six million Tibetans, a land traditionally free and independent.

In 1950, Radio Beijing announced that "The task of the People's Liberation Army for 1950 is to liberate Tibet." China then invaded Tibet, saying that Tibet historically was part of China.

The facts are these. At the time of China's invasion, Tibet was essentially an independent country. It had a defined territory, system of government, tax base, currency, its own postal system, and its own army.

Nevertheless, the invasion occurred, Tibet fell to the Chinese, and 2 years later, a 17-point agreement was imposed on the Tibetan Government by the Communists. The Chinese maintained that the Dalai Lama supported China's actions in Tibet and "acknowledged" that Tibet was in fact part of China.

Yet eight years later, in 1959, after a Tibetan uprising at Lhasa and its savage suppression by the Chinese, the Dalai Lama and 100,000 followers fled to India. After his escape, the Dalai Lama repudiated the 17-point agreement, stating it was forced upon the "Tibetan government and people by the threat of arms."

Since then, the Dalai Lama has become an international symbol of peace, and his intent to reclaim a free Tibet a cause for many.

Despite the efforts of the Dalai Lama, since its invasion, China has sought to re-create Tibet in its own image, by force if necessary. According to FreeTibet.org …

- It is estimated that since 1950, 1.2 million Tibetans have been killed by the Chinese.

- Long-term Chinese settlement in Tibet has been encouraged, with the result that Tibetans are in the minority in many areas.

- Chinese has replaced Tibetan as the official language.

- Young Tibetans are being re-educated about their cultural past, with references to an independent Tibet being omitted.

- Mining and mineral extraction have become among the largest economic activities in much of Tibet, and at least one half of Tibet's forests have been logged since Chinese occupation.

In 1988, the Dalai Lama put forward the "Strasbourg proposal," which called for autonomy for Tibet rather than independence. Although it was rejected by the Chinese, the following year the Dalai Lama received the Nobel Peace Prize.

Tibet remains an occupied country and liberation but a dim hope. As the Swedish Human Rights Delegation to China and Tibet said in October 1994, "Since the

Chinese government perceives demands for independence as a formidable threat to national unity, it sees repression as the only means of dealing with (the problem)."

The Xinjiang Province

Xinjiang covers fully one sixth of China's total land mass. It became a Chinese province in 1881, but even as late as the establishment of the Chinese republic in 1912, Xinjiang remained more or less independent of the central government. Rebellions in 1936, 1937, and 1944 further lessened Chinese rule. Late in 1949, though, Xinjiang capitulated to the Chinese Communists' invasion without a struggle.

As it did with Tibet, China sent native Chinese to Xinjiang in order to reinvent the population in the Chinese mold. In the 1950s and 1960s, the central government sent massive numbers of Chinese to Xinjiang, drastically altering the population balance; the Chinese are now approaching numerical parity in the region. The percentage of ethnic Chinese in the population has grown from 6 percent in 1949 to 40 percent at present.

Beijing has long claimed to be confronted with "religious extremist forces" and "violent terrorists" in Xinjiang, a largely Muslim area. It is true that much like Tibetans, the Uighurs in Xinjiang have struggled for religious and cultural survival in the face of the mass influx of Chinese immigrants, as well as the harsh repression of political dissent. Some have resorted to violence in a struggle for independence.

Nevertheless, according to the New York–based Human Rights Watch, "Chinese authorities have not discriminated between peaceful and violent dissent. Their fight against 'separatism' and 'religious extremism' has been used to justify widespread and systematic human-rights violations against Uighurs, including many involved in non-violent political, religious, and cultural activities."

Reliable Resources

At every meeting of the Shanghai Five—an informal association of China, Kazakhstan, Kyrgyzstan, Tajikistan, and Russia, set up in 1996 at China's initiative—China emphasizes the need to prevent cross-border "activities undermining national sovereignty." One focus of the Shanghai Five is cooperation to counter Islamic radicalism in the Xinjiang region. Beijing has received ample assurances from the Shanghai Five that Xinjiang opposition groups will not be allowed to operate.

In the 1990s, the Turk peoples of Xinjiang grew increasingly discontent with Chinese rule. Rioting by pro-independence Muslims broke out in 1997, and China subsequently increased the number of troops in the region.

Then, after September 11, 2001, the Chinese government charged that Uighur groups had links with the Taliban in Afghanistan and were supported from abroad by other radical Islamist organizations. According to Human Rights Watch, "China has used these claims to justify ruthless repression in Xinjiang against religious activities, personnel and individual believers in what are known as 'campaigns to rectify social order.'"

Today, Xinjiang remains the only province in China where execution of political prisoners is common. Among conflict watchers, Xinjiang is now one of the most closely scrutinized areas on Earth.

China and Russia

After the founding of the People's Republic, Chinese leadership was concerned with ensuring national security, consolidating power, and developing its economy. To those ends, it formed a united front with the Soviet Union.

Mao traveled to Moscow to negotiate the 1950 Sino-Soviet Treaty of Friendship, Alliance, and Mutual Assistance. Under this agreement, China gave the Soviet Union certain rights in return for military support, weapons, and large amounts of economic and technological assistance. China acceded, at least initially, to Soviet leadership of the world Communist movement and took the Soviet Union as the model for development.

But the relationship would quickly be strained. In the late 1950s, disputes over ideology, borders, and economic development caused the rift. During the 1960s, this ideological dispute deepened and spread to include territorial issues, culminating in 1969 in bloody armed clashes along the long Russian-Chinese border. Both sides drew back from the brink of war at the last minute.

This seesaw relationship was down in the 1970s as Beijing began a rapprochement with Washington as a counterweight to the perceived threat from Moscow, but up again in the 1980s, when Soviet leadership changes provided openings for renewed diplomacy.

After the fall of the Iron Curtain, however, things turned icy once again. China was the last large Communist nation on Earth (albeit a Communist in capitalist clothing), and the Russian Federation, with its emphasis on democracy, rattled Beijing.

The countries flip-flopped again in 2000, when Russia's lower house of parliament (the Duma) ratified a groundbreaking treaty with China that aimed to end decades of suspicion and border conflicts between the two nuclear-armed neighbors.

The treaty prohibited the two countries from launching nuclear strikes against each other or even targeting one another with such weapons. It also recognized Beijing's "sovereignty" over Taiwan and pledged Russian support of Chinese military operations in any conflict over the island, which potentially would involve the United States.

China and the United States

China's relations with the other superpower, the United States, have followed a similarly uneven course. Chinese leaders expressed an interest in possible economic assistance from the United States during the 1940s, but by 1950, Chinese-American relations were openly hostile.

The Korean War was a major reason for this because it contributed to the United States policy of *containing* the Chinese threat through a trade embargo and travel restrictions, as well as through military alliances with other Asian nations.

After the Soviet Union's invasion of Czechoslovakia in 1968 and the border clashes with the Soviets in 1969, China decided that its major threat was the Soviet Union rather than the United States, and thus sought a closer relationship with Washington. President Richard M. Nixon thereafter made his dramatic trip to China in 1972.

def•i•ni•tion

Containment is a foreign policy strategy that was pursued by the United States after World War II, wherein America pursued a plan of long-term, patient, and firm containment of Communist expansion.

As the Chinese began to open up their billion-person market to the West, relations continued to thaw. The United States granted China the trading status of Most Favored Nation, and in 2000, China joined the World Trade Organization.

Yet the lesson of the Soviet Union and China must be kept in mind. Countries who are your friend can easily become your enemy. Countries promote what they believe to be their best interest. China and the United States had good relations at the turn of the millennium because China wanted access to the West's technology and the West wanted access to China's vast market. That could change at any time, for any number of reasons. Today's friend is tomorrow's foe.

> **Landmine!**
>
> Jack Spencer, a defense analyst and fellow at the Heritage Foundation, claims the Chinese military is preparing itself for a future war with America. "Of course China is narrowing the technological gap. They are in the midst of a major military buildup that is driven by the belief that the United States will be its primary future competitor," Spencer told Newsmax.com.

The Old Guard Versus the New Guard

Since the founding of the Communist regime in 1949, Chinese political life has been dominated by the Chinese Communist Party. A dictatorial, brutal, repressive regime, the party is dominated by (mostly) old-school hardliners who are loath to share power.

That monopoly on power was threatened for the first time ever in 1989 with the fall of the Iron Curtain. The wave of democracy that was lapping over the world found a beachhead in Tiananmen Square, the center of Beijing, and thus the center of China.

In 1989, students—seeing how students in other Communist countries were changing their world by large, peaceful demonstrations, and who had long wanted to change China, too—decided that the time was right to take on the old guard.

In April and early May 1989, students and intellectuals began to occupy Tiananmen Square. The students understood that world attention would soon be focused on China because of Soviet President Mikhail Gorbachev's upcoming visit to China at the end of May. Because Gorbachev had opened the Soviet Union to democracy, the students believed that occupying the square prior to his arrival could help bring about similar democratic reforms in China.

The movement quickly gained speed. Thousands upon thousands of people began to join the students. On May 13, workers joined, and a hunger strike began. The students were becoming more and more persuasive in their calls for radical reform. Soon, more than a million people filled the square.

The scene inside Tiananmen Square was too much for the Chinese hierarchy. The movement was perceived as a threat to their power. According to secret transcripts smuggled out of Beijing 10 years after the event, the Associated Press quoted Communist Party Chairman Deng Xiaoping saying at a meeting at the Party Central Office, "A tiny minority is exploiting the students; they want to confuse the people and throw the country into chaos. This is a well-planned plot whose real aim is to reject the Chinese Communist Party."

Because power corrupts, and absolute power corrupts absolutely, the Communist Party of China was determined to retain its stronghold on power and use whatever means necessary to crush the rebellion. On May 18, Deng told a high-level party meeting that "After thinking long and hard about this, I've concluded that we should bring in the People's Liberation Army and declare martial law in Beijing."

Deng was encouraged by several members of his inner circle, including Wang Zhen, who said, "The students are nuts if they think this handful of people can overthrow our party and our government." On May 20, Deng declared martial law in China. The students still didn't dissipate. In fact, they called on the party leadership to resign.

On June 4, 1989, Deng had seen enough. He ordered Chinese troops to kill Chinese civilians. Troops moved into Tiananmen Square and opened fire on the demonstrators. The brutal action killed hundreds, and thousands were arrested in a nationwide crackdown.

According to the Associated Press, "Two days after the violent crackdown, Deng reportedly defended the decision in a Central Politburo Standing Committee meeting. 'If we hadn't been firm with these counterrevolutionary riots, if we hadn't come down hard, who knows what might have happened? … If the plots of the people who were pushing the riots had gotten anywhere, we'd have had civil war.'"

Although the scene inside Tiananmen Square was remarkable, maybe the most remarkable sight of the democracy movement was that of a lone man bravely walking in front of, and thereby stopping, a line of tanks.

However, despite his bravery, the man didn't change history, and the issues that sparked those mass protests across China in 1989 still plague the country today: general dissatisfaction with the party, increased demands for democracy, and the widening gap between the rich and the poor. If political freedom does not catch up with economic freedom, the resulting dichotomy in the country could be disastrous.

The Least You Need to Know

- The Communist revolution created the split with Taiwan.
- The Chinese have brutally repressed Tibet.
- They have done the same thing in Xinjiang.
- China and Russia have had a hot/cold relationship.
- China and the United States have a relationship of mutual convenience.
- The Tiananmen Square massacre might foreshadow what is to come in China.

Cain and Abel: India and Pakistan

In This Chapter

- ◆ Kashmir in conflict
- ◆ Three wars and the birth of Bangladesh
- ◆ Sikh separatists in India
- ◆ The nuclear option
- ◆ An opening

India and Pakistan are home to two of the world's largest populations. India has more than 1 billion people to feed, clothe, and house every day, and Pakistan has 150 million of its own. They have gone to war three times so far, they detest one another, and now both countries have the bomb. Is it any wonder that many analysts believe that if there ever will be a nuclear war, these are the countries who will have it?

To understand the depth of this conflict, you must examine the main conflict in Kashmir and the wars it has spawned, as well as the nuclear capacity of both countries.

India and Pakistan are locked in a potentially dangerous conflict.

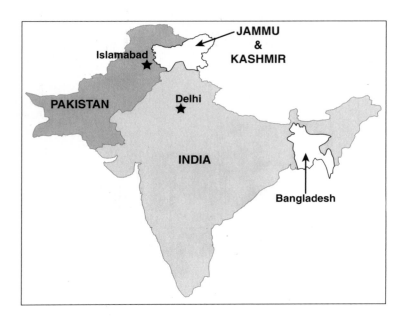

The Indian Subcontinent

The Indus Valley civilization is one of the oldest in the world, going back at least 5,000 years. Aryan tribes invaded in about 1500 B.C.E. and merged with earlier inhabitants to create what is now known as Indian culture. Arab invasions began in the eighth century, and Turkish ones started in the twelfth century.

By the late fifteenth century, European traders had begun to rise in influence in the region, and in the nineteenth century Britain had assumed political control of virtually all Indian lands.

Peacekeepers

Mohandas Gandhi is often referred to as "Mahatma" Gandhi, but that is not his name. The people of India gave that moniker to him. It means "great soul."

Mohandas Gandhi invented nonviolent resistance as a way to rid the Indian subcontinent of foreign rule once and for all. It was a long but ultimately successful campaign, and in 1947, independence was achieved. Thereafter, the subcontinent was divided into the large Hindu state of India and the smaller Muslim state of Pakistan. This dichotomy—two states, two religions, and two people—has led to bloodshed, war, poverty, and strife.

Pakistan Versus India

The people of Pakistan, being overwhelmingly Muslim, always wanted independence, not only from the British, but also from India. Their wish was realized on July 18, 1947, when the British Parliament passed the Indian Independence Act, creating two new countries—India and Pakistan. The act also provided for the complete end of British control over Indian affairs. Pakistan took the opposite route, not surprisingly, choosing to become part of the British Commonwealth of nations.

It was after independence that the full extent of the differences between the two new countries would become apparent.

Roots of War

The first issue that they had to deal with was their long border with one another. It was agreed that a Boundary Commission would be set up to delineate the borders between India and Pakistan. The British government appointed a Boundary Commission to demarcate permanent borders. The boundaries had to be fixed in such a manner that areas which were predominantly Muslim went to Pakistan, whereas the Hindu ones went to India. This was not always readily apparent, nor easy to do.

In an almost frantic hurry, the commission divided districts, villages, farmlands, water, and property into the two new countries. Thousands of people were caught in the middle, and the result was that many hastened across the border to one side or the other, leaving their homes, land, and personal property to seek refuge.

The Legacy Project, a global exchange on the lasting consequences of the tragedies of the twentieth century, reports that the ensuing war and violence caused by the partition of the subcontinent cost more than one million lives. Some 3.5 million Hindus and Sikhs were forced to move from Pakistan into India, while

Reliable Resources

There are 750 million Hindus in the world, and most of them live in India.

about 5 million Muslims migrated from India to Pakistan. Overall, the demographic shift was the first of many causes that resulted in extreme bitterness between the two countries.

Kashmir Becomes a Problem

Adding to the tensions was the issue of what to do with the following three areas:

◆ Junagadh

◆ Hyderabad

◆ Kashmir

Junagadh was (and is) a Hindu-majority area, but its leader was a Muslim. Although the leader wanted to join to Pakistan, a *plebiscite* was held, and the state chose to join India.

def•i•ni•tion

A **plebiscite** is a direct vote in which a population exercises the right of self-determination.

Hyderabad also had a Muslim ruler of a Hindu-majority populace. Rather than join either country, his plan was to gain independence for his state. After more than a year of negotiations, India finally decided to send its army into the region and Hyderabad became part of India in 1948.

The real problem was, and is, Kashmir, whose subjects were roughly 80 percent Muslim. Its Hindu leader, Maharaja Hari Singh, had also wanted Kashmir to remain independent, but the large Muslim population wanted to become part of Pakistan.

In 1948, frustrated and nervous, the Muslims in Kashmir revolted. Singh then fled to New Delhi (in India) and there agreed to place Kashmir under the dominion of India in exchange for military support and the promise of a referendum on independence. Indian troops thereafter flew to Kashmir to engage the rebels, who by then were being supported by Pakistan.

def•i•ni•tion

When a fact exists, whether it is legal or not, it is said to be **de facto**. For example, when two countries are in a de facto state of war, they are waging war, whether one country has actually declared war or not.

A cease-fire was arranged in 1949, and the cease-fire line created a *de facto* partition of the region. The central and eastern areas of Kashmir came under Indian control as the Jammu and Kashmir states, whereas the northwestern quarter came under Pakistani control as Azad Kashmir and the Northern Areas.

Although a U.N. peacekeeping force was sent in to enforce the cease-fire, and remains there to this day, the dispute was never resolved. A U.N. resolution, adopted after the war, allows the people of Kashmir to join either India or Pakistan. The United Nations urged both countries to allow the people of Kashmir to choose which country they wanted to join by holding a plebiscite; to this day the plebiscite has not been held.

The Indian position today is that Kashmir belongs to India because of the Instrument of Accession signed by Maharajah Hari Singh, which handed over the "princely state" to India. Pakistan maintains that Kashmir is a heavily Muslim region, and if allowed to determine its own path via a vote in a plebiscite, it would become part of Pakistan.

Whatever the case, the seeds of animosity had been firmly planted, only to intensify over the years.

Act Two

In 1965, Pakistan sent guerrilla forces into the Indian part of Kashmir. Their mission was to stir up a rebellion that would either oust the Indians or at least force the issue back onto the international agenda. The Pakistani forces, however, were unable to round up sufficient support among the Kashmiri population, and by August fighting had spread.

A process of escalation culminated in a full-scale Indian offensive against Pakistan in Kashmir, and between September 6 and 23, the parties engaged in a full-scale war. A U.N.-brokered cease-fire took effect thereafter, and in January 1966, President Ayub Khan of Pakistan and Prime Minister Lal Bahadur Shastri of India met at the invitation of the Soviet government and agreed to the mutual withdrawal of troops to the positions held before the war.

In Concert with Bangladesh

While the Kashmir conflict simmered, a new problem was brewing for Pakistan in the late 1960s and early 1970s: the emergence of the East Pakistan independence movement.

After Pakistani parliamentary elections gave the East Pakistani separatist party a majority in the 1970 elections, Pakistan refused to acknowledge these demands for greater autonomy in the East. So, in March 1971, fed-up East Pakistani leaders proclaimed the independent state of Bangladesh.

Pakistani forces were called in to suppress the revolt—without much success. In the ensuing civil war, Pakistani troops murdered an estimated one million Bengalis (the largest ethnic group in Bangladesh) in one of the largest genocides of the twentieth century. More than 10 million more Bengalis took refuge in India.

On December 3, 1971, India, which had provided secret aid to the Bangladesh independence movement, began a large offensive against Pakistan in support of the Bangladeshi cause. The U.N. Security Council voted in support of Bangladesh's independence and called for a cease-fire. On December 17, 1971, almost 100,000 Pakistani troops surrendered to Indian forces in Bangladesh. Another war was over. In 1974, Pakistan formally and finally recognized the independence of Bangladesh.

Reliable Resources

The end of the war left Bangladesh in shambles. Soon afterward, Bengali Ravi Shankar, a good friend of ex-Beatle George Harrison, casually asked Harrison to help with a benefit concert for Shankar's home country. Shankar was hoping to raise about $25,000. Harrison took it to the next level, renting out Madison Square Garden and getting Bob Dylan, Eric Clapton, and even Ringo Starr, among others, to come out and play in the Concert for Bangladesh. The first ever rock benefit for a cause had just occurred.

In 1972, India and Pakistan signed the Simla Agreement, which called for a bilateral solution to the Kashmir issue. Although the Simla Agreement reaffirmed the Line of Control between Pakistani and Indian administered Kashmir that was arrived at after the 1947 war and eased tensions, theirs was an uneasy truce.

Sikhing Freedom

Besides Muslims and Hindus, this part of the world also contains many Sikhs. And, apparently like every other ethnic group or religion discussed in this book, the Sikhs, too, want a land to call their own and are willing to kill people in order to get it. Since 1973, Sikh separatists in the Indian state of Punjab have campaigned to secede from India and form an independent state. Their fight has often been a violent one.

The insurgency in the state of Punjab originated in the late 1970s when an age-old fear in the Sikh community—that of being absorbed into the Hindu fold—re-emerged more strongly than ever before. One of the leaders of this revivalist movement was Sant Jarnail Singh Bhindranwale, a politically ambitious Sikh preacher. Bhindranwale and his followers soon became a source of mayhem and disruption in Punjab.

> ### Reliable Resources
>
> The essence of being a Sikh is that one lives one's life according to the teachings of the Sikh gurus, devoting time to meditating on God and the scriptures, and doing things to benefit other people. Sikhs believe that there is a single, all-powerful God, who created the universe and everything in it. Sikhism emphasizes social and gender equality, and stresses the importance of behaving altruistically.

In 1984, Bhindranwale and his followers took over the Golden Temple complex in Amritsar, Punjab. This temple is Sikhism's most holy of shrines. Indian Prime Minister Indira Gandhi responded by ordering the Indian army to get them out. Negotiations failed, and so Gandhi ordered the army to storm the temple.

A variety of army units, along with substantial numbers of paramilitary forces, surrounded the temple complex. Demands to surrender were met with gunfire. After a day-long siege and firefight, the Indian army successfully regained control of the temple. According to the Indian government, 83 Indian army personnel died and 249 were injured in the battle. Almost 500 Sikhs were also killed and 86 injured.

Needless to say, the massacre at the Golden Temple inflamed the Sikh community. In retaliation, that same year, Indian Prime Minister Indira Gandhi was assassinated by her Sikh bodyguards. In the reprisal's reprisal, mobs massacred Sikhs throughout India.

Things seemed to be finally settling down until one September day in 1995. That was the day that Beant Singh, India's chief minister of Punjab, was killed when a powerful plastic explosive near one of his convoy of sedans exploded just as he was stepping into his bulletproof car. The blast killed Singh and 15 others instantly, injured 14 more, shattered windows in the capital, and was heard 2 miles away.

It's not surprising that Singh was murdered; he was both despised and a symbol of Indian control over Punjab. According to *Time* magazine (September 11, 1995), "Singh's tactics were often ruthless. There were complaints of human rights abuses: More than 120 court cases involving more than 450 policemen [were then] pending against the Punjab police. Corruption and nepotism were rampant, and the Singh administration had 17 high court indictments against it."

India shows no signs of giving in to the demands of the Sikh separatists. As in Kashmir, India seems resigned to protecting its territories, damn the consequences.

Nuclear Roulette

The real problem today on the Indian subcontinent is not that India and Pakistan have so far failed to resolve their differences over Kashmir, that they have two of the largest populations on Earth, or that they hate each other. No, the problem now is that they both have nuclear weapons; the same dispute that might have killed 10,000 people yesterday could well kill more than a million people today.

Briefing Book

On May 18, 1974, India detonated its first nuclear device, saying that it was for atomic research and not weapons. Why it did so is a matter of some debate, but the fact is, it did. India thereafter began an inexorable climb up the nuclear mountain in search of the plutonium at the end of the rainbow.

Why did it go down the nuclear road? Having a nuclear bomb forces other countries to think twice. That is as true for the United States and Russia as it is for India. The deterrence effect of having a nuclear weapon cannot be underestimated. India understood and wanted this.

Now it is true that India has legitimate security concerns, not just from Pakistan, but from other countries, too. In an interview with the Deccan Herald News Service, former Indian Prime Minister I. K. Gujral explained India's security concerns. According to Gujral, the Indian coastline is nearly 7,000 miles long and is in an area that is "heavily nuclearized." Moreover, Gujral says the U.S. military base in Diego Garcia sits in the Indian Ocean, and is also home to nuclear weapons. Gujral also pointed out that warships, submarines, and aircraft carriers with nuclear weapons constantly sail in the Indian Ocean.

Even more disturbing, in India's eyes, is that after the disintegration of the Soviet Union, the United States, being the world's sole superpower, has abused its strength against much smaller and more venerable nations, Iraq, Yugoslavia, and Afghanistan to name but three examples.

So it was of little surprise that India's tests of nuclear weapons in 1998, were popular among Indians. The *Times of India* reported that 91 percent of Indians approved of the tests. Fully 82 percent further believed India should build nuclear weapons.

A typical analysis of why so many in the third world supported India's bold move was written by Nawab Khan in the *Iran Times*. In his piece, titled "Nuclear Tests, Why Not India?" Khan wrote:

The argument that Western powers are democratic and hence their nuclear arsenals are under strict control and can never be misused are not quite convincing. American democracy did not prevent it from dropping the atomic bomb twice on Japan. The lesson to be learnt from the Pokharan nuclear blasts is that there cannot be one law for the haves and another for the have-nots.

Yet not everyone was so enthusiastic. India and Pakistan, after all, had already had three wars. So, if the five nuclear tests conducted by India at Pokharan were not bad enough, that they were followed three weeks later by six nuclear explosions conducted by Pakistan was worse. Both countries now had the bomb.

Landmine!

In 1966, the year the United States had the greatest number of nuclear weapons in its stockpile, the number of warheads it had available was 32,193.

You Started It!

According to an article by M. V. Ramana and A. H. Nayyar published in *Scientific American* titled "India, Pakistan and the Bomb," both countries had actually been working on their nuclear programs practically since independence. India's first prime minister, Jawaharlal Nehru, stated in 1948 that India should "develop (atomic energy) for peaceful purposes." Nehru also believed, though, that "if we are compelled as a nation to use it for other purposes, possibly no pious sentiments will stop the nation from using it that way."

Like many countries that developed nuclear capabilities, for Indian leaders, India's nuclear program gave the country political clout and a sense of joining the modern world. Accordingly, for the next 20 years, India built and operated nuclear reactors, mined uranium, and extracted plutonium.

Reliable Resources

After the 1965 India-Pakistan War, many Pakistani politicians wanted to get a jump-start on their nuclear program. Pakistani Foreign Minister Zulfikhar Ali Bhutto put it bluntly when he stated that if India ever developed an atomic bomb, Pakistan would, too, "even if we have to eat grass or leaves."

When India finally tested its bomb in 1974, the news was, not surprisingly, greeted with enthusiasm in India and apprehension abroad. Western countries retaliated by cutting off any further nuclear assistance and restricted the export of nuclear technologies and materials to nations, such as India and Pakistan, that refused to sign the Nuclear Non-Proliferation Treaty.

Because these two countries are so linked (whether they like it or not), once India entered the nuclear game, Pakistan was sure to follow, and it did. Pakistan operated its first nuclear reactor in 1965, and opened its first commercial reactor in 1970.

Pakistan made up for its lack of trained nuclear scientists by shipping more than 600 scientists and engineers to the West for training. Pakistan was therefore able to get its nuclear research laboratories in place by the mid-1960s.

Success for Pakistan finally came in 1979 when it enriched a small amount of uranium, a process necessary for isolating the "bomb-usable" isotope uranium 235. Since that time, it is estimated that Pakistan has developed enough uranium to arm between 20 and 40 nuclear bombs.

Pakistan's bid for nuclear parity with India was bolstered in the spring of 1990, as events in Kashmir threatened to erupt into another full-scale war. According to a 1993 *New Yorker* article by Seymour Hersh, U.S. surveillance satellites detected a convoy of suspicious trucks moving toward an air base as the latest Kashmir crisis accelerated.

Reliable Resources

Pakistani Islamic funda- mentalist Qazi Hussain Ahmad declared in 1993: "Let us wage jihad for Kashmir. A nuclear- armed Pakistan would deter India from a wider conflict."

This information was relayed to India by the Americans, and a worried India therefore decided to recall the troops it had amassed at the border. Pakistan concluded that its nuclear weapons were a strong deterrent. Indian officials never acknowledged the story; doing so could be construed as a sign of weakness.

Whatever the case, this event led India to double its efforts to make a usable bomb, a plan encouraged by the rise of Hindu nationalism in India. The Bharatiya Janata Party (BJP), an ultra-nationalist party that had long called for India to acquire nuclear weapons, came to power in 1998. It ordered nuclear tests immediately, giving Pakistan a reason to do the same.

The First-Ever Nuclear War?

The subcontinent now had all the necessary ingredients for a nuclear war: a contentious and ongoing conflict in Kashmir, extremist pressures, possession and development of nuclear bombs, inadequate fail-safe precautions to avoid unauthorized use of these weapons, geographical proximity, and jingoistic leaders.

Evidence of just how bad things can be now that both countries have the bomb was seen in November 2001 when suicide terrorists stormed the Indian parliament building in Delhi. Twelve people were killed, including the five attackers. It is believed that the terrorists were Pakistanis demanding a free Kashmir.

Both countries sent massive amounts of troops to the Kashmir border. India accused Pakistan of coddling terrorists, with an external affairs minister saying, "Like the United States in the case of Taliban, we have launched a comprehensive diplomatic offensive to apprise the international community of Pakistan's active role in fomenting terrorism on Indian soil."

Envoys from both countries were recalled, and plans for war were underway. The question this time was far more serious—would they go nuclear? Somehow, cooler heads prevailed, and both countries backed off from war when Pakistan took concrete steps to reign in those responsible.

What Does the Future Hold?

Although both countries had certainly been bellicose, they also seemed to realize the enormity of the disaster that awaited them had they continued down the slippery slope toward yet another war now that both were nuclear nations. That is likely why they agreed in 2004 to try and find peaceful solutions to their thorniest of issues—Kashmir and nuclear weapons.

In January 2004, Indian Prime Minister Atal Bihari Vajpayee and Pakistani President General Pervez Musharraf released a joint statement declaring that the two countries would hold comprehensive, bilateral discussions. The statement said, in part, that they would explore "possible options for a peaceful negotiated settlement of [all] issue[s]" and that such discussions "should be explored in a sincere spirit and purposeful manner."

> **Peacekeepers**
>
> If anything positive can be gleaned from the almost mind-numbing violence evidenced throughout this book, it is that peace usually requires brave leaders taking bold actions in new and unexpected ways. The willingness of the leaders of India and Pakistan to engage in meaningful dialogue regarding the difficult issues they face is exactly that type of action. As they say, you don't make peace with your friends, you make peace with your enemies.

Certainly this was a large concession on India's part, as it is in control of Kashmir. In return for this gesture of good faith, President Musharraf agreed to "restore normalcy and cooperation between India and Pakistan" while also agreeing to implement confidence-building measures. In addition, the two sides agreed that the proposed talks should also include discussions for avoiding nuclear war (India has a "no-first-use" policy; Pakistan does not).

In January 2005, India's chief of the army staff, General N. C. Vij, announced that, in an effort to further normalize relations with Pakistan, India would be reducing the number of troops it stationed along the border in Jammu and Kashmir. Later that summer, the two sides entered talks centered on nuclear issues, the idea being to create a pact mandating that each tell the other about pending nuclear tests.

Will such comprehensive talks bear fruit? We can only hope so. The lives of more than one billion people depend on it.

The Least You Need to Know

◆ Kashmir has long been a problem on the Indian subcontinent.

◆ India and Pakistan have fought three wars, one of which created Bangladesh.

◆ Sikh separatists cause India additional pressures.

◆ India and Pakistan are engaged in peace talks so as to peacefully settle the issue of Kashmir while also reducing nuclear tensions.

Chapter 16

Religious and Ethnic Animosity in Indonesia

In This Chapter

- ◆ From authoritarian rule to East Timor's independence
- ◆ Problems in Sulawesi
- ◆ Killing in the name of God in Kalimantan
- ◆ Aceh's independence movement
- ◆ The Bali bombings

Indonesia is not only the world's fourth-most-populous nation and one of the world's most populous Muslim nations, it is also the world's largest archipelago, containing more than 13,000 islands—of which 3,000 are inhabited. Only one of its islands has captured popular imagination—Bali.

And, with more than 300 tribal and ethnic groups and 250 different languages, the country is beset with interethnic and inter-religious hatred. Even the largely predominant Muslim religion is characterized by regional variations.

Indonesia is a vast archipelago.

The End of Colonialism and the Rise of Democracy

After winning independence from Spain in 1581, the Netherlands became one of the world's major seafaring powers. A Dutch fleet entered Indonesian waters in 1596, and in 1602 the United East India Company was formed. The city of Jakarta became the Indonesian capital of the burgeoning spice trade, and the company would go on to rule Indonesia for two hundred years.

def•i•ni•tion

An **archipelago** is any sea or broad sheet of water interspersed with many islands or with a group of islands.

In the nineteenth century, Indonesia saw the replacement of company rule by Dutch government, as well as the transformation of Java (the main island) into a colonial society that spread throughout the *archipelago*. The modern state of Indonesia is a nineteenth-century creation.

Independence Day

Japan invaded China in 1937, and in 1942, the Battle of the Java Sea resulted in the Japanese defeat of a combined British, Dutch, Australian, and U.S. fleet. On March 9, 1942, the Dutch government surrendered Indonesia to the Japanese.

Although Japanese occupation was a watershed in Indonesian history, Japanese control of Indonesia would not last long. As its war effort became more desperate, Japan announced in 1944 that Indonesia would become independent. This announcement was a vindication for the Indonesian nationalist leader, and soon-to-be first president, Achmed Sukarno, and his Communist allies.

Sukarno believed that the new country should have a strong presidency and a constitutional form of government. This was agreed to, although many in the country's large Muslim population had misgivings about forming Indonesia as a secular state. Nevertheless, Sukarno formally declared the nation's independence on August 17, 1945.

The Rise of Suharto

Ruling such a vast, populous, heterogeneous country would prove, and not for the last time, to be a difficult thing to do. By 1965, Indonesia had become an unstable place. Sukarno was a despotic ruler who instituted martial law in 1957. His ruling party (PKI) aroused the hostility of many Islamic groups, as well as the military. In addition, the United States and China had used Sukarno and Indonesia to wage a bloody proxy war. So, many despised Sukarno's rule.

By 1965, the population had fallen into two camps—those supporting Sukarno and the ruling PKI and others who supported Major General Suharto. On September 30, 1965, an attempted coup d'état occurred. Although unsuccessful, it proved how disliked Sukarno had finally become, and eventually it would lead to his displacement from power.

In the wake of the coup's failure, there was a violent reaction. Many in the country wanted to be rid of the PKI. By December 1965, mobs were engaged in large-scale rioting and killings. Paramilitary groups carried out a war against the PKI. Estimates of the number killed vary widely; 300,000 dead is believed to be an accurate number.

The end result of this conflict was that Indonesia would get itself a new leader, yet another strongman, General Suharto. Suharto's military government was, if nothing else, a stable one. Given the instability of the Sukarno years, that alone was a salve for the Muslim country. After Suharto took power, he solidified his power base and ruled with an iron will. Rebellion had become sporadic and, until recently, unsuccessful.

> **Reliable Resources**
>
> In the 1983 movie *The Year of Living Dangerously*, Mel Gibson plays an Australian reporter assigned to Indonesia during the calamitous summer of 1965. Linda Hunt played the local who helped him, and she won an Academy Award for best supporting actress (although she played a man!)

> **Landmine!**
>
> The elimination of the PKI was one of the bloodiest events in postwar Southeast Asia.

Revenge of the Sukarnos

However, with stability came repression. Suharto would repressively govern Indonesia for the next 30 years. He remained in power until 1998, when charges of corruption were leveled against him and his family. Coupled with the ongoing crisis in East Timor (see the following section) and an economic crisis throughout Southeast Asia, the Indonesians had had enough. Massive rioting, strikes, and protests finally forced Suharto out, and soon brought new elections.

When Indonesians went to the polls to vote for a successor to the ousted Suharto, they chose a woman, Megawati Sukarnoputri, who had few visible talents as a politician, except for one—Sukarno was her father.

As the heir to Indonesia's first family, the 54-year-old matriarch was reluctantly pushed into politics by opponents of the dictatorship who hoped to use the Sukarno name to rally support. Although her family had been ousted from power by Suharto, it remained part of Jakarta's elite.

What "Mother Mega" found upon taking office was a country bursting at the seams, what with Suharto's ability to crush opposition now gone. Separatist rebellions in some regions and ethnic and religious violence in others showed that the hodgepodge of thousands of islands that became a nation-state only because of their common colonization by Holland was now threatening to disintegrate. But Sukarnoputri proved not to be the person to solve such vast problems. In September 2004, a former general, Susilo Bambang Yudhoyono, defeated the incumbent to become the nation's next president.

> **Reliable Resources**
>
> Sixty percent of the Indonesian population is educated only through elementary school.

East Timor Gains Independence

East Timor became a colony of Portugal in the sixteenth century and remained so until 1975. In 1974, Portugal decided that all of its territories should have the right of self-determination, and in 1975 representatives of several East Timorese political groups were invited to attend conventions to that end.

But before a decision could be made, the Portuguese authorities withdrew from the country after violent uprisings in East Timor. Thereafter, in November 1975, the Revolutionary Front for an Independent East Timor (Fretilin), a Marxist group, declared the independence of the Democratic Republic of East Timor.

For Indonesia, this was an alarming development. On one hand, having a Communist regime in its neighborhood was thought to be a national security threat. The Indonesian government decided that if Portugal was unable to reestablish effective control over its colony, it would be necessary for Indonesian forces to restore order. On the other hand, the Communist movement proved to be an awfully handy reason to invade and annex the small country.

Indonesia sent in an army of 10,000, and in December 1975, the establishment of a provisional government of East Timor was declared. Indonesia declared that the people of East Timor had requested Indonesia "to accept East Timor as an integral part of the Republic of Indonesia." Indonesia thereafter incorporated East Timor as part of Indonesia. The slaughter of East Timorese during the 1975 Indonesian invasion foreshadowed the ruthless manner in which Indonesia would come to govern the former Portuguese colony.

Indonesia thereafter began a long and harsh campaign of subjugation and pacification against the East Timorese. Through the late 1970s and 1980s, accounts of military repression and mass starvation repeatedly emerged from the country. An estimated number of as high as 200,000 of East Timor's inhabitants died as a result of the armed occupation.

Landmine!

According to the Federation of American Scientists, "as many as 60,000 Timorese were killed in the initial assault, out of a total population of about 600,000."

The World Takes Notice

Indonesia's highly questionable annexation of East Timor naturally became the subject of much international debate, and East Timor became the focus of two U.N. Security Councils. Security Council Resolution 384 (1975) called upon "all States to respect the territorial integrity of East Timor as well as the inalienable right of its people to self-determination." It further called upon "the Government of Indonesia to withdraw without delay all its forces from the Territory." Indonesia ignored the resolutions.

By the 1990s, discontent with Indonesian rule escalated sharply among the younger generation of East Timorese, particularly those born after the island's forced annexation of 1975. With the disintegration of global communism by this time, it was this emerging militancy of East Timorese youth, far more than the remnants of the Marxist Fretilin group, which posed the greatest threat to Indonesia's rule.

In November 1991, peaceful youths were marching in a pro-Fretilin political demonstration in the East Timorese capital of Dili. Video of the event taken by participants caught Indonesian troops firing upon the marchers. At least 70 protesters were shot or clubbed by the troops. The inflammatory video was smuggled out of East Timor, and for the first time in a long time, the plight of the Timorese became world news, showcasing what was widely seen as mass murder by the Indonesian army.

The growing resentment of Indonesia's rule became more evident in November 1994 during the Asia-Pacific Economic Cooperation meeting. At that meeting, roughly 30 East Timorese climbed over a fence surrounding the U.S. Embassy in Jakarta and occupied the embassy compound for 2 weeks, demanding the release of a Timorese resistance leader. They asked President Clinton, who was attending the summit, to intercede on behalf of the East Timor people. At the same time, rioting in the region of Dili left four people dead, leading to additional clashes with police.

World sympathy was further aroused by the award of the 1996 Nobel Peace Prize to exiled East Timorese independence leader Jose Ramos Horta and Dili's Bishop Carlos Ximenes Felipe Belo.

Change Is in the Air

With the demise of the Suharto regime in 1998, and the emergence of Megawati Sukarnoputri, efforts to resolve this conflict came to the fore. U.N.-sponsored talks on East Timor gained new momentum; both sides agreed to discuss an Indonesian plan to offer special status for East Timor, which was more than any previous government was willing to concede.

In May 1999, Indonesia, Portugal, and United Nations Secretary General Kofi Annan signed an agreement in New York, which would grant the right of self-determination to East Timorese through a plebiscite. The historic agreement called for Indonesia to be responsible for ensuring a peaceful environment in East Timor so that the voting process could take place as scheduled.

The Plebiscite

At the end of August 1999, despite an intense climate of fear, a healthy 98.6 percent of all East Timorese registered voters went to the polls. During the five days that it took the United Nations to count the ballots, Indonesian-backed violence escalated, and thousands of civilians fled to the hills and mountains. In the end, the East Timorese voted overwhelmingly for independence.

The agreement had stated that "all sides must lay down their arms and subsequently disarm," but this was easier said than done. Immediately after the vote, the Indonesian military and its militia brethren began to attack and destroy the East Timorese population and infrastructure. Estimates are that 70 to 80 percent of Dili's businesses were destroyed, and half of all homes were burned to the ground.

After 10 days of turmoil, and under intense international pressure, President Clinton suspended all U.S.-Indonesian military ties on September 11, 1999. On September 15, the Security Council endorsed the deployment of an Australian-led peacekeeping force to East Timor.

The international pressure proved to be too much, and the Indonesian military finally began to withdraw from the country it had occupied for nearly a quarter century. U.N. peacekeeping forces took control.

As all parties realized that the ruined country was not quite ready for full independence, the United Nations created the United Nations Transitional Administration for East Timor. UNTAET was established to administer the region and institute a transitional government during the transition period. To that end, UNTAET works in close cooperation with the East Timorese.

Finally, on January 30, 2002, United Nations Secretary General Kofi Annan invited the leaders of all 189 U.N. member states, as well as the pope and Switzerland, to attend a May 20 ceremony marking the full independence of East Timor. Its mission completed, UNTAET folded up shop, and East Timor was finally free.

> **Reliable Resources**
>
> "Today we suspended all military sales, and continue to work to try to persuade the Indonesians to support the United Nations' operation to go in and help to end the violence and secure the safety of the people in East Timor."
>
> —President Bill Clinton, September 11, 1999

Papua, a.k.a. Irian Jaya

Irian Jaya is the easternmost island in the Indonesian archipelago and forms half of the island of New Guinea. The island reportedly was discovered during the 1800s by a Portuguese spice merchant who named the island Papua (the Malay word for curly-haired people). Today, the eastern half of the island is Papua New Guinea, a territory that was administered by Australia until it gained independence in 1975.

Reliable Resources

Irian Jaya's 2.4 million people represent only one hundredth of the Indonesian population, but in land area, it is the largest and one of the most resource-rich parts of Indonesia. Its people are the poorest of all Indonesians.

The western half is called Irian Jaya—Glorious West Guinea—by Indonesia, which took over from Dutch rule in the early 1960s. With the handover to Indonesia, Irian Jaya was promised eventual self-determination, but, typically, that never occurred.

As a result, the Free Papua Movement (or OPM) emerged in opposition to Indonesian rule and has waged a battle for independence that has lasted for 30 years. In 1996, the OPM attracted international attention when it kidnapped more than 20 people. Two were killed during a rescue operation by Indonesian special forces. The next year, OPM took control of the streets of Jayapura, and thousands of people gathered in the capital, demanding independence.

The pressure on the Indonesian government to give the people of this mostly Christian territory a greater voice in their own future was mounting. In response, new President Megawati Sukarnoputri decided to grant the province a far greater degree of autonomy than ever before.

The new laws went into effect on January 1, 2002. The main changes, as summarized by BBC regional analyst Nicholas Nugent, were …

- The government allowed the province to change its name to the preferred name of Papua.

- The Papua flag was allowed to fly next to, although lower than, the Indonesian flag.

- The Papuan provincial government was allowed to retain most of the revenue from oil and gas production as well as from mineral and forestry activity. Given the province's enormous natural reserves, this compromise was worth hundreds of millions of dollars.

Landmine!

President Megawati Sukarnoputri's father, Indonesia's first president Sukarno, first promised autonomy to the region nearly 40 years ago.

Maybe surprisingly, many Papuans rejected the package. OPM demanded nothing less than a plebiscite on full independence, along the lines of that held in East Timor in 1999. But the government, fearing that the people of Papua would follow the Timorese precedent if given the chance, ruled out an independence referendum for the province.

The likelihood that this long simmering conflict would end peacefully diminished greatly after pro-independence leader They Eluay went missing. The 64-year-old Eluay was later found dead, suffocated in his overturned car. Indonesian police ruled the death a murder.

> **Landmine!**
>
> In 2002, in Jakarta, Muslims in the city's central square called for a jihad against Christians in the Moluccas. One man held a sign that read "Tolerance Is Nonsense, Slaughter Christians."

Sulawesi

Central Sulawesi has been described as a remote and backward province. Farming and fishing are the occupations of most people who live there, and the economy is of little significance. As in the Moluccas, the Christians and Muslims here have lived side by side in peace. But in 1998, all that changed when religious violence erupted in the small town of Poso. And, as with the Moluccas, a seemingly insignificant event turned neighbors into killers.

It was nothing more than a stupid drunken fight between a Christian and Muslim youths that was the catalyst for the violence and rioting that ensued. After a period of relative calm, violence again broke out in 2001. By the time the insanity subsided this time, Poso was practically destroyed. An estimated 1,000 people were dead, and many more Christians were no longer welcome there.

The actual cause of the animosity and violence is a matter of speculation. Some say that it is a result of similar fighting in the Moluccan Islands to the East. Christians say it is because of a rise in Islamic fundamentalism. No one is really sure.

Kalimantan

Violence has erupted on the island of Borneo, too. Ethnic and religious riots broke out in the Indonesian-controlled side of Borneo, called Kalimantan, in late December 1996. In this case, it was a matter of two different tribes battling one another—the ethnic Christian Dayaks versus immigrant Muslim Madurese.

The immigrants arrived as part of a resettlement program that lasted for 40 years, until 2000. The program was unwelcome by many as the government was accused of ignoring the local Dayaks. It seems evident again that the end of the Suharto rule created an opening for this long-festering feud to break out in full.

Although several peace agreements were signed following the first clash, none held. Rioting continued to take place as Madurese men went on a rampage that included the burning down of a Catholic school. The fighting between the Dayaks and the Madurese then spread to other parts of the Kalimantan province. Murder and rampage begat revenge and retribution on both sides.

Government officials said the body count from one "incident" stood at around 500, nearly all of them Madurese, adding, however, that the death toll could be as high as 1,000 as uncounted bodies lay rotting in houses and fields. Local Christian church leaders have calculated the number of missing Madurese in the thousands.

> **Landmine!**
>
> According to a CNN.com report on Indonesia, "Before Indonesia's former Dutch colonial rulers outlawed headhunting in the late nineteenth century, the Dayaks were widely believed to be cannibals. In traditional Dayak belief, consuming the flesh of an enemy endows the eater with the victim's strength."

Indonesia's military then cracked down on both groups. Although the Army has successfully taken control of many of the most problematic areas, in the interior, beyond the military checkpoints, Dayaks continue to hunt for Madurese.

Hopefully, the recent peace agreements signed by the two tribes signal an end to this violent conflict.

Aceh

On December 27, 1949, the Dutch left Indonesia, including the province of Aceh. The Republic of Indonesia was born. The problem here is that even though Aceh had never formally been incorporated into Dutch colonial possession, upon the creation of Indonesia, Aceh was made part of the new country.

Subsequently, the Indonesian government annexed Aceh. Since annexation, the Acehnese have continued to resent what they consider foreign occupation. The Aceh independence movement was born.

Aceh Merdeka (Free Aceh)

Recognizing the problem, the Indonesian government gave Aceh the status of "special territory" in 1959. This conferred upon it a high degree of autonomy. But even so, the desire for an independent Islamic state did not die.

In 1976, the Aceh Merdeka movement ("Free Aceh") was founded. In the 1970s, Indonesian authorities arrested members of the group and shut down their activities until 1989.

> **Reliable Resources**
>
> Another issue for the Acehnese is Indonesia's resettlement policy. Most of Indonesia's population lives on the island of Java. The government helps Java's overcrowding by migrating residents to other islands, including Aceh. In Aceh, many of the residents are now primarily Javanese transmigrants.

Escalation

The conflict has turned increasingly brutal. According to *Human Rights Watch*, "By mid-2001, so many killings were taking place in Aceh of people suspected of belonging to Aceh Merdeka that it was difficult to keep an accurate tally." It adds, "There is ample evidence that Indonesian forces deliberately and systematically employ executions to deter villagers from supporting (the independence movement)."

By the same token, Human Rights Watch adds, "[Rebel] abuses include killings of suspected military informants, as well as of family members of police and military personnel, unlawful detentions, forced expulsions, and other terrorizing of non-Acehnese; destruction of property, including homes, and systematic extortion."

In 2002, peace talks were at a stand-still and as the new year dawned, the governor of Aceh province declared that the region had implemented Islamic "sharia." The strict Muslim code provides rules on alcohol, dress, and personal conduct, but also in theory demands amputation for theft and execution for adultery.

Accord

In August of 2005, years of bloodshed (estimated dead: 15,000) gave way to peace as the Indonesian government signed a peace treaty with the Aceh rebels. What caused such a turnaround? Was it bold leaders being brave? Was it a cynical, calculated "lesser of two evils" conclusion? No. Here, the impetus to reach a peace accord was new: a natural disaster. The devastating tsunami that destroyed much of the Aceh province on December 26, 2004 created an opening that heretofore had not been present.

Reliable Resources

On December 26, 2004, a magnitude 9 earthquake occurred about 150 miles off the Aceh coast, in the Indian Ocean. It was the largest earthquake in the world since 1964 and was soon followed by a 7.3 magnitude aftershock. These quakes spawned a giant wave, called a tsunami, which raced across the Indian Ocean, the Bay of Bengal, and the South China Sea.

Traveling at speeds in the open ocean of up to 300 miles per hour, the tsunami hit Indonesia hardest, but also damaged coastal areas in Sri Lanka, Myanmar, Thailand, Malaysia, and the Maldives. Hours later, the huge wave hit the coast of Africa, damaging parts of Kenya, Tanzania, and Somalia.

Although it is difficult to say exactly how many people died, it is estimated that the number is somewhere around 150,000, the vast majority being in Indonesia generally and Aceh specifically.

The tsunami was so devastating that it forced the two sides to enter into what turned out to be seven months of peace talks so that the overwhelmed region could peacefully receive aid. The peace agreement was signed in Helsinki, Finland, as the former-Finnish President Martti Ahtisaari, mediated the agreement. Relevant parts of the treaty included the following:

◆ An immediate end to hostilities

◆ Amnesty for members of Free Aceh

◆ An agreement by the rebels to surrender their arms

◆ Increased self-government and autonomy

◆ An agreement by the government to cut troops and police numbers in the region in half

◆ An agreement that 70 percent of the province's oil and gas revenue would stay in the province

It was hoped that the accord could signal a way to settle other longstanding disputes in the country, too. According to Umar Juoro, a political scientist at the Center for International Development Studies in Jakarta (*Christian Science Monitor*, August 15, 2005), "If we can deal with Aceh, it means that autonomy could work in Indonesia without splitting the country apart. It's an important lesson."

And it is a lesson that was not lost on the leadership. With the country suddenly awash with billions of dollars in foreign aid to assist with tsunami relief, the government tried to capitalize on this rare confluence of goodwill and flush coffers triggered by tragedy.

According to the *Christian Science Monitor*

> Indonesia … has made more of its post-tsunami opportunity to make peace. The tragedy has created a space for political dialogue and has mobilized billions of dollars in long-term reconstruction funds. … "This means that funding is available for the peace process and there's an enormous amount of creativity and 'by the seat of their pants' thinking within the government about how to make this agreement work," [said] Sidney Jones, head of the International Crisis Group in Jakarta.

Hopefully it won't take another natural disaster for other Indonesian disputes to find similar resolution.

Trouble in Paradise

A little before midnight on October 12, 2002, on the Indonesian tropical island of Bali, Islamic terrorists detonated a bomb outside a busy, popular nightclub. About 15 seconds later, a car bomb exploded in the same area. At that same moment, a third bomb exploded outside the American consulate in Bali.

The War on Terror had arrived in Bali.

The first bomb was hidden in a backpack, and the suicide bomber died in the blast. The car bomb was hidden in a white van and was detonated by remote control, leaving a crater 3 feet deep. The embassy bomb did little damage.

In all, 202 people died, including 88 Australians, 38 Indonesians, and 26 Brits. The rest of the dead were from a dozen other countries.

It was quickly suspected that the group Jemaah Islamiyah, a radical Islamist group linked to al-Qaeda, was responsible for the blasts. Abu Bakar Bashir, one of the leaders of the group, denied involvement, alleging that the United States had exploded the bombs.

But on April 30, 2003, a member of Jemaah Islamiyah was arrested and charged with being the "mastermind" behind the attacks. Amrozi bin Haji Nurhasyim was charged with buying both the van and the explosives used in the bombings. A few months later, he was found guilty and sentenced to death.

In September, a second suspect in the Bali bombing, Imam Samudra, was also sentenced to death for his part in the attack. Samudra said that the bombings were part of a jihad, quoting the Koran: "Fight in the path of Allah against people who are fighting Muslims."

A third man, Amrozi's brother, Ali Imron, was sentenced to life in prison; and a fourth man, Mukhlas, brother to Amrozi and Ali, was sentenced to death in October, 2003. In March, 2005, a fifth man, Abu Bakar Bashir, was found guilty of conspiracy in the bombings and sentenced to two and a half years in prison.

Al-Qaeda and Indonesia

Because of its vastness, as well as its Islamic ties, there was widespread belief in Washington that al-Qaeda had bases in Indonesia. And, as the U.S. War on Terror began, Washington found Indonesia to be a hard country to deal with. Washington was frustrated by the unwillingness of the Indonesian security forces to rein in Islamic militants.

This is so, despite the fact that the head of Indonesia's National Intelligence Agency said that al-Qaeda members had been fighting on the island of Sulawesi. Apparently, the militant Islamic organization Laskar Jihad had links with al-Qaeda and was responsible for sending in thousands of armed fighters to Sulawesi to support local Muslims.

Even this is not surprising, considering that Indonesian General Abdullah Hendropriyono admitted in late 2001 that international terrorists, including Osama bin Laden's al-Qaeda network, have training camps on Sulawesi.

If Indonesia didn't have enough conflict already, a war against the United States is the last thing it needs.

The Least You Need to Know

- Suharto's authoritarian rule clamped down on conflicts.
- East Timor is finally free.
- The isle of Irian Jaya wants to be free.
- Aceh got its independence.
- Islamic terrorists brought their holy war to Indonesia when they blew up discos in Bali.

Chapter 17

More Asian Atrocities

In This Chapter

- Burma's heroine
- Sri Lanka's long civil war
- An Islamic insurgency … in Thailand?
- Nepal

Conflict is born of many mothers. Asia, being one of the most densely populated parts of the planet, has learned that overpopulation can often create conflict; countries with too many mouths to feed might look with envy and ill will toward their neighbors' resources.

Conflict also arises when one group thinks that its philosophy can care for the people better than that of another group. It might also come about when competing countries lay claim to the same parcel of land. And finally, let's not forget the vices of power and greed as potential causes. When it comes to conflict, Asia has it all!

Asia: Little room to expand.

Burma's Close Shave with Democracy

A largely rural, densely forested country, Burma (or Myanmar, as it is also known) is adorned with ample symbols of Buddhism, manifested most vividly by the thousands of pagodas and Buddhas throughout its ancient towns. Yet this peaceful vision of the Buddha couldn't be more discordant with modern Burma.

Burma is ruled by a military junta, which has a history of gross human-rights abuses, including the forcible relocation of civilians and the widespread use of child labor. The military controls key Burmese industries, and corruption is a hallmark of the black-market economy. The armed forces are also said to traffic in heroin.

The Savior?

Aung San Suu Kyi is the daughter of the late Burmese nationalist leader, General Aung San. According to the BBC, after attending school in the Burmese capital of Rangoon, Suu Kyi went on to live in India and then moved to Britain for her university education, where she met and married an Englishman.

In March 1988, Suu Kyi went back to Burma alone to attend her ailing mother. At the same time, as they had throughout the world, student protests were breaking out in Burma, demanding democracy.

On August 8, 1988 (8/8/88), the famous 8-8-88 mass uprising began in Rangoon and spread to the entire

> **Reliable Resources**
>
> The excellent movie *Beyond Rangoon* tells the story of these chaotic days in Burma, through the eyes of Patricia Arquette's character, an American doctor stuck in the country during the crisis.

country, drawing millions of people to protest against the government. On August 26, Aung San Suu Kyi addressed a half million people in a mass rally in Rangoon, calling for a democratic government.

Inspired by the nonviolent campaigns of Mahatama Gandhi and Martin Luther King, Aung San Suu Kyi began to organize nonviolent rallies throughout Burma, calling for free elections.

On September 18, 1988, Suu Kyi was placed under house arrest and held without charges or trial. The next year, despite her continuing detention, her National League for Democracy party won a landslide victory in the general elections by securing 82 percent of the vote.

As can be expected from what you've read so far in this book, the military junta that ruled Burma refused to recognize the results of the election. In protest to her continued detention, Suu Kyi went on a hunger strike, and many of the elected NLD representatives fled the country, maintaining a government in exile. In 1991, while still under house arrest, Aung San Suu Kyi was awarded the Nobel Peace Prize. In the meantime, many Western governments have enforced sanctions against Burma until the military government steps down.

Reliable Resources

Nobel Peace prize winners include the following:

1906	President Teddy Roosevelt
1919	President Woodrow Wilson
1964	Martin Luther King
1973	Henry Kissinger
1979	Mother Theresa
1983	Polish leader Lech Walesa
1984	South African Bishop Desmond Tutu
1989	Dalai Lama
1990	Mikhail Gorbachev
1998	U.N. Peacekeeping Forces

Amazingly, although he was nominated in 1937, 1938, 1939, 1947, and 1948, the most famous symbol of peace and nonviolence in the twentieth century, Mahatma Gandhi, never won the Nobel Peace Prize.

Indeed, the military junta continues to wage war against its own people. Violence against various groups have forced more than a million refugees to flee Burma.

Asia's Hero

Finally, in 1995, after six years in jail, Aung San Suu Kyi was released, only to be put under house arrest again in September 2000. Although she was able to live at home, her phone was disconnected and she was unable to travel freely. In fact, when her husband Michael died of cancer in 1999 in Britain, she was unable to leave Burma, fearing the junta would never allow her back into her country.

In October 2000, Suu Kyi entered into talks with the ruling military junta, aimed at ending the country's political deadlock. And in 2002, she was again released. In 2004, *Time* magazine nominated 20 people to be named "Asia's Hero." The list included everyone from the Dalai Lama to Yang Liwei (China's first man in space). Voted on by the readers of *Asia Time*, the runaway winner was Aung San Suu Kyi.

According to *Time* (October 4, 2004):

> For her steadiness and her steadfast belief in the powers of democracy and peaceful protest, 40.4% of voters nominated Aung San Suu Kyi as Asia's Online Hero for 2004. The daughter of Aung San, an independence leader who helped free Burma from colonialism under the British in 1948, Aung San Suu Kyi rose to the fore of the pro-democracy movement, only to see it violently suppressed in the early 1990s by Burma's ruling military junta. She has spent most of the time since then under house arrest, locked up in her family home on University Avenue in the Burmese capital of Rangoon, but remains a beacon of hope for her people. In 1991 she was awarded the Nobel Peace Prize, and remains the only living recipient of that award incarcerated.

Trouble in Paradise

In Sri Lanka, a small island off the coast of India, Hindu Tamils are the majority in the northern part of the country, but are a minority in the country overall (accounting for only 12 percent of the population). Buddhist Sinhalese are the majority.

The Tamils are violently demanding (what else?) independence. The Tamils believe that because they have their own history, traditions, culture, and language, they deserve their own homeland. The problem is that Sri Lanka is a very small place.

The most powerful Tamil group in Sri Lanka, the LTTE, began its armed conflict with the Sri Lankan government in 1983. Often called the Tamil Tigers, the group utilizes a traditional guerrilla/terrorist strategy to forward its aims—the group's elite Black Tiger squad conducts suicide bombings against various Sri Lankan targets, and all rank-and-file members carry a cyanide capsule so they can kill themselves should they ever get caught before their mission is accomplished.

In 1987, the Sri Lankan government went on a major military offensive against the Tigers, ignoring objections and warnings by the Indian government that it would intervene if it thought the Tamils were being starved. (India has a population of about 55 million Tamils.)

In July 1987, India and Sri Lanka signed an accord in an attempt to settle the dispute by giving greater autonomy to the Tamils and including an Indian peacekeeping force that would disarm the rebels. At first, the LTTE was game to the accord.

The accord broke down in 1989 after opposition by some Sinhalese natives who turned violent. In 1990, India withdrew its troops, and civil war was again on. Since then, the LTTE has turned out to be a very active, very violent group, as evidenced by the following:

- ◆ In 1991, it assassinated Indian Prime Minister Rajiv Gandhi.

- ◆ In 1993, a suicide bomber attacked and killed Sri Lankan President Ranasinghe Premadasa.

- ◆ In 1996, they exploded a massive truck bomb at the Sri Lankan Central Bank and another at the Colombo World Trade Center the next year.

- ◆ In 2000, they murdered C. V. Goonaratna, the Sri Lankan minister for industries.

- ◆ They have also attacked several ships in Sri Lankan waters, including foreign vessels. They also attack trains, buses, and power stations.

According to the BBC, "The government says its strategy is to defeat the Tigers militarily while simultaneously pursuing a constitutional settlement to Sri Lanka's troubles. The Tigers say they will not stop their struggle until they have secured an independent homeland."

Although the elections held in 2001 were the most violent in recent Sri Lankan history—17 people were killed on polling day alone—somehow cooler heads soon prevailed. Not long after the election, the Tigers declared a short-term cease-fire.

The government followed suit. Norway then entered the picture and negotiated a more permanent cease-fire agreement. The preamble of that cease-fire agreement is remarkable given the long-standing animosity between the parties:

> The overall objective of the Government of the Democratic Socialist Republic of Sri Lanka (hereinafter referred to as the GOSL) and the Liberation Tigers of Tamil Eelam (hereinafter referred to as the LTTE) is to find a negotiated solution to the ongoing ethnic conflict in Sri Lanka.

> The GOSL and the LTTE recognize the importance of bringing an end to the hostilities and improving the living conditions for all inhabitants affected by the conflict. Bringing an end to the hostilities is also seen by the Parties as a means of establishing a positive atmosphere in which further steps towards negotiations on a lasting solution can be taken.

The deal held. For three years, the civil war was in abeyance while the government and the Tamil Tigers tried to iron out their differences. Although various incidents threatened the cease-fire, and although peace talks started and collapsed, somehow, the cease-fire held.

The biggest threat to the cease-fire occurred on August 12, 2005, when Sri Lankan Foreign Minister Lakshman Kadirgamar was assassinated in his home by a sniper's bullet. The government declared a state of emergency, and police arrested 12 ethnic Tamils, although the Tigers denied involvement in the assassination.

According to Bloomberg.com (August 13, 2005), "The attack threatens a 2002 cease-fire that sparked the longest period of peace in the island's 20-year civil war, and a three-year expansion of the nation's $20 billion economy."

Islamic Separatists in the Land of Buddha

Thailand has a tradition of being the most peaceful country in Southeast Asia, one populated by a vast Buddhist majority (about 95 percent). Buddhist monks in orange robes are everywhere, and by and large the general Buddhist population endeavors to be like Buddha—peaceful, selfless, compassionate, and "right thinking." Whereas Judaism, Christianity, and Islam worship God as the creator, Buddhists focus on the spiritual development of the individual and do not pray to a God, per se. They see Buddha as a man like themselves who achieved enlightenment, and they strive to achieve it as well through right living.

Reliable Resources

The Kingdom of Thailand draws more visitors than any other country in Southeast Asia with its irresistible combination of breathtaking natural beauty, inspiring temples, renowned hospitality, robust cuisine and ruins of fabulous ancient kingdoms.
—The Lonely Planet Guide to Thailand

Maybe that is why it was such a shock when it became clear in January 2004 that the wave of attacks that had been occurring the previous few years in southern Thailand were not being perpetrated by criminals but rather by Islamic separatist militants. Their issue? Having their own homeland, of course. The Islamic Pattani United Liberation Organization (PULO) alleges that Thailand illegally incorporated the predominantly Islamic southern tip of the country 100 years ago and presently illegally rules it using "colonial repression."

Although there had previously been sporadic calls and movements for Islamic independence in the three southern Muslim-dominated provinces, for the most part the activity had been more criminal (drug smuggling to raise money and so on) than revolutionary. This really began to change after September 11, 2001.

Since then …

- An unexploded truck bomb was found next to a large hotel in southern Thailand in November 2001.

- In December that year, police checkpoints in southern Thailand were attacked and five policemen were killed.

- On June 10, 2003, police broke up a terrorist cell, thwarting plans to bomb various embassies in Bangkok.

- On January 4, 2004, an army depot south of Bangkok was attacked, four army officers died, and a cache of weapons was stolen.

- Soon thereafter, the terror campaign intensified as a series of bombs ripped through different populated areas in the southern part of the country. Government officials warned that Islamic terrorists were planning to plant more bombs as part of their ongoing terror campaign.

Since the attacks began in earnest in January 2004, the southern insurgency has killed more than 900 people, mostly by either drive-by shootings or small bombings.

In response, the government declared a state of emergency in the South and passed tough new laws intended to quash the insurgency. The measures allow authorities to search suspects without warrants, keep suspects for up to 30 days without charges, and tap telephones.

Round and round they go, and where it stops, nobody knows.

Nepal

Nepal is one of the most remote areas of the world. It is a distant land north of India where the tallest mountains on Earth sit—K-2, Mt. Everest—among the Himalayas. The Nepalese people are poor and poorly educated, and the country was run by a hereditary monarchy for most of its known history. Then the revolutionary democratic wave that swept the world in 1991, drowning the Soviet Union in its wake, found a beachhead even in distant Nepal. Revolution brought democracy. Nepal converted to a constitutional monarchy and elected its first prime minister in the early 1990s.

Although the Communist Party of Nepal won and briefly formed a government in 1994, it was dissolved shortly thereafter and the Communists fell from power. Stung by their electoral defeats, the Communists went underground in 1996 and began to organize an insurgency. What were they upset about?

◆ Continued extreme poverty

◆ Government corruption

◆ Political instability

Meet the New Boss, Same as the Old Boss

On February 13, 1996, the rebels (who looked to Chinese despot Mao Tse-Tung for their inspiration) began what would become a decade-long guerilla war against the government with a series of bombings. Promising equality and prosperity, as Communists do, the insurgency grew in popularity with Nepal's poor and disadvantaged. Fed up with both their sorry lot in life and a new political system that seemed no better than the old one, rural Nepalese accepted the Maoist rebels' promises of a better life. The rebels wanted nothing less than to overthrow the government and institute a revolutionary Marxist system of, by, and for the peasants, by whatever means necessary.

The rebels have become as powerful a guerilla group as there is in Asia, rivaling the Tamil Tigers in Sri Lanka. It is estimated that they have as many as 15,000 active members, and many parts of Nepal are now under their control. Their methods are brutal, kidnapping being one of their favorites. Once, for example, they kidnapped hundreds of children for a weeklong "re-education" in Maoist ideology. More than 12,000 people have been killed to date during the insurgency.

> **Reliable Resources**
>
> "The Maoists may not yet have the strength to win their 'People's War' but they are too strong to lose it."
>
> —BBC News, June 6, 2005

Fiddling While Rome Burns

It is against this dire backdrop that the Nepalese government has been mostly at a loss as to what to do. Political instability was the only constant throughout the late 1990s, with governments forming and falling with regularity. But in 2001, when the Maoist rebels called for a general strike, the entire country came to a standstill.

But that was the least of Nepal's problems that year. In June, 2001, a stoned and drunk Crown Prince Dipendra shot and killed his parents—the Nepalese king and queen—as well as seven other royal family members before turning his gun on himself and committing suicide. After the king was murdered in this palace massacre, his brother assumed the constitutional throne. The next month, Bahadur Deuba became the new prime minister of the country, heading the eleventh government in 11 years.

The new king, King Gyanendra, assumed power in the middle of this crisis and responded by sacking the elected government in 2002, consolidating power for himself, and thereafter, appointing various hand-picked prime ministers. Yet his heavy-handed response (including declaring various states of emergency) shows no appreciable results insofar as dealing with the rebels goes. The civil war continues, peace talks between the rebels and the government have failed, and a cease-fire ended with gunfire.

At the present time, it seems that neither side is strong enough to defeat the other. The rebels control the hinterlands and the government controls the major cities of Katmandu and Pokhara. So don't expect an end to this conflict any time soon.

The Least You Need to Know

- ◆ Aung San Suu Kyi is Burma's brave heroine.
- ◆ Sri Lanka's long civil war was interrupted by a 2002 cease-fire agreement.

◆ Islamic insurgents are staging terrorist actions in southern Thailand.

◆ Maoist rebels and government forces continue to fight to a standstill in Nepal.

Part 5

Europe

Europe has been the center of more violence and conflict in the past 100 years than any other place on Earth. World War I, World War II, the Cold War, and the Northern Ireland conflict have raged in Europe.

Today, the War on Terror is being fought in Europe, too. Both Britain and Spain have been victims of terrorist bombings. Russia has problems aplenty with her many neighbors, the Balkans have recently been the scene of a bloody conflict, and simmering animosities linger throughout the land.

Trouble in the Stans

In This Chapter

- ◆ Uzbekistan
- ◆ Kazakhstan
- ◆ Kyrgyzstan
- ◆ Turkmenistan
- ◆ Tajikistan

When the Soviet Union disintegrated in 1991, five republics in Central Asia declared their independence and began to chart their own respective courses. These countries—Kazakhstan, Kyrgyzstan, Uzbekistan, Tajikistan, and Turkmenistan—are commonly referred to as the "Stans." But, instead of peace and prosperity, independence in this remote corner of the world has more often brought conflict and corruption.

The Stan Land

Former Soviet republics such as Latvia and Lithuania benefited from the relative prosperity and stability that followed their adoption of democracy and capitalism. The Stans took a different path, and ended up with far different results. They are beset by corrupt dictatorships, rabid unemployment and poverty, few civil liberties, little rule of law, and a growing threat of Islamic fundamentalism.

Independence has more often brought conflict and corruption to the "Stans."

Although each of the five Stan states half-heartedly attempted to create market-driven democracies in the wake of the Soviet collapse, they were largely unsuccessful. Only Tajikistan has a government with leaders different from those who ran things during the Soviet era. The rest of these countries are still run by the same people who were in charge under the old Soviet Communist system, and so reforms that became common throughout the rest of the ex-Soviet empire, such as a free press or private property rights, are largely absent in the Stans.

Instead, what you find is political repression, subjected populations, environmental contamination, a thriving drug trade, and widespread corruption.

Yet, at the same time, these countries have significant resources at their disposal. The Stans are thought to have the third-largest oil and gas reserves in the world. Moreover, due to the universal education that

Reliable Resources

Long before becoming part of the Soviet Union, the Stans were part of other large empires. Not only were they part of the empire founded by Alexander the Great, but so, too, were they part of the great Mongolian Empire created by Genghis Khan, as well as a central player in India's Moghul Empire.

was part of the old Soviet system, they can also boast near-universal literacy, with many people in the region being multilingual, and a large percentage of the college-educated population being scientists, doctors, and engineers.

Yet despite these attributes, there are two overriding emerging problems that threaten the stability (such as it is) of the entire region—the rise of Islamic fundamentalism and potential environmental disasters.

The Rise of Islamic Fundamentalism in Central Asia

Because central Asia is an area on the brink—one that is largely Muslim, is near Iraq and Afghanistan, and has many needs—it is a region that could easily come to the forefront of the West's conflict with radical Islamists. Why? Because the main economic result of the fall of the Soviet empire on this region has been widespread poverty and unemployment, and if the past is prologue, we know that when people become hungry, they are far more likely to turn to radical solutions.

Although the Stans have long been Islamic, it traditionally has been a more secular sort of Islam, more of cultural glue than a radical religion. But that began to change throughout the 1990s for two reasons:

1. The collapse of the Soviet Union meant that the lid that had been placed on both religion and expression finally came off. As such, people were finally able to express deep-seated religious and social feelings that had been repressed for decades.

2. As indicated, the economic problems that emerged from the fall of the Soviet Union became more and more acute, so people began turning to the promises of fundamentalist Islam.

According to Alexei Malashenko, scholar-in-residence at the Moscow Carnegie Center, and an authority on Islam in Central Asia, the reason for the rise of radical Islam in this part of the world is that "Nothing works. People exist in poverty under oppressive regimes. So, what is there left for the desperate to turn to? Only fundamentalist Islam, that promises a viable state and paternalistic social justice" (*Time* magazine, September 13, 2000).

As a result, the entire region is becoming more radicalized. In Tajikistan, for instance, it was the Islamic militants who opposed the government and created a civil war that killed an estimated 500,000 people.

The rise of militant Islam in the area has also been fueled by the emerging presence of the U.S. military in the region. During the Afghan campaign, the United States was able to secure acceptance of increased American military presence in the Stans for the purpose of staging and supporting the war. As a result, an American military buildup began.

Since then, various governments throughout Central Asia have allowed the United States access to their military installations to conduct the War on Terror. Their reasons for doing so are threefold:

♦ First, because they are undemocratic, repressive regimes, these governments concluded that befriending the last remaining superpower could only help them stay in power.

♦ Second, there were strong financial incentives for allowing the U.S. military to use their airbases.

♦ Finally, these governments figured that a U.S. presence could be a bulwark against the threat of Islamic radicalism as well as ever-increasing drug trafficking, the issues considered to be two of the main security threats in the region.

The result is that a growing radical Islamic population is now sitting atop one of the latest outposts in the War on Terror, creating a potentially combustible situation.

Environmental Apocalypse?

Because of their remote location, the Stans were a favorite spot for the Soviet Union to locate environmentally suspicious activities. For instance, poorly secured, leaking radioactive waste dumps were located throughout the region, causing illness in their wake. These sites were quite crude—radioactive materials dumped in pits and then simply bulldozed over—and today are not only environmental disasters waiting to happen, but also an easily accessible cache of radioactivity for *dirty bombs* for those so inclined.

def•i•ni•tion

A **dirty bomb**, also known as a "Radiological Dispersal Device" (RDD), is a weapon that combines a conventional explosive like dynamite with radioactive material. The potential lethality of such a bomb depends upon the size of the conventional explosive used, the type of radioactive material, and the weather.

Such issues are not isolated, either in terms of location or importance. Because of the interrelated geography of the region, environmental concerns can and will have significant repercussions on the stability and economy of all of Central Asia. Should seasonal landslides cause either toxic waste or uranium from abandoned mines to flow into the local rivers, for just one example, entire water supplies, economies, and populations could be at risk. And that is just one of many looming environmental disasters that could create both widespread panic and conflict.

For a better understanding of just how these various trends are changing the different countries in this region, let's take a closer look at each.

Uzbekistan and Islam

With a population of 26 million, Uzbekistan is the largest of the Stan countries, and certainly one of the most repressive regimes in all of Central Asia (which is saying a lot). It is a country that so intimidates and brutalizes its own people that the possibility of civil war is very real indeed. And if the Islamic rebels were to win that civil war, expect to see a fundamentalist Islamic state along the lines of Iran emerge.

Because of its proximity to Afghanistan and Pakistan, and the willingness of the government to ally itself with the United States, Uzbekistan has become a major American ally in the War on Terror. Yet the "War on Terror" has also become a useful catch phrase that the Uzbek government can throw around to intimidate, torture, and harass opponents of the regime, whether those opponents are actual terrorists or not.

Indeed, the United Nations has characterized torture in the country as "systematic." According to Human Rights Watch, Muslim prisoners especially have been treated harshly: beaten with fists and metal rods, subjected to electric shock and cigarette burns, raped, and in one case, according to an autopsy, immersed in boiling water.

Moreover, says Human Rights Watch, "Prisoners are forced to sign statements begging President Islam Karimov for forgiveness, renouncing their faith, and incriminating themselves as terrorists. Prisoners who refuse are punished with beatings, time in punishment cells, and even new criminal prosecutions."

Which is not to say that there are not real terrorists in Uzbekistan. There are. The Islamic Movement of Uzbekistan (IMU) was originally focused on overthrowing the secular government of President Karimov and creating in its place a fundamentalist Islamic state. However, shortly before 9/11, the UMI declared that its stated goal was nothing less than the creation of an Islamic state for all of Central Asia.

Landmine! _____

In 2004, the U.S. State Department concluded that Uzbekistan had failed in the human rights commitments mandated by the U.S.-Uzbek Bilateral Agreement. As a result, the State Department cut off $18 million in aid to the country. That same year, however, the U.S. Department of Defense pledged $21 million in new military aid to Uzbekistan.

Certainly there is ample reason to find the situation in Uzbekistan abysmal. There is no freedom of association, or assembly, or religion, or press. There is no independent judiciary, few jobs, the drug trade is rampant, and torture and repression are widespread, begging the question: What can be done to change things here, if anything?

The answer is, not much. Although Russia continues to carry significant influence in the region, and although the United States is growing in influence, neither country seems to have much sway over the Karimov government, with the Uzbek president seemingly concluding that the two great powers need him more than he needs them; Russia needs the gasoline deals it has in place with Uzbekistan, and the United States needs the Uzbek military bases.

The upshot is that the Uzbekistan government is able to introduce laws and measures that seem to beg for civil unrest and armed conflict. Karimov has banned all Islamic political parties, for example, and Muslim men with long beards tend to disappear and are never heard from again.

Needless to say, these sorts of arbitrary actions fuel the fire of conflict, and the world saw what may be the future of Uzbekistan in May 2005. It was then that peaceful demonstrations broke out in the Uzbek province of Andijan when thousands of people joined together to protest the repressive government's actions and policies. The Uzbek government responded by having the police fire into the crowd. Estimates of the number of dead range from a government figure of 169 to an opposition party figure of 745.

If full-scale civil war ever does erupt in this far-off country, you will know why.

Kazakhstan Has Issues

Whereas the threat of radical Islam and torture are the bugaboos of Uzbekistan, in Kazakhstan it is corruption and repression that are the greatest threats to stability.

Bribery is so commonplace in this country that when Americans go there to adopt orphans, they are told by American authorities to bring cash to pay off everyone from social service workers to politicians, taxi drivers, and airport personnel. On a grander scale, Kazak President Nursultan Nazarbayev (the only president the country has ever had) has been, according to Radio Free Europe/Radio Liberty, responsible for a "dismally high level of corruption." Thus, while criminal charges in the West for stealing millions from the Kazakh people were pending, Nazarbayev got a law through the Zazakhstani legislature granting him lifetime powers and immunity from prosecution.

At the same time, the government harasses supporters of Kazakhstan's opposition political parties, via criminal prosecutions, confinement, and threats of losing one's job. The co-founder of the Democratic Choice of Kazakhstan (DVK) had to disavow his opposition to the government as a precondition for his release from prison in 2003.

Yet it is not hard to understand why the government wants to retain power and the opposition wants to grab it. Some estimates suggest that Kazak petroleum reserves could rival those of Saudi Arabia, which has an estimated 30 billion barrels of oil remaining. Kazakhstan may have as much as 50 billion barrels below ground! If these estimates prove accurate, and if this oil ever begins to be pumped from the ground, the entire global balance of power could shift to this remote region.

Reliable Resources

The underpaid scientist opens the fridge door and pulls out a Tupperware box containing vials of anthrax for me to inspect. Behind us a row of ancient refrigerators hold vast quantities of plague. The scientist pulls out a tray of diseases, then accidentally whacks the fragile glass vials as she puts them away. One of her colleagues gasps in fear. Everybody in the room freezes. Nobody dares to breathe.

Welcome to this former Soviet biological weapons laboratory in Kazakhstan, abandoned by Moscow when the USSR collapsed in 1991, and now a Plague Research Institute.

—*The Sunday Herald* (Scotland), September 21, 2003

Kyrgyzstan Coup D'état

Askar Akayev was the president of Kyrgyzstan at the time of its transition from communism, and, as became the norm in Central Asia, the ex-Communist leader became an authoritarian president willing to kill and imprison his rivals to retain power. Akayev was ostensibly re-elected several times throughout the 1990s, but by the late 1990s, his fraudulent maneuverings and elections caused the Clinton administration to demand reform.

But September 11 changed Kyrgyzstan, just as it changed the rest of the world. With Central Asia suddenly thrust into the forefront of geopolitics because of the region's proximity to Afghanistan, Iraq, and Pakistan, reform became far less important than geography, and the Bush administration engaged Kyrgyzstan to join its War on Terror. The upshot was that the United States was able to land on a Kyrgyz beachhead for incursions into Afghanistan and Iraq, and President Akayev was able to consolidate power once again.

But it appears that Akayev may have stolen an election, too, many in March 2005. It was then that another obviously fraudulent election resulted in even a *greater* majority for the highly unpopular leader, with his party gaining 69 of 75 seats in parliament, 2 of which were won by Akayev's son and daughter.

Outraged, in late March 2005, thousands of Kyrgyz protesters stormed the capital and the government building, effecting a coup d'état and causing Akayev to flee the country. According to *USA Today*, March 25, 2005, opposition leader Kurmanbek Bakiyev was named acting president and stated, "Freedom has finally come to us."

Turkmenistan

In 2003, the U.S. State Department contracted with your author to visit Turkmenistan to give a series of lectures throughout the country. Of the many countries I have been to, it was, by far, both the scariest and the strangest.

Turkmenistan sits on the border of Afghanistan and Iran. Because my visit was not long after the Afghanistan war, and during the time the United States was building up for the Iraq war, prior to leaving I was concerned for my safety, thinking that either rebels or terrorists might target a State Department speaker.

I should have known better, given the part of the world to which I was traveling. It was not rebels that ended up scaring me, but rather, the repressive Turkmenistan government. There were police huts seemingly on every other corner, and soldiers watched everything that everyone did. The autocratic megalomaniac president of the country, Saparmyrat Niyazov, has plastered his picture and statue everywhere, the idea apparently being that he, too, is always "watching" you.

Traveling there was what it must be like to travel to another isolated, odd, backward country—North Korea. And like Kim Jong Il of North Korea, Niyazov, too, has created a very strange country based on a "cult of personality."

How strange? Consider:

♦ Niyazov renamed himself Turkmenbashi—"Father of all Turkmen."

♦ He also renamed the months and days in the Turkmen calendar after his family members, and the city of Krasnovodsk was renamed Turkmenbashi, too.

♦ His picture is on all denominations of the Turkmen currency, and the vodka.

♦ The horse on the Turkmenistan coat of arms was replaced with his favorite horse.

♦ On Sunday, the entire country stops and studies the holy book—called the Holy Ruhknama—written by, you guessed it, Niyazov.

♦ Ballets, operas, cruises, libraries, and hospitals outside the capital of Ashgabat have been banned.

♦ A statue of Niyazov made from gold sits in the capital square and rotates every 24 hours—so that it is always facing the sun.

Given that Niyazov has created one of the most repressive, and certainly the most isolated, regimes in all the Stans, it is not surprising that in November 2002, there was an attempt on his life. Niyazov survived and used the event to further promote himself and clamp down on any suspected rivals.

Reliable Resources

In the past, the [Turkmenistan] government has arbitrarily detained and imprisoned civic and politically active individuals and their associates, razed their houses, and locked them up in psychiatric institutions. Judging from his track record, President Niyazov is likely to use the assassination attempt as a pretext to lash out at any opponents, real or imaginary.

—Erika Dailey, director of the Open Society Institute's Turkmenistan Project

Tajikistan Civil War

Tajikistan is a small, mountainous country. According to the CIA World Factbook, "60 percent of [Tajikistan's] people … live in abject poverty. Tajikistan's economic situation remains fragile due to uneven implementation of structural reforms, weak governance, widespread unemployment, and the external debt burden." So no, things are not much better in this last of the Stan countries.

In fact, for much of the last decade, things were decidedly worse in Tajikistan than almost anywhere else in Central Asia due to the Tajik civil war. Almost from the time it became independent in 1991, and until 1997, Tajikistan faced a major war between the Moscow-backed central government and the Islamic United Tajik Opposition (UTO).

The UTO wanted to turn the country into an Islamic state. They thus began their attacks in the southern part of the country, where they had more support. By 1996, the rebels were being aided by the Taliban, who were, at that time, still in control of the country next door, Afghanistan.

The fighting over the years between the rebels and the government was intense and bitter, with predictable results: More than 500,000 people died, and some 1.2 million became refugees. Finally, in late 1996, extensive United Nations negotiations paid off when the Tajik government signed a cease-fire agreement with the rebels. Peaceful elections were finally held in 1999.

> **Landmine!**
>
> In 1911, an earthquake created a colossal earthen dam 10,000 feet up in the Pamir Mountains of Tajikistan. Behind this natural dam now sits a lake that is 50 miles long and a mile wide.
>
> Earthquakes frequent this region, and U.N. experts believe a quake of 7.5 or more will likely dislodge the dam. The resulting flood would be, according to a United Nations report, "the worst disaster in recorded history." The United States Army Corps of Engineers predicts that the ensuing flood would travel through several countries and threaten the lives of five million people.

The Future of the Stans

Despite all the challenges they face today, the Stans are ripe for even more problems in the future. From the rise of fundamental Islam to the lack of fundamental human rights, the region is a simmering cauldron of conflict.

According to Alexei Malashenko of the Carnegie Moscow Institute (*Time* magazine, September 13, 2000)

> We must recognize the radical Islamic opposition [in this region] as an eternal factor. We must engage this factor into mainstream political processes. Once fanatics and plain bandits are isolated from recognized political forces, they

either wither, or get wiped out. This is the only way to contain extremism. But it'll be a long time before we come to that, if ever. Meanwhile, we'd better brace for major trouble.

The Least You Need To Know

- Two emerging problems in the Stans are rising Islamic fundamentalism and potential environmental degradation.

- The Islamic threat is greatest in Uzbekistan.

- Kazakhstan sits atop some of the largest oil reserves in the world.

- Like many countries in Central Asia, Kyrgyzstan has opened its military bases to the U.S.-led War on Terror.

- Turkmenistan is ruled by a strange megalomaniac.

- Tajikistan suffered from five years of civil war.

Chapter 19

The Balkan Mess

In This Chapter

- ◆ The players and their politics
- ◆ The rise of Slobodan Milosevic
- ◆ The Croatian and Bosnian wars
- ◆ The Dayton Accords
- ◆ Mass murder in Kosovo
- ◆ Milosevic's downfall

There was a time, just before the beginning of the horrific wars within what would soon become the "former Yugoslavia," when things were much different. The country was on the brink of European Union membership, and its people took vacations. Yugoslavia was the freest and most economically advanced of all the communist countries.

You may recall that during the Cold War, much of the world was divided into two camps—the West (or democratic countries) and the East (Communist countries). Eastern bloc countries were those that were part of the Soviet Union's Warsaw Pact and sphere of influence—countries such as East Germany, Poland, Romania, and Czechoslovakia.

Yugoslavia was different because it was the only communist country not under Soviet domination. But upon the disintegration of Yugoslavia, things went downhill fast. Instead of peace and prosperity, the country was plunged into war and poverty. After the Cold War ended, ethnic animosities took precedence, and the region broke out in the worst violence Europe had seen since World War II. Ethnic cleansing, murder, rape, and torture became commonplace.

Today, with the possible exception of Slovenia, all parts of the former Yugoslavia are now far, far behind former Eastern bloc countries such as Hungary and Poland, countries that once envied the Yugoslav standard of living. Today, the Balkan countries that make up what was once Yugoslavia lay in ruins. Genocide can do that.

Hence the term—
Balkanization.

Break Out Your Scorecard

To understand the Balkan mess, the first thing you must do is know who the players are. When you can tell them apart (and it can sometimes be a bit confusing), understanding this conflict becomes much easier.

You Say Slavonia, I Say Slovenia

In 1914, Austria-Hungary invaded Serbia, triggering World War I. After the war, the Balkan countries of Croatia, Slovenia, Vojvodina, Serbia, Montenegro, and Macedonia joined forces to form a new country called "The Kingdom of Serbs, Croats, and Slovenes." Smartly, the name was soon changed to Yugoslavia. As time went by, the main three groups that would make up Yugoslavia were the Serbs, the Croats, and the Bosnians.

In 1945, the Communist Party, under Josip Tito, came to power. During his presidency, Tito walked a fine line between the two superpowers, and remained unaligned with either the West or the Soviets. Besides being a tightrope artist, Tito was also a tyrant, and when he died in 1980, long-simmering resentments between the many nationalities that made up Yugoslavia came to the surface.

After Tito's death, the Yugoslav presidency became a post that rotated between nine elected members of the government. In 1986, a Communist Party *apparatchik* named Slobodan Milosevic got his turn in the seat. The vision he would begin to espouse was that of a "Greater Serbia"—a land untainted by foreign blood or other Balkan blood. It was a vision that would lay to waste an entire region.

def•i•ni•tion

Under Communist rule, loyalty to the party was one of the most respected traits. An **apparatchik** was an unquestioningly loyal subordinate or bureaucrat.

Serbia

The Serbs are the bad guys. With a population of almost 10 million, compared to Croatia's 5 million and Bosnia's 4 million, the Serbs were the dominant force in the old Yugoslavia and wanted the same power in the new region. They were in a far better position to create that, too, because, as Yugoslavia disintegrated, the Yugoslav People's Army generally followed orders from the Serbs, and thus, Milosevic. Therefore, almost by default, he became the dominant player in the region.

The problem for Milosevic was that Serbs didn't just live in Serbia—they lived in Bosnia (the so-called Bosnian Serbs), as well as other areas in the region. His desire for a Greater Serbia threatened Croatia and Bosnia because Greater Serbia, if it were ever to be, would be carved partially from those countries.

Needless to say, Slovenia and Croatia were alarmed at Milosevic's grand plan, and as such, declared themselves independent of Yugoslavia in June 1991. This signaled the end of Yugoslavia as the world had known it.

Slovenia

Slovenia has a population of less than two million, and few of them are Serbs. So when the country declared independence from the crumbling Yugoslavia on June 25,

1991, Milosevic did not care. Slovenia's independence had no impact on his Greater Serbia plan.

Croatia

Croatia immediately followed suit, declaring its independence on the next day, June 26, 1991. Milosevic was also prepared to let Croatia have its independence, if it was willing to give up Slavonia, a region with a heavy Serb population. (Note: Slavonia and Slovenia are different.) Croatian President Franjo Tudjman was, like any president of any country, unwilling to simply give part of his country away to the dictator next door. Conflict became inevitable.

Bosnia

Bosnia was created out of desperation. Despite opposition from other member states in the European Union, Germany had formally recognized the new states of Slovenia and Croatia in December 1991. Other EU countries soon followed. For Bosnia, this was a disaster.

The new political landscape left what remained of Yugoslavia as a Serbian-dominated state—a situation intolerable for Muslims in Bosnia, who had lived amicably with Serbs and Croats in Bosnia for 40 years, but who suddenly became a vulnerable minority in a state ruled by Serb nationalists. Bosnia thus wanted to become independent too, to protect its large Muslim population from the newly ethnocentric Serbs.

A vote on Bosnian independence was held in early 1992, but the Bosnian Serbs decided to boycott the vote as they did not want to be separated from their Serb brothers in Serbia. Yet even so, because Muslims made up about 65 percent of Bosnia's population, the election resulted in an overwhelming vote for independence.

So the stage was now set for a massive war. Milosevic, and his much better-armed Yugoslav army, was ready to attack Croatia and Bosnia to both reunite all Serbs and kill any non-Serbs (that is, Muslims).

The Great Dictator

Slobodan Milosevic was born in 1941 near Belgrade. His was not a happy childhood. His father left home just after World War II and committed suicide in 1962. He was brought up by his mother, a strict Communist schoolteacher.

At university, Milosevic met Mira Markovic. She so believed in her Slobo that she often boasted that one day he would be as glorious a leader as Comrade Tito himself. Little did she know that Milosevic would turn out to be the opposite of the beloved Tito.

Milosevic then began a long, slow climb up the Communist Party ladder. By 1986, he had become head of the Serbian Communist Party. It was the issue of Kosovo that transformed Milosevic from a dull bureaucrat into a jingoistic politician.

Landmine!

Milosevic's mother also committed suicide, in 1972. He also had an uncle who committed suicide. In all, three very close relatives of the Serbian leader killed themselves.

"No One Will Ever Beat You Again!"

According to BBC News, "In 1987, Milosevic was a middle ranking and virtually unknown Yugoslavian communist official who was sent to calm local Serbs who had been complaining about abuses by the ethnic Albanian population in Kosovo. When he got there, he was greeted by an angry crowd that was being beaten by the mainly Albanian Kosovo police."

Milosevic gave a fiery speech and, according to the BBC, "uttered the words that transformed him from apparatchik [into a hero], telling the frightened Serbs: 'No one will ever beat you again!'" The result was amazing. State television began broadcasting the remarks around the clock. Newspapers analyzed the event, and suddenly, Milosevic came to symbolize the resentments Serbs had felt during Tito's reign; they thought that their interests had always come last since Tito was a Croat.

By lifting the lid on the long-standing taboo of ethnic rivalries, Milosevic was able to use the event as a springboard to reinvent himself. Serbian nationalism became his calling card, and his newfound popularity allowed him to soon take control of the Serbian state.

As the BBC put it, "In 1989, on the anniversary of the historic battle of Kosovo Polje, Milosevic gathered one million Serbs at the site of the battle to tell them to get ready; changes were coming. He then began to arm and support Serb separatists in Croatia and Bosnia and to prepare his own army for the battles ahead. The Balkans' long nightmare of civil war was beginning."

The Croatian War

After Milosevic was firmly in control of Serbia, it was clear to all concerned that his aspirations were far greater than merely leading his country into the post–Cold War world. He obviously aimed to take over other Serb-dominated areas by force if necessary. As he said at the time, "We believe that Serbs have the legitimate right to live in one country. If we must fight, then by God, we will fight!"

When Croatia declared independence, it set off an immediate war with Serbia. Serbs were no small minority in Croatia at the time, and many believed in Milosevic and his grand plan. Encouraged and armed by Serbia, Serb guerrillas inside Croatia were quickly able to take control of about one third of Croatia, driving out members of other ethnic groups in the process.

In May 1995, the Croatian army went on a major offensive, bent on gaining back Croatian territory it had lost in 1991. The Croat army entered Krajina Serb enclaves inside Croatia, and either expelled or murdered the Serb residents. Three months later, Croatian troops had retaken the disputed territory and had sent more than 100,000 Serbs fleeing.

The Siege on Sarajevo

Following Croatia's lead, Bosnia declared independence in April 1992, and violence immediately broke out there, too. Milosevic vowed to defend the Serbs living in Bosnia. But he didn't need too much help: Serbs inside Bosnia, the "Bosnian Serbs," already controlled the military. In fact, since 1991, Radovan Karadzic (a former psychiatrist) had been creating a renegade army within Bosnia with the support of Milosevic. In 1992, under Karadzic's leadership, Bosnian Serb nationalists began a systematic policy of "cleansing" large areas of Bosnia of non-Serbs.

Serbia then began to do its part by attacking the main Bosnian city of Sarajevo, shelling the city from hilltop positions above. In an orgy of murder, the Serbs took the ancestral lands of the Muslim population and sent hundreds of thousands of Muslims fleeing. This became the largest refugee movement in Europe since World War II as Muslims fled to other parts of Europe.

The Serbs were indiscriminate in their killing. They shot and bombed hotels, schools, hospitals: even mourners in graveyards were killed. All the while, governments in the West continued to do little to stop the bloodshed.

Peacekeepers

In 1984, before the insanity, Sarajevo hosted the Winter Olympics. The city, adorned with cafés, restaurants, pubs, shows, theaters, and public art, put on a magnificent party. Three-time defending world champion Scott Hamilton won gold in men's figure skating, and East German Katarina Witt won gold on the ladies' side. The British ice dancing team of Torvill and Dean amazed crowds and judges with nine perfect sixes to take the gold.

In August 1992, television began to display images of Muslims in Bosnia in newly built Serbian concentration camps. Alarmed by this and other evidence of Serbian "ethnic cleansing," the United Nations created a War Crimes Tribunal, the first such tribunal since Nuremberg.

Despite the atrocities (or maybe because of them), the war raged on and by 1993, Serbs controlled almost two thirds of Bosnia. The Croats, whose war with Serbia had spilled over to Bosnia, had taken over nearly one third of the country.

Genocide

In May 1993, the United Nations designated six U.N.-protected "safe areas" in Bosnia, all of which were Muslim areas that had been under siege by the Bosnian Serbs. U.N. peacekeeping forces were to provide limited military protection and assist in humanitarian aid efforts to those who could get there.

In the summer of 1995, Serb forces began to attack these safe havens. Ethnic cleansing had come to Srebrenica. Srebrenica was supposed to be the world's first U.N. safe area, but safe was the one thing it was not. The worst case of genocide in Europe since World War II would occur there. In July 1995, the Bosnian Serb army staged a violent takeover of the small spa town and its surrounding region. During a period of five days, the Bosnian Serb soldiers separated Muslim families and systematically murdered more than 7,000 men and boys.

After the fall of the Srebrenica "safe area," the international community finally seemed to realize that if this war didn't end soon, it could spill over into the rest of Europe—thereby possibly creating a much larger conflagration. NATO threatened air strikes against Bosnian Serbs if they attacked any of the remaining safe areas in Bosnia. Ignoring the warning, they launched attacks against the "safe areas" of Zepa, Bihac, and Sarajevo.

On August 30, 1995, Operation Deliberate Force began against Bosnian Serb military targets. Air attacks continued until September 14, dropping more than 1,000 bombs on Serbian targets.

Apparently, military might is the only thing Slobodan Milosevic understands. After three weeks of being brutally shelled by NATO, the Serbian strongman agreed to peace talks, but not before more than 200,000 people had died in the fighting.

The Dayton Accords

In December 1995, President Milosevic of Serbia, President Alija Izetbegovic of Bosnia, and President Franjo Tudjman of Croatia met in Dayton, Ohio, under the prodding of the Clinton administration.

From the outset, the outcome of the negotiations was in doubt. So intransigent were the warring parties that on the last day, as President Clinton put it, "Our American negotiators had their bags packed and were ready to head home without an agreement." However, the Balkan leaders finally decided to make peace. They did so because the alternative was too terrible: more war, ethnic cleansing, mass graves, refugees, economic ruin, and international isolation.

The Dayton Peace Accords that they signed did several things:

- ◆ It affirmed Sarajevo as the capital of Bosnia.

- ◆ It carved Bosnia into two autonomous and ethnically based entities separated by a demilitarized zone.

- ◆ It rewarded the Serbs for their aggression by giving them 49 percent of the territory of Bosnia. The Bosnians received the remaining 51 percent of their own country.

Shortly after the accords were signed, a NATO-led peacekeeping force of 60,000 soldiers (called SFOR) arrived in Bosnia. SFOR maintained the cease-fire and forced the parties to pull back their forces and weapons from the demilitarized zone. Nearly all heavy weapons were placed under SFOR supervision, and many were destroyed. More than 100,000 soldiers were demobilized.

SFOR also stopped the widespread killing of civilians and restored security to Sarajevo. Virtually all prisoners of war were released. SFOR moved to take down internal checkpoints, and, although far from perfect, freedom of movement improved. The force was downsized to 20,000 troops by 2002.

One would think that this should be the end of the story. But it's not—not in the Balkans. Although the fighting was over in Bosnia, Milosevic had already set his sights on another minority, the Albanians living in the Kosovo region of Serbia.

Kosovo

Beginning in 1997, Serbians began a systematic mass murder of Albanians in Kosovo. Serbian forces also expelled the majority of Kosovar Albanians from urban areas. Those who remained behind were used as human shields.

It was also reported that the Serbian forces stole personal belongings and documentation, telling the Albanians they would never return to Kosovo. Hundreds of villages and thousands of homes throughout the region were burned to the ground.

Kosovar Albanians also allege that Serbian forces systematically executed ethnic Albanian men—ranging from as young as 14 to 59. Mass graves found later confirmed this.

Serbian forces also allegedly burned bodies in an apparent attempt to destroy forensic evidence of their crimes.

Rape also became a staple of the Serbian form of war:

◆ Kosovar Albanian women have stated that they were raped repeatedly by Serbian soldiers.

◆ Serbian forces especially focused on raping young Kosovar Albanian women.

◆ Numerous Kosovar Albanians have also claimed that they were gang raped by the Serbs.

NATO, having intervened in the Balkan atrocity once already, finally decided that it would have to act again. In March 1999, wave after wave of NATO warplanes and missiles struck Serbia, pummeling army barracks, power plants, and air defenses in an effort to force Slobodan Milosevic to cease his genocide of Kosovo Albanians.

The NATO attack came after months of diplomacy failed to end a year of fighting that left more than 400,000 homeless in Kosovo. The campaign took far longer than anyone had anticipated—11 weeks—but in the end, Serbia capitulated. Although Milosevic withdrew his troops from Kosovo, he still didn't admit defeat.

Serbia's infrastructure was destroyed, and its economy was in ruins, but Milosevic tried to turn the devastation to his advantage. In a propaganda campaign waged through the state-controlled media, he styled himself as the rebuilder of the nation.

Thankfully, the End

By the time Milosevic called elections in the fall of 2000, the country was already crippled by sanctions and poverty. Milosevic was finally being seen by his countrymen for what he was—a genocidal murderer.

But his undoing came when he refused to recognize the election victory of an opposition leader. Hundreds of thousands of people took to the streets and went on strike. Important allies of Milosevic then dropped their support, including the Serbian Orthodox Church.

Ten days after the election, protesters stormed the parliament and the state television station, setting both buildings on fire. Policemen joined the protesters, and the country unraveled. It was finally the end for Slobodan Milosevic.

Milosevic was arrested soon thereafter and sent to the International War Crimes Tribunal in the Hague, Netherlands where he was set to be tried. The 66 charges included crimes against humanity and genocide for actions in Bosnia, Croatia, and Kosovo. During the trial, Milosevic acted as his own lawyer and argued, according to C-Span.com, "that his arrest was unlawful, that the tribunal is illegal, and that NATO committed the war crimes in Serbia while he himself was a peacemaker."

The Least You Need to Know

- The former Yugoslavia was made up of many conflicting nationalities.
- The Bosnian War saw horrendous atrocities.
- The Dayton Accords ended the war between Bosnia, Serbia, and Croatia.
- Kosovo was the last place in the Balkans where ethnic cleansing took place.

Chapter 20

The Russian Bear

In This Chapter

- ◆ The Russian revolutions
- ◆ Poisoning the Ukraine
- ◆ Breakaway Chechnya
- ◆ Radical Islam in the Caucuses
- ◆ Russia and the West

For much of the last century, Russia (then known as the Soviet Union, or the USSR) was one of the most feared countries on Earth. Seemingly indifferent to the desires of the rest of the world, and aided by a huge nuclear capacity, the USSR was a country few wanted to tangle with, including the various republics that it encompassed.

However, the breakup of the Soviet Union in 1991 unleashed forces that continue to affect life there to this day. Long-forgotten feuds were apparently not so forgotten, and conflicts that lay dormant for years, once again rose to the surface.

Russia is simply too vast to discount for long.

Russian History 101

The defeat of the Russian Empire in World War I created the opening for a Communist revolution in Russia. Vladimir Lenin (1870–1924) led his *Bolsheviks* to power in 1917, creating the first Communist state in history. Lenin was able to harness power despite a bloody civil war, famine, and an unknown path toward an untried communism.

def•i•ni•tion

The **Bolsheviks** (meaning "majority") split from the original Russian Socialist movement in 1903, and developed into a small, organized, revolutionary, Marxist group. In November 1917, they took over a country torn by civil war. Upon gaining power, the Bolsheviks renamed themselves the Communist Party of the Soviet Union (CPSU).

Lenin ruled Russia until his death in 1924, and was succeeded, after a three-year power struggle, by Josef Stalin. Stalin proved to be one of the most ruthless, despotic leaders of the entire twentieth century; a feat not easy to achieve. Upon seizing power in the Soviet Union, Stalin quickly took measures to make his reign absolute by expelling and demoting his most hated rivals from the party.

Believing that the West might attack the USSR at any moment, Stalin began to militarize his country and solidify his power. Beginning in 1934, he also began to purge the country of supposed enemies, and his grip on power tightened even more. Internal concentration camps for those who opposed the state became a fixture of life inside the Soviet Union, and both party members and citizens alike were afraid to question Stalin or his policies.

The "cult of personality" that blossomed around Stalin would not only lead some countrymen to revere him (or fear him, as the case may be), but also would ingrain Russians for generations to come with the idea that the good leader is probably an authoritarian leader.

During World War II, the Soviet Union emerged as a formidable world power. The Russian forces resisted the German advance and eventually overwhelmed them, reaching Berlin in April 1945. Thereafter, with his troops already in place, Stalin was able to control, either directly or indirectly, most of Eastern Europe. When the war ended, he immediately began to establish Communist rule in these countries.

Reliable Resources

Who was the most murderous person of the twentieth century? It is hard to say. Hitler can probably claim the top prize—between those killed in the war he started, as well as those killed in concentration camps and other forms of intentional murder he sanctioned, probably 34 million people died because of him. Stalin comes in a close second, having caused the deaths of probably 20 million people.

The Cold War

As a result, the postwar world was suddenly divided between East and West. The East was dominated by communism, the USSR, and puppet states such as Poland, Hungary, Czechoslovakia, and East Germany. The West was led by democracy, the United States, and European allies such as Great Britain, France, Italy, and West Germany.

Fearing this newfound Soviet strength and its dominance over Eastern Europe, the West decided to enter into a mutual defense commitment in 1949, and the North Atlantic Treaty Organization (NATO) was born. NATO was intended to counter what was now being called the "Iron Curtain."

Peacekeepers

From Stettin in the Baltic to Trieste in the Adriatic, an "Iron Curtain" has descended across the Continent. Behind that line lie all the capitals of the ancient states of Central and Eastern Europe: Warsaw, Berlin, Prague, Vienna, Budapest, Belgrade, Bucharest, and Sofia; all these famous cities and the populations around them lie in what I must call the Soviet sphere, and all are subject, in one form or another … to control from Moscow. The safety of the world, ladies and gentlemen, requires a unity in Europe….

—Winston Churchill, Westminster College, Fulton, Missouri, March 5, 1946

The newly emerging Cold War was named that because, unlike a "hot" war, the two combatants rarely squared off directly against one another. Rather, they operated in a series of proxy battles intended to either strengthen their team or harm the other. The number of actual conflicts that occurred during the Cold War (1946–1991) is numerous, but the major ones are these:

- **The Berlin Airlift.** After World War II, Germany was divided into four zones administered by four nations: the United States, Great Britain, France, and the Soviet Union.

  In June 1948, the Soviet authorities, claiming "technical difficulties," halted all traffic by land and by water into or out of the Western-controlled section of Berlin. In response, the West chose to airlift in supplies. For the next 11 months, the Berlin airlift sustained the city's two and a half million residents.

- **The Berlin Wall.** In an effort to stem the tide of people escaping Communist East Germany, the East German government, on August 12, 1961, decided to close the Berlin border. The next day, just after midnight, East German troops erected barbed wire barricades and roadblocks.

  Construction of the concrete Berlin Wall began five days later. Eventually, the wall would use guard dogs, machine-gun nests, floodlights, and observation towers to keep people in. From 1961 to 1981, almost one thousand East German citizens were killed by East German troops in attempts to escape, and tens of thousands were imprisoned for planning to do so.

- **The Bay of Pigs.** On March 17, 1960, President Eisenhower asked the CIA to "organize the training of Cuban exiles [for] a possible future date when they might return to their homeland," invade, and take out Castro. President Kennedy inherited the dubious plan, was never committed to it, waffled when it began, and when it was launched, saw it turn into an utter disaster as Cubans killed or captured the American forces in a matter of hours.

  After the Bay of Pigs, relations between the United States, Cuba, and the Soviet Union deteriorated rapidly. It is speculated that it was Kennedy's indecisiveness during the Bay of Pigs that encouraged new Soviet leader Nikita Khrushchev to send missiles to Cuba soon thereafter.

- **The Cuban Missile Crisis.** For 13 days in October 1962, the world stood on the brink of nuclear annihilation as the United States attempted to get the USSR to withdraw nuclear warheads it had placed in Cuba.

President Kennedy, after receiving advice that ranged from the continued use of diplomacy to preemptive air strikes to a blockade of Cuba, finally settled on the latter. Soviet ships carrying more missiles were turned away, the missiles that remained were soon removed, and a bigger crisis was averted.

Détente

In 1968, the virulent anti-Communist Richard Nixon was elected president of the United States. Whatever else can be (and has been) said about President Nixon, it cannot be said that he did not understand international relations. Among the things he realized was that the Cold War was dangerous business for all concerned. So just as he had decided to go to China, he also decided to warm relations with the Soviet Union. He called his plan *détente*.

def•i•ni•tion

From the French, **détente** is the relaxation of strained relations or tensions.

The results were the SALT I (Strategic Arms Limitations Talks) and Anti Ballistic Missile (ABM) treaties, opening the decade of the 1970s on a positive note. And although SALT II followed, the Soviet invasion of Afghanistan in 1979 ended the decade on a very sour note. With the election of Ronald Reagan the next year in the United States, the Cold War was back with a vengeance.

It is yet unknown whether Reagan actually intended to bankrupt the Soviet Union, or if that was simply a byproduct of his plan to massively increase American defense spending. Either way, it worked. The Soviets were unable to match either American resolve or its deep pockets throughout the massive arms buildup the United States undertook in the 1980s. Cracks in the Soviet system finally began to emerge.

In 1985, Mikhail Gorbachev came to power in the Soviet Union. Understanding that his country was unable to continue along on the course it had been following, Gorbachev began to steer a radically new path for his country. In 1986, he ended economic aid to Soviet satellite countries. That same year, Reagan and Gorbachev resolved to remove all intermediate nuclear missiles from Europe.

Gorbachev's plan was twofold. In an attempt to unleash his society, he introduced *glasnost* (openness). And in an attempt to revive his moribund economy, Gorbachev introduced *perestroika* (restructuring). What he didn't anticipate was that his attempts to modernize communism would inadvertently unleash forces that would change the world.

def•i•ni•tion

To counter NATO, the Soviet Union created the Warsaw Pact in 1955. Participating countries included Albania, Bulgaria, Hungary, East Germany, Poland, Rumania, and the USSR. In July 1991, all members agreed to end the 36-year alliance.

In 1989, Hungary declared its independence from the Warsaw Pact. In November of that year, the Berlin Wall fell. In December, Communist governments in Czechoslovakia, Bulgaria, and Rumania fell. In 1990, Germany reunited.

In late 1991, Mikhail Gorbachev resigned as head of the Soviet Communist Party, and on December 25, 1991, he resigned the presidency of the USSR. Unable to cow its many republics into subservience any longer, the Soviet Union itself soon splintered into 15 independent republics.

Postscript

After 74 years, the USSR faded into history, not with a bang, but with a whimper. The Soviet Empire was over, and the Cold War had finally ended. Although Russia would inherit the Soviet mantle, it was largely symbolic. Russia was now seen for what it might have been all along: a *third-world* country with a large army and nuclear weapons.

def•i•ni•tion

In politics, the so-called first world refers to the highly developed industrialized nations often considered the Westernized countries of the world. The second world refers to the Communist nations as a political and economic bloc. The **third world** is the aggregate of the underdeveloped nations of the world. Some people even refer to a fourth world, meaning a group of nations, especially in Africa and Asia, characterized by extremely low per capita income and an absence of valuable natural resources.

Even before the end of the USSR, the new Soviet president, Boris Yeltsin, had set about creating an entity to replace it. On December 8, 1991, Russia, Ukraine, and Belarus signed an agreement to form the Commonwealth of Independent States (CIS), also sometimes known as the Russian Federation. After the Soviet Union collapsed, other nations joined the CIS.

I Want to Get Away

The largest factor contributing to conflict in the old Soviet Union today is the desire of many of the former Soviet republics to be free and the insistence from Moscow that they remain part of the Russian Federation.

This tension was first seen in May 1989, before the dissolution of the USSR, when the three Baltic republics of Estonia, Lithuania, and Latvia declared their sovereignty. The three tiny republics continued to push for separation from the USSR for 19 months.

On January 13, 1991, the Soviet Union sent troops and tanks into the breakaway republic of Lithuania. But a mere nine months later, after the collapse of the USSR, the Soviet parliament acknowledged the independence of the three Baltic republics and the troops were withdrawn.

Seeing what the small Baltic countries were able to do, many other republics followed suit and declared their independence. Some became independent states when the USSR was finally dissolved, whereas others remained a part of the Russian Federation—some unhappily so.

Reliable Resources

During World War II, some Ukrainians hailed the advancing Nazi army as liberators. But the Germans' genocidal policies against the Jews, as well as its deportation of ethnic Ukrainians to work in Germany, convinced most Ukrainians that the Germans were no liberators and so fought against the Nazis. It is estimated that upward of seven million Ukrainian civilian died in World War II.

Orange Revolution in the Ukraine

In 1922, the Soviet Union annexed Ukraine. Ukraine's marriage with the USSR was never a good one, and the republic declared its independence from the Soviet Union in 1991 after the fall of communism. The Ukraine did, however, join other Soviet republics to form the Commonwealth of Independent States (Armenia, Azerbaijan, Belarus, Georgia, Kazakhstan, Kyrgyzstan, Moldova, Russia, Tajikistan, Ukraine, and Uzbekistan.)

The Orange Revolution

In 2004, Russian-backed Prime Minister Viktor Yankovych was in a pitched electoral battle with opposition leader Viktor Yushenko. The tone of the election was especially bitter, with charges of cronyism, media bias, election fraud, and intimidation flying freely. Certainly the stakes were high because the winner would become Ukraine's third president since independence, and Yushenko was a distinctly pro-Western candidate.

The results of the November runoff election seemingly gave the presidency to Prime Minister Yankovych, but opposition leader Yushenko, his supporters, and international observers cried foul, demanding a new vote amid charges of election fraud. Exit polls certainly favored Yushenko, and vast instances of voter fraud were apparent to most international observers.

Yet Prime Minister Yankovych was officially declared the winner, sparking a nation-wide crisis. Yushenko and his supporters refused to abide by the "results" of the election and began to engage in civil disobedience: sit-ins, demonstrations, strikes, and so on. They also adopted the color orange as their symbol of unity, because it was the color of the Yushenko electoral materials. Demonstrations with hundreds of thousands of people in Kiev's central square became a common sight.

In early December 2004, the Ukrainian Supreme Court sided with Yushenko, invalidated the previous election results, and ordered a new runoff. The day after Christmas, Ukrainians again took to the polls to vote for a new president. This time, there were far fewer charges of electoral fraud and Yushenko was declared the winner on December 28.

The "orange revolution" had been a success, but it was not without its casualties.

Who Poisoned Viktor Yushenko?

The general election leading up to the disputed runoff was no less acrimonious than the runoff, and in September 2004 challenger Yushenko came down with a viral infection, acute pancriatis, and—get ready for this—"chemical substances which are not normally found in food products" (according to the clinic where he was seen). Someone had poisoned Viktor Yushenko.

> **Landmine!** _____
>
> Dioxin is a well-known carcinogenic. In addition, it causes developmental problems, reproductive problems, and has been linked to birth defects, diabetes, lung problems, skin disease, low sperm count, and miscarriage.

To see his face before and after the poisoning is to see the effects of the poison dioxin. Before, he was a ruggedly handsome political candidate. But after, he was a gray, pockmarked, scarred, gaunt man. Blood tests revealed that Yushenko had more than 1,000 times the normal amounts of dioxin in his system. Who slipped him the poison and how they did it remains a mystery.

Chechnya

Chechens are a Muslim people who live in the Caucasus Mountains. The Chechens have long engaged in struggles against Russian rule both before and after their surrender to tsarist Russia in the mid-1800s.

The Chechen region was made a Soviet republic in 1936. But after the Chechens collaborated with the invading Germans during World War II, Stalin expelled many of them to Kazakhstan, charging them with disloyalty. Needless to say, actions such as these, and others, never endeared the Russians and the Chechens to each other.

The 1994 War

Russia, although accepting its new world order, was yet unwilling to lose all of its republics. Chechnya is one republic that Russia decided must remain part of the federation. Nevertheless, under the leadership of Dzhokar Dudayev, Chechnya declared full independence in 1993, leading to civil war in that republic, as well as several Russian-backed attempts to overthrow Dudayev in 1993 and 1994.

Tensions between the Russian and Chechen governments continued to escalate, and by late 1994, the Russians had decided that they needed to crush the Chechen separatist movement. Russian troops were sent to Chechnya in late 1994 to end the rebellion.

But this Russian army was not the old Soviet war machine. With paydays rare and food scarce, Russian troops were already suffering from low morale. That they were disinclined to attack their countrymen in the Chechen capital of Grozny made matters worse.

Earlier in the year, Moscow had begun to fund and support Chechen rebels who were opposed to President Dudayev. These forces eventually joined the Russian troops, and together they launched a clandestine, poorly organized, and badly executed attack on Grozny in November 1994.

By December, Russian forces were pummeling Chechnya with massive aerial bombardments. But the aerial attacks did not have the desired effect. Rather than capitulating to the clearly superior air power of Moscow, the Chechens dug in. And as so often happens in these "precision-bombing" campaigns, many bombs missed their mark, killing an untold number of civilians. This, in turn, was reported by Russian journalists. In Moscow, opposition to the war was growing.

Russian President Yeltsin then sent in thousands more troops. But unlike the Russians, the Chechens believed in their cause. Said Chechen Foreign Minister Shamsedin

Yusef, as quoted by BBC News, "They cannot kill every Chechen. There are one million of us, and every one of us will fight." What the Chechen guerilla army lacked in organization and training it made up for in tenacity and intensity.

Moscow finally ordered a massive bombardment of the capital of Grozny in a last-ditch effort to root out the rebels. Tanks and soldiers rolled into Grozny in a show of strength.

However, the following days proved to be a military setback for the Russian forces. In a "David versus Goliath"–like scenario, Chechen guerilla units used hand grenades to destroy the lead tanks in Grozny's narrow streets. The tanks following behind were forced to halt, and thus they became sitting ducks; the guerillas picked off the Russian tanks and soldiers one by one. Thousands of Russian soldiers are believed to have been killed in the first days of the battle for Grozny.

> **Peacekeepers**
>
> One way the Chechens fought the Russians was by mobilizing entire villages to prevent the passage of Russian tanks.

> **Reliable Resources**
>
> How demoralized was the Russian army in Chechnya? One U.S. military survey reported that Russian soldiers had taken to selling their arms to the rebels in exchange for alcohol. Chancellor Helmut Kohl described the events as "sheer madness," and "journalists reported appalling human rights abuses being carried out by both sides."

Russia reacted by increasing its firepower. Journalists reported that the Russian artillery was targeting apartments, homes, and civilians; and Grozny was rocked by the magnitude and severity of the attack. Russia was, in effect, attempting to raze the city.

But the Chechens struck back, and by the third day of the assault, had repulsed the attack. And so, only a few days after its offensive, Russian forces began to withdraw from Chechnya.

But the war wasn't over. Russian forces would return, apparently opting for a war of attrition. Eventually, Grozny began to fall to the Russians under the weight of the attack.

Although Russian military forces took key buildings in the capital, Chechen rebels kept up their guerilla attacks. Russian soldiers were now facing an enemy they rarely saw and a population who despised them. The invaders grew disheartened.

By May 1995, about two thirds of Chechnya and most of the main towns were controlled by Russian forces. Yet, the Chechen rebels continued to inflict heavy damage on the invaders, operating from bases hidden in the mountain region.

Eventually, the Russian forces had to concede defeat in the face of a Chechen rebel force that refused to be contained or have itself crushed. Following a peace deal in August 1996, the troops who had entered the territory to keep it part of the Russian Federation withdrew, leaving behind about 10,000 dead and a country in ruin.

Estimates vary on the total number of casualties caused by the war. Russian Interior Minister Kulikov claimed that fewer than 20,000 civilians were killed, whereas then-Secretary of the Russian National Security Council Aleksandr Lebed asserted that 100,000 had been killed and 240,000 injured. International organizations estimate that up to 500,000 people fled Chechnya during the war.

Round Two

The Russians might have won the battle, but they lost the war. What began as a war of independence for many Chechens turned into a jihad for many others in this Muslim enclave. Radical Islam was able to make strong inroads as a reaction to Russian atrocities and imperialism.

Indeed, many Chechen commanders who started as pro-independence, essentially nonreligious figures increasingly turned to radical Islam as the war continued. And they did so, not just because it might have appealed to them, but also for the far more *realpolitik* reason that doing so enabled them to obtain money, troops, and the moral boost needed to sustain their fight.

def•i•ni•tion

Realpolitik is politics based on practical and material factors rather than on theoretical or ethical objectives.

The rising influence of Islam in this region was demonstrated in 2000 when the first of what would be many Chechen suicide bombers struck a Russian army barracks. Heretofore, suicide bombers had been seen only in the Middle East. But ever since the first suicide bombing in Moscow, more attacks have followed. According to senior analyst Tomas Valasek, "Qoqaz.net reports that at least 500 Muslim Chechens volunteered for martyrdom on these suicide missions."

Suicide bombers again attacked Russia in 2004, but with a twist. This time two Chechen women boarded Russian civilian airliners and blew them up in mid-air.

Surprisingly, this rise of radical Islam, and the events of September 11, actually played into Russia's hand. All of a sudden, the Chechens were no longer "freedom fighters" but rather Osama bin Laden–like terrorists. Russia was able to use these attacks as a pretext to "fight terrorism." In 2001, Russian air strikes targeted Chechen communications and infrastructure while ground troops poured into Chechnya again, a clear sign that Russia once again was mobilizing to reassert its military and political authority in the region.

And now, whereas the Chechen army was once seen in the West as rebels with a cause, the American War on Terrorism changed all that, too. It became clear to Russia-watchers that Russian President Putin was able to extract a promise from U.S. President Bush that the West would ignore Russian carnage in Chechnya in exchange for Russia's help in America's latest war.

But that didn't change the Chechen point of view. Chechen rebels would continue to demand independence.

Russian School Siege

On September 1, 2004, Chechen separatists stormed Beslan school number one in Russia and took more than 1,000 children and adults hostage. According to the BBC, the hostages were all taken to the school gym, where "the floor was peppered with mines and bombs connected by cables. Bombs were taped to the walls and suspended from the ceiling. Two larger devices were placed in the basketball hoops. Periodically the attackers fired their guns to terrify the hostages and placed children along the windows to act as human shields."

Russian special forces surrounded the school and tried to negotiate with the terrorists who were demanding a Russian pullout from Chechnya. On the second day of the siege, 26 hostages were freed, but the hostage takers also refused to allow food or water into the compound. Temperatures inside the building rose, and hostages began to get ill and faint. Some drank their own urine to stave off dehydration.

On Friday, the third day of the crisis, one of the bombs around the gym exploded as one of the terrorists was attempting to rewire it. This caused a second bomb to go off, and then the panicking, barbaric terrorists blew the roof of the gym, causing it to collapse on the hostages. Chaos ensued, including, inexplicably, the use by Russian troops of flame-throwers. Hostages and hostage takers began to run, and the hostage takers began to shoot the children. Russian forces then stormed the building, along with parents who had already armed themselves. A firefight ensued.

About two hours into the siege, Russian troops blew holes in the walls of the school compound in order to help the hostages escape, and they did escape—bloody, thirsty, petrified. Later, hundreds of dead children were found in the rubble of the gymnasium. Thirty-one of the 32 hostage takers were dead, as were 331 hostages. Seven hundred people were injured.

More Crises in the Caucasus

Chechnya, although Russia's biggest problem, is by no means its only one.

The Rose Revolution

Another of the ex-Soviet Union's so-called "color revolutions" (orange in Ukraine, rose here in Georgia) occurred in November 2003. As with the orange revolution in the Ukraine, the precipitating factor for ferment in Georgia were the results of a disputed parliamentary election.

A bit of background: Eduard Shevardnadze joined the Soviet Communist Party in 1946 and eventually became the party boss in the republic of Georgia by the early 1970s. Between 1985 and 1990, he was the Soviet foreign minister. After the collapse of the USSR in 1991, Shevardnadze returned to a newly independent Georgia, where he was hailed as a hero. Shevardnadze was installed as president of Georgia in 1992, was elected president in 1995, and was reelected five years later.

But despite the fact that Shevardnadze can rightfully claim a significant hand in such monumental accomplishments as the rise of democracy in the old Soviet Union and the reunification of Germany, his administration was increasingly seen by Georgians as corrupt and ineffective, unable to stem rising poverty.

Parliamentary elections in November 2003 were widely seen as corrupt, too. Opposition candidate Mikhail Saakashvili seemed to have won handily, but the results gave the election to Shevardnadze's party. Opposition candidates called for mass civil disobedience and new elections. Huge rallies sprang up across Georgia, demanding that Shevardnadze step down.

In response, the Georgian president sent soldiers to the streets of the capital of Tbilisi. Tensions rose, and so did the rose. Rather than fight, demonstrators gave red roses to the soldiers, many of whom laid down their arms.

Protests reached their apex on November 22, 2003, as the illegitimate parliament convened. Opposition leader Saakashvili and his supporters stormed the parliament building armed only with roses. Interrupting a speech by Shevardnadze and holding a long-stemmed red rose above his head, Saakashvilli shouted "Resign!" Shevardnadze was forced to flee the building with his bodyguards.

Although Shevardnadze attempted to declare a state of emergency, his actions answered the old question, "What if they had a war and nobody came?" Georgia's military refused the president's orders, Shevardnadze resigned, and 100,000 people in the streets of Tbilisi rose in joy.

The Dagestan Rebellion

In 1999, a number of Islamic rebels started a guerilla war in Dagestan, a republic in the Russian federation, demanding independence. As journalist Sara K. Miller relates in her account of the history and conflict in Dagestan, the rebels were a small, internationally funded militia whose numbers included Arabs and Africans, as well as Dagestanis and Chechens.

The rebels declared Dagestan's independence and a holy war against Russia. In response, Dagestan's neighbor, Chechnya, declared a state of emergency. Russia initially relied on an air offensive to combat the rebels, but ground troops were introduced soon thereafter.

And of course, refugees began to pour out of Dagestan. But international aid organizations were unable to help much as the rebels were not averse to kidnapping or killing relief workers. The end result of all of this is that this conflict is far from over.

The Rise of Islamic Fundamentalism

The big fear for Russia is that this outbreak of fighting in Dagestan, coming as it has on the heels of the fighting in Chechnya, might mean that the Caucasus and Central Asia are turning toward radical Islam. It is, in fact, a regional problem.

In Central Asia, the former Soviet states of Kyrgyzstan, Uzbekistan, and Tajikistan are also battling Islamic groups lodged in the mountainous region where the borders of the three republics converge.

Poverty and the collapse of the Soviet government, combined with the opening of the borders, have enabled radical Arab missionaries to spread their message in this area. These clerics, part of the fundamental *Wahabi* tradition, are opposed to the more traditional Islam that has long been practiced in the region.

The growth of radical Islam in this area is a cause for deep concern. One reason is that this form of Islam provides a reason to fight, and fighting, as we have seen, produces refugees. Refugees, unable to pursue their professions, are often forced into poverty. And poverty provides another reason to fight, to wit: If communism didn't work, and capitalism didn't work, maybe Islam is the answer! That many people are disillusioned with the corruption and poverty plaguing the former Soviet republics makes puritanical Islam even more inviting.

def•i•ni•tion

Wahabi is the most fundamental form of Islam. It was practiced by both the Taliban in Afghanistan and by Osama bin Laden.

Russia and the West

Throughout most of the twentieth century, Russia and the West stood ready to do battle with one another. Even though they became allies during World War II, because they faced a common enemy, Russia was still the West's enemy.

The breakup of the Soviet Union in 1991 began to change that perception. Russian Presidents, first Mikhail Gorbachev, and later Boris Yeltsin and Vladmir Putin, began to make peace overtures to the West, needing, as they did, Western capital. Old Warsaw Pact countries began to join NATO. Russian and American nuclear arms were greatly reduced. Things seemed to be getting better.

But it might not stay that way. Russia is a huge country with vast resources. Nationalism runs high there, and this is especially true with Vladmir Putin as president—a man who wants to restore former Soviet glory to Russia. To expect it to remain a second-tier country for long is unrealistic. Russia will likely rise again, and it might well become the West's biggest problem.

Putin

Russian president Vladmir Putin graduated from Leningrad State University in 1975 and joined the KGB. He was later stationed in East Germany, and then joined the faculty of his alma mater after the collapse of the Soviet Empire. Later, he joined the administration of Russian president Boris Yeltsin, including heading the successor agency to the KGB.

Putin was named prime minister by Yeltsin in 1999, although being the unknown that he was, few expected him to succeed in the position. But then, on New Year's Eve 1999, Yeltsin resigned and named Putin president of Russia. Four months later, Putin was elected to the position, and reelected in 2004. He has proven to be a very capable, strong politician.

Putin has endeavored to re-attach modern Russia to its powerful Soviet past, and in the process, has limited democracy in Russia. For example, he changed the system whereby regional governors are elected. Instead, under his new system, governors are nominated by the president and voted on by regional legislatures. This is a plan opposed by both Boris Yeltsin and Mikhail Gorbachev. He has been a significant player on the international stage, and has taken a hard-line stance on the question of Chechnya.

Reliable Resources

On April 25, 2005, Putin gave a speech in which he said that the collapse of the Soviet Union was "the greatest geopolitical catastrophe of the century," apparently forgetting World Wars I and II, and the Holocaust, among others.

Maybe the tough Putin can best be understood with this quote. When asked by Western journalists why he wouldn't negotiate with Chechen rebel leaders, he said, "Why don't you meet Osama bin Laden, invite him to Brussels or to the White House and engage in talks, ask him what he wants and give it to him so he leaves you in peace? You find it possible to set some limitations in your dealings with these bastards, so why should we talk to people who are child killers? No one has a moral right to tell us to talk to child killers."

The Least You Need to Know

- Russia was in conflict with the West for most of the twentieth century.
- The peaceful orange revolution in the Ukraine brought Viktor Yushenko to power.
- Chechen rebels are terrorists.
- Radical Islam is making large inroads in the Caucuses and Central Asia.
- Russia and the West might duel yet again.
- Vladmir Putin is a tough cookie.

Chapter 21

Northern Ireland Imbroglio

In This Chapter

- ◆ A history of Ireland
- ◆ Irish troubles
- ◆ The Good Friday Peace Agreement
- ◆ The IRA renounces violence

The current state of the world can be depressing. From one country to the next and one region to the next, people somehow seem to find new and better ways to kill one another. And in this orgy of violence, it might seem that there is no light.

But there is. If anything good can come from all this conflict and hate or from all this war and death, it is that peace is possible. No, it's not easy, and yes, it is rare. But it is possible. The bitter antagonists in Northern Ireland are heroic evidence of that. They are the light.

How the Irish saved their civilization.

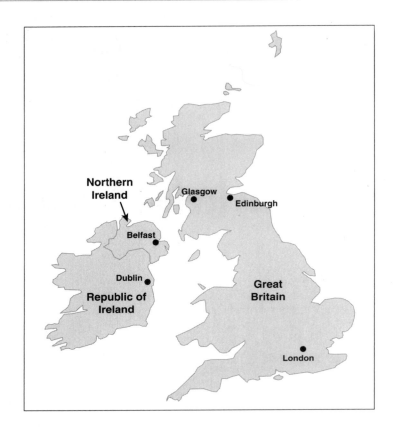

The Roots of the Problem

The first British involvement in Ireland began in 1169, when Anglo-Norman troops arrived in County Wexford. During the next 500 years, English rulers attempted to colonize Ireland, moves that precipitated numerous rebellions by the Irish over the years.

Reliable Resources

The traditional Irish alphabet uses only 18 letters: the 5 vowels (*a, e, i, o, u*) as well as the consonants *b, c, d, f, g, h, l, m, n, p, r, s,* and *t*.

By the sixteenth century, the English, a mostly Protestant bunch, were able to expand their power over the weaker Ireland. As such, religious persecution of Catholic Irish grew. This was especially true after the accession of Elizabeth I, a Protestant, to the English throne in 1558. By 1691, with the victory of Protestant English King William III over the Irish forces, Protestant supremacy began to dominate life in much of the British Isles as the British grip and occupation of the predominantly Catholic Ireland tightened.

Catholics in Ireland suffered greatly under British occupation. In fact, there were laws enacted that …

- Prevented Catholics from bearing arms.

- Denied them the right to hold public office.

- Restricted their ability to get an education.

When combined with the Act of Union, passed in 1800, which legally joined England and Ireland as one, Catholic rights became an oxymoron. The island was now officially governed by London.

Home Rule

Understandably, many Irish wanted to govern themselves, and the campaign for "home rule" was begun in the 1870s. Home Rulers wanted a separate Irish government. Yet not all Irish were Home Rulers. In the northern part of Ireland, which was predominantly Protestant, the people wanted to remain part of the British Empire. Wanting to remain in union with England, they were called, quite naturally, "Unionists."

On the other side were the "Nationalists," those who wanted to have their own nation—a free Irish state. In 1916, these Irish Nationalists stormed the General Post Office and other key buildings in Dublin and proclaimed the formation of an Irish *republic*. But the uprising failed. The subsequent execution of most of the leaders led to the emergence of Sinn Fein, the Nationalist Party that would dominate Irish politics for years to come.

In the 1918 general election, Sinn Fein demanded full freedom for Ireland and no union with Great Britain. On this platform, it beat the Unionists, who supported continued governance from London. Emboldened by this mandate, Sinn Fein boycotted the British Parliament the next year, instead declaring the formation of its own Irish Parliament.

def•i•ni•tion

According to Merriam Webster, a **republic** is "a government in which supreme power resides in a body of citizens entitled to vote and is exercised by elected officers and representatives responsible to them and governing according to law."

At the same time, Sinn Fein's military wing, the Irish Republican Army (IRA), began a violent struggle for independence from Great Britain. Led by Michael Collins, they began a terror campaign throughout Ireland.

The Partition of Ireland

The campaign worked. The British government relented and, in 1920, passed the Government of Ireland Act. The act partitioned Ireland into two areas—southern Ireland and Northern Ireland—with the intention that both would be given limited powers of self-government but would remain part of the United Kingdom.

This partitioning would have a lasting impact on Ireland. By creating two separate parliaments—one in the North and the other in the South—the British effectively pitted Ireland against itself. And it was done deliberately. The British knew that Northern Ireland had plenty of Protestants who still supported a union with Great Britain.

So in 1921, Sinn Fein and British officials signed the Anglo-Irish Treaty, which created an Irish Free State over the 26 southern counties. Although the south was finally free of English rule, the partition left Irish Catholics in the six northern counties cut off from their countrymen, subject to British rule, and dominated by a Protestant majority.

The partition was unacceptable to some Irish Nationalists, who demanded nothing less than a united, independent Ireland. How opposed was the IRA to partition? They even killed Michael Collins, a signer of the treaty.

The Troubles

In the 1960s, the Catholic population in the North, inspired by the civil rights movement in the United States, began to agitate for change. In 1966, Nationalist councilor Austin Currie squatted in a house in the village of Caledon, setting in motion a tragic chain of events, which became known throughout the world as the Northern Ireland Troubles.

Reliable Resources

Currie squatted in protest to the fact that an unmarried Protestant woman could get housing while many Catholic families remained on the public-housing waiting list. Discrimination in housing and an unfair voting system were two of the main grievances of the Catholic community.

Currie's actions instigated a widespread campaign for civil rights in the province. Although it was intended to be a peaceful campaign, the pro-British unionists viewed it as a covert attempt to destabilize the status quo. There was a violent reaction.

Violence Erupts

The feelings of frustration, acrimony, and humiliation that had been pent up over these many years finally found an outlet. Attacks by the IRA against the Nationalists began in earnest, and the Nationalists fought back. Now it was clear: Catholic was against Protestant, north was against south, England was against Ireland, and Unionists were against Nationalists.

Groups bombed each other's government installations, and, as community tension grew, arson attacks and incidents of intimidation reached a frightening level. In Belfast, entire streets of homes were torched as mobs went on wild rampages. In Londonderry, the police were almost overwhelmed by rioters. The crisis led to the greatest population movement in Western Europe since the end of World War II as thousands of families fled the violence in Northern Ireland.

Britain responded by sending troops to restore order, suspending the Northern Ireland government, and assuming control of the territory. But, as hostilities continued, the British, caught between rival Protestant and Catholic communities, themselves became the targets of violence.

Although Catholics initially welcomed the army, the relationship deteriorated swiftly when soldiers began to search Catholic homes looking for nationalists. The Troubles worsened.

Sunday, Bloody Sunday

On January 30, 1972, British troops opened fire on a group of Irish demonstrators, killing 13 of them. A fourteenth victim later died of his wounds. The incident became known as Bloody Sunday and became one of the defining moments of the Troubles.

But Sunday wasn't the only bloody day. Violence came every day of the week now in Northern Ireland. According to official statistics, the death toll in Northern Ireland from 1969 to 1997 was 3,228.

> **Reliable Resources**
>
> Well it was Sunday, bloody Sunday
> When they shot the people there
> The cries of thirteen martyrs
> Filled the Free Derry air
> Is there anyone amongst you
> Dare to blame it on the kids?
> Not a soldier boy was bleeding
> When they nailed the coffin lids!
>
> —John Lennon/Yoko Ono, February 1972; *Some Time in New York City,*
> Apple Records

But statistics alone cannot begin to tell the tale of woe suffered by the peoples of Northern Ireland who lived with, among other things:

- The bombing of pubs
- Car bombings
- Firebombings
- Assassinations
- Extortion
- Train bombs
- Subway bombs
- Kidnappings

> **Landmine!**
>
> On March 1, 1981, an IRA prisoner, Bobby Sands, began a hunger strike to protest his status as a common, rather than a political, prisoner. His eventual passing by starvation, and the death of nine fellow IRA inmates, sparked more outrage and riots, and brought increased sympathy for the IRA's drive for a united Ireland. While on his deathbed, hunger striker Bobby Sands was elected to the British Parliament.

Both Nationalist and Unionist politicians were targeted, and the IRA twice came close to killing the entire British cabinet—in a bomb explosion at the Conservative Party conference and in a mortar bomb attack on the prime minister's home at 10 Downing Street.

At the height of the British presence, in 1972, a massive British police and army presence was deployed in Northern Ireland. Some 21,000 soldiers were stationed there, yet the Troubles would continue for the next decade.

The Good Friday Peace Accords

The search for peace in Northern Ireland has gone on longer than the Troubles themselves. Efforts have ranged from pleas to the terrorists to lay down their arms to complex interparty and intergovernmental discussions.

The problem with any proposal is that a division in Northern Ireland exists that some thought too wide to bridge. Many Catholics wanted to become one with the rest of Ireland, whereas the majority of the Protestants wanted to remain in union with Great Britain. How could a solution connect this seemingly insurmountable divide?

Certainly people were trying. In 1972, three young children were killed when a terrorist getaway vehicle crashed into them after the driver had been shot by soldiers. The "Peace People" organization was formed as a result. The group drew thousands of people who demanded an end to violence. In 1977, the group's leaders, Mairead Corrigan and Betty Williams, were awarded the Nobel Peace Prize.

> **Peacekeepers**
>
> In 1972, the first direct attempt to broker peace took place. Sinn Fein leader Gerry Adams, then in jail, was released and flown with other senior republicans to London to take part in secret talks with the British Northern Ireland secretary of state, William Whitelaw. Although the result was but a short IRA cease-fire, a new day had dawned.

Throughout the late 1970s and early 1980s, attempts to end the violence continued, with little to show for it except more death. Finally, according to the *Washington Post*, in 1985, there was a breakthrough. The United Kingdom and the Republic of Ireland (ROI, or the southern part of Ireland) signed an agreement that "gave the ROI an oversight role on behalf of Catholics in Northern Ireland." The deal was a breakthrough as it established for the first time ever "the Irish government as a legitimate player in Northern Ireland politics."

With the door open, British leader John Hume and Sinn Fein president Gerry Adams held secret talks in 1988 aimed at finding a political solution to the problems. The talks continued, off and on, for several years until at last, in 1993, they announced the "Downing Street Declaration."

The deal stated that Sinn Fein could be a partner in any talks on the future of Northern Ireland if it renounced violence. Importantly, the declaration also stated that the British and Irish governments would support the democratic wish of the majority of people in Northern Ireland, whether it be a continued union with Britain or a united Ireland.

And then, on August 31, 1994, the amazing occurred: The IRA called a cease-fire. This enabled the talks to get serious. Six months later, in February 1995, the Irish and British governments announced their "Frameworks for the Future"—a document that outlined in general terms what any overall settlement might look like.

However, nothing comes easy in this most intractable of conflicts. Over the next 24 months, there was disagreement over disarmament and the lack of an IRA cease-fire. A new wave of bombings threatened to derail the peace process.

The IRA had become increasingly frustrated at what it considered to be a general lack of progress in the talks. Convinced that the British government would never deliver, the IRA ended its 18-month truce and blew up Canary Wharf in London.

But British Prime Minister John Major was clearly committed to this process by now, and vowed it would continue with or without Sinn Fein. When actual settlement negotiations began, in the absence of an IRA cease-fire, Sinn Fein was locked out.

Meet George Mitchell

In 1996 an international body was formed to help end the deadlock. Chaired by former U.S. Senator George Mitchell, the group endeavored to come up with a comprehensive plan to solve the many issues that threatened peace. The first thing Mitchell did was to offer a compromise to end the stalemate, suggesting that Britain drop its insistence that the IRA begin disarming before entering negotiations.

Then in May 1997, Tony Blair became Britain's prime minister. In one of his most important acts, Blair offered Sinn Fein entry into the talks if it would agree to a cease-fire. Sinn Fein agreed, and in the summer of 1997, Nationalists joined Unionists at Stormont Castle in Belfast, Northern Ireland, to decide the future of region.

Reliable Resources

George Mitchell comes from humble beginnings. His father was a janitor, and his mother worked in a textile mill. Even so, in 1980, Mitchell had worked his way into a position to be appointed to the U.S. Senate to complete the unexpired term of Senator Edmund S. Muskie. Mitchell was elected to a full term in the Senate in 1982, and in 1989 he became the Senate majority leader (until he retired from the Senate in 1995).

Pathway to Peace

The parties knew that any agreement would have to do two things. First, if there was to be no overall political union between North and South (and that seemed increasingly unlikely as a majority in the North wanted to remain with Britain), the agreement would nevertheless have to reassure the Catholics that the ROI would still play an important role in the life of Northern Ireland. The agreement also needed to reassure Northern unionists that Protestant Northern Ireland would not be dominated by the ROI.

This was one of the thorniest of issues—how to create an all-Ireland body that still respected Protestant ties to England. It was a balancing act to be sure. Unionists accepted the need for some sort of north-south structure, but they resisted any sort of powerful all-Ireland institution that might give the ROI too strong a say in Northern Ireland affairs while also weakening links with Britain.

Nationalists, on the other hand, viewed an all-Ireland structure as critical to a deal. If the ROI was going to dilute its claim to Northern Ireland, they believed that a strong all-Ireland council needed to be set up to ensure stability.

In addition to the British and Irish governments, 9 other parties were included in the talks at Stormont, including, for the first time in 75 years, the IRA and the Unionists.

An Agreement Is in Sight

As could be expected, the talks were contentious and were repeatedly marked by one side or the other walking out, threatening to quit, and actually quitting, as well as by breakdowns in negotiations, violence threatening future negotiations, and stalemates.

A frustrated, but equally committed George Mitchell then set a deadline. Either an agreement would be reached, or there would be no peace and negotiations would end. Within a week, Mitchell proposed a draft settlement.

Negotiations then reached a fever pitch. Both Prime Minister Tony Blair and Irish leader Bertie Ahern flew in for crisis meetings with the political parties. But even so, the mood was optimistic. As the days dwindled down to hours, that optimism increased in spite of the difficulties which had to be overcome.

According to the *Washington Post*, "By midnight on April 10, 1998, after 21 months of negotiations, the politicians had in their hands an agreement that no one thought they would ever see. The historic Good Friday Agreement created a new form of self-rule for Northern Ireland. The Accords would give the minority Catholics in Northern Ireland a far greater voice in their affairs and end direct British rule over the area—all while meeting Protestant demands that the province remain a part of Britain."

The Agreement

Specifically, the groundbreaking 69-page deal struck at the Stormont set out a new constitutional framework and proposals for an assembly and other complex issues. The main details included …

- **Constitutional changes.** The agreement explicitly recognized the principle of majority rule as a method to determine any change in Northern Ireland's status. It also stated that Articles 2 and 3 of the Irish constitution were to be changed (articles that called for reunification). The new formula ended the Irish territorial claim to Northern Ireland but recognized formally its Nationalist identity.

- **Institutions.** A new 108-member assembly, elected by proportional representation, would come into effect. The new body would have full legislative and executive authority on issues. Safeguards would be put in place to ensure that all sections of the community could participate and their rights would be protected by a bill of rights.

- **North-South reinforcement**. A civic forum was to be established, composed of representatives of business, trade union, and voluntary sectors. A new North-South ministerial council, which was to be made up by the first minister and deputy of the Assembly and Irish ministers, would be created. Meeting twice a year, it would deal with matters of common interest.

Thus, there would be a new Northern Ireland Assembly, a North-South Council, and a British-Irish Council.

No, the agreement wasn't all or nothing. Neither side won, nor did either side lose. As the Belfast Telegraph political analyst Barry White puts it, "Haven't you learned over the past 30 years, that if the population is divided 60–40 in its loyalty to Britain and Ireland, that means that its institutions must incorporate a bit of both? Most of us would wish that things were different, and that we could be all British or all Irish, but we can't. It is something we have to accept, like it or not."

Peacekeepers _____

April 10, 1998 (Associated Press): "Critically, the new Belfast assembly will be expected to cooperate formally with the Irish Republic in a North-South council of law-makers. This measure is considered essential to win support from the north's Catholics, who generally favor the unification of Ireland. But the Protestant bloc appeared to have won a substantial concession because the Belfast assembly will have the right to approve decisions taken by its members in the cross-border council."

White continues:

> To my mind, the Agreement sets up a governmental framework in Northern Ireland that could develop in one of two directions. It could consolidate Northern Ireland's position in the UK, mainly by getting the Republic to drop its territorial and psychological claim, or it could swing us in the direction of a united Ireland, if these cross-border bodies get us thinking that links with the Republic could be more advantageous than links with Britain.
>
> In other words, the Agreement gives us the freedom to expand our horizons and drop our obsession with exclusiveness, either British or Irish. We can be either or both, without having to make any excuses or to regard ourselves as second class.
>
> We happen to live in (an area) where the majority want to be part of the U.K., but we could change, or the majority could change. What's wrong with that?

Yes indeed, what's wrong with that? And the best part is that no one has to die if someone changes his or her mind now.

The plan was put to a vote. In 1998, following nearly 30 years of bloody conflict, the people of Northern Ireland voted overwhelmingly in favor of the Good Friday Peace Agreement. Peace had finally come to Northern Ireland.

Postscript

On July 28, 2005, the Irish Republican Army formally announced that it was renouncing the use of violence and would disarm, thereby ending its 90-year war to oust Great Britain from Northern Ireland. In a statement released to the press, the IRA said, "The leadership has formally ordered an end to the armed campaign.

All Volunteers [the IRA's name for their soldiers] have been instructed to assist the development of purely political and democratic programs through exclusively peaceful means."

Said IRA party leader Gerry Adams, "There is a time to resist, to stand up and to confront the enemy by arms if necessary. In other words, unfortunately, there is a time for war. There is also a time to engage, to reach out, to put the war behind us all. … This is that time."

The Least You Need to Know

- Irish history is replete with sadness.
- The Troubles caused the worst bloodshed in modern Irish history.
- The Good Friday Peace Agreement is a historic document.
- The IRA renounced the use of arms and ended its decade-long war.

Chapter 22

Smoldering European Conflicts

In This Chapter

- Spain's terrorist threat
- London subway bombing
- Armenia and Azerbaijan
- Cyprus divided

The twentieth century was a century marred by violence from Europe. Both World War I and World War II began, and largely took place, there. The Cold War was also mostly a European phenomenon. Even the late-century conflict in the Balkans was a European affair. More recently, al-Qaeda terrorist attacks have occurred there. Europe and war tend to go hand in hand.

In the modern world, then, Europe is always a concern. The fear today is that even the smallest of conflicts, conflicts that would barely be a concern elsewhere in the world, must be handled properly and contained swiftly because they are in Europe. No one wants the Continent to again be the spark that lights the world.

Europe ruined the last century for the rest of us.

Madrid Train Bombings

The global terror war hit home in Spain on the morning of March 11, 2004, when 10 bombs blew up 4 commuter trains during the height of rush hour in Madrid, killing 191 people and injuring 1,460. Although Spain had suffered smaller terrorist attacks at the hands of Basque separatists over the past half-century, the March 11 Madrid bombings (also known as 3/11 or M-11) were the worst terrorist attacsk in Spanish history. And this, despite the fact that three additional bombs failed to go off that day.

Spanish authorities initially thought that the bombings were the work of the Basque separatist group ETA, but further analysis revealed the bombers likely were Islamic terrorists:

◆ The explosives were not the type usually used by ETA.

◆ ETA also typically warned of pending attacks and took credit after they occurred. Neither was true here.

◆ The sheer size and complexity of the bombings were far greater than anything ETA had ever attempted.

◆ A stolen van parked outside the rail station contained tapes of the Koran in Arabic.

◆ The March 11 attacks came exactly 30 months after the September 11 attacks, and both used public transportation systems to inflict great loss.

Though it is difficult to say exactly why the Madrid attack occurred, facts indicate that they were likely a response to the Iraq War and an attempt to influence the outcome of Spanish elections. If so, it accomplished its aims.

The Madrid bombings came at the end of a Spanish election that was turning on the question of whether Spain should continue to assist in the American invasion and occupation of Iraq. Going into the last few days of the election (the train bombings occurred on one of the last days of campaigning) it was thought that the ruling conservative party would retain power. However, probably because of the terrorist attacks, the anti-war Socialist Worker's Party won a plurality of the vote.

Reliable Resources

"We reserve the right to retaliate at the appropriate time and place against all countries involved [in assisting the U.S.-led invasion of Iraq, *especially Britain, Spain, Australia, Poland, Japan and Italy."*

—Statement issued by Osama bin Laden, October, 2003

New Prime Minister José Luis Rodríguez Zapatero formed a government, and one of his first decisions was to pull Spain's troops out of Iraq.

London Calling

That a qualitatively different sort of terrorist enemy was on the loose in Europe became painfully even more obvious on July 7, 2005, when a coordinated series of four bomb attacks struck London during rush hour. Eerily reminiscent of the Madrid train attacks, the London subway bombings killed 52 people.

Three bombs exploded almost simultaneously on three different London Underground trains, and a fourth blew up a double-decker bus about an hour later. The attacks were the result of four Islamic suicide attackers and were the worst bombing in London since World War II.

Two weeks later to the day, four more explosions occurred on three Underground trains and a bus, but apparently due to a mistake, only the detonators of the bombs went off and no one was hurt. All four suspected bombers were subsequently arrested by Scotland Yard.

Why did they do it, and then attempt to do it again? One of the reasons given for the war in Iraq by President Bush was that by attacking terrorists "over there" the West would not have to fight them "over here." That faulty, tortured logic was laid bare after the Madrid and London bombings.

Indeed, in September of 2005, Osama bin Laden's right-hand man, Ayman al-Zawahiri, said in a taped message played on *Aljazeera* television that al-Qaeda had the "honor" of carrying out the attacks in response to Great Britain's foreign policy.

The reason for the bombings, al-Zawahiri said, was because of "the British Crusader's arrogance and against the American Crusader's aggression on the Islamic nation for 100 years." In addition, al-Zawahiri denounced England's "crimes in Afghanistan and Iraq."

def•i•ni•tion

Launched in 1996, **Aljazeera** is the Arab-world equivalent of CNN. With 30 bureaus around the globe, the network provides the Islamic world with a distinctly Eastern view of world events.

This was the second time that al-Zawahiri had publicly commented on the London bombings. Earlier in September 2005 he said in a taped message that the bombings were proof that the battle had now been brought to "the enemies' land."

So much for the latest reason for the Iraq War.

Armenia Versus Azerbaijan

Between 1915 and 1917, Russia occupied most of Armenia. But the Bolshevik victory in Russia ended Russia's involvement in World War I, and Russian troops also left Armenia. Similarly, immediately after the chaotic Bolshevik revolution, Armenia's neighbor Azerbaijan declared its independence from the Soviet Union. Neither country wanted anything to do with the big Russian bear.

However, the bear wanted them. Azerbaijan was reconquered by the Red army in 1920, and annexed into the USSR in 1922. Armenia, seeing its neighbor Azerbaijan fold so quickly, decided not to fight. In November 1920, the Armenian government made a political agreement with the communists to enter into a coalition government.

Then, for reasons that are still difficult to decipher, the Soviet Union created the Nagorno-Karabakh Autonomous Region within Azerbaijan in 1924. It did so even though 94 percent of the region's population was Armenian, and the land sits on the border between the two countries. Just as easily, Nagorno-Karabakh, with its largely Armenian population, could have been made part of Armenia. But it wasn't.

Nevertheless, even though the region is Armenian, it became part of Azerbaijan. If one thing is clear, it is that governments are loathe to give up their land, even when keeping that land makes no sense.

Seventy years later, after the collapse of the Soviet Union, both countries finally got their chance to be independent. Azerbaijan declared its independence from the collapsing Soviet Union on August 30, 1991. The next month, more than 99 percent of voters in Armenia also voted to free themselves from the Soviet Union. Both countries were finally free from the Russians.

However, they were not free from each other. Since 1988, Azerbaijan and Armenia have been feuding and fighting over Nagorno-Karabakh. Not surprisingly, the majority of the population of Armenian Christians wanted to secede from the predominantly Muslim Azerbaijan and join with Armenia. Azerbaijan would not hear of it.

In 1988, Armenian legislators in the Nagorno-Karabakh region voted to unify with Armenia. Azerbaijanis responded by killing more than 100 Armenians, and war erupted. Refugees then began to pour out of both Armenia and Azerbaijan as the minority populations in both places came under attack.

Soviet President Mikhail Gorbachev then attempted to solve the problem by granting greater autonomy to Nagorno-Karabakh itself while also granting Azerbaijan authorities greater powers. But this balancing act satisfied neither Armenians nor Azerbaijanis. The fighting intensified. In September 1989, Azerbaijan began an economic blockade of Armenia supply lines through its territory.

In 1991, another referendum was held by Armenians in Nagorno-Karabakh, who decided that they wanted to be associated with neither

> **Reliable Resources**
>
> According to a March 8, 2002, BBC News report, "Armenia has seen great changes since the breakup of the Soviet Union in 1991. Once dubbed the Soviet 'silicon valley,' Armenia's economy collapsed when the Soviet market disappeared. It has also suffered from a trade blockade imposed by neighboring Turkey and Azerbaijan after the dispute over Nagorno-Karabakh erupted."

> **Landmine!**
>
> In 1992, after taking over the Nagorno-Karabakh Region, Armenian rebels expelled all Azerbaijanis. In 1993, they captured the province of Kelbacar, looting and burning the capitals and most of the villages of these regions as they expelled the inhabitants from that area, too.

of these countries, opting instead to create an independent state. Nevertheless, Armenia decided to go on the offensive. It sent in large numbers of troops and tanks to the disputed region and soon took control of it, as well as large parts of Azerbaijan. All-out war was the result.

In 1994, after more than 30,000 people had died and 1 million Azerbaijanis had been displaced by the violence, a truce was called. At the time, forces of both Armenia and the "Republic of Nargono-Karabakh" (a government unrecognized by anyone on the outside) occupied the disputed lands, as well as parts of Azerbaijan.

In 2001, even though nothing had changed in the conflict, the United States lifted a ban on aid to Azerbaijan that it had placed during the Nagorno-Karabakh conflict. Why was the ban finally lifted? Because Azerbaijan provided airspace and intelligence following the September 11 attacks on the United States.

Coincidentally, earlier that year, the United States sponsored talks between the parties in Florida and Paris. Nothing came of those talks. Armenia still controls the region, and the economies of both countries are severely damaged after years of war and changing economic trends.

Cyprus

To understand why Europe could be engulfed in a war over this tiny island, you need to appreciate that the vast majority of Cypriots are of Greek descent, whereas a significant minority are Turkish. If you add that the country was run by Britain for almost 100 years, you begin to see why it is a recipe for conflict.

Under the British, the Greek Cypriot population began to call for union with Greece and an end to British rule. To that end, in 1955, a Greek Cypriot separatist organization (EOKA), began a campaign of (you know it by heart now) terrorism. Tension and terror mounted, especially after British authorities deported the spokesman for the Greek Cypriots.

Of course, no conflict would be complete if there wasn't another side that wanted something totally different. The Turkish minority had their own ideas, namely, that the island should be partitioned. Under this plan, North Cyprus would house the Turks and South Cyprus would be Greek.

Cyprus is too small for continued division.

Negotiations in 1955 among Britain, Greece, and Turkey started, broke down, and went nowhere. In 1959, though, a settlement was finally reached after four arduous years of talks. The agreement provided for Cypriot independence from Britain, along with constitutional guarantees by the Greek Cypriot majority that were supposed to protect the Turkish Cypriot minority.

But the best-laid plans of mice and men often go awry. Cypriot Turks felt like second-class citizens in their own country, and large-scale fighting between the Greeks and Turks erupted several times in the 1960s. The clashes got so bad that a U.N. peace-keeping force was sent in.

1974

The major event in this struggle occurred in 1974, when the president of Cyprus, Archbishop Makarios, was deposed in a coup orchestrated by Greek Cypriot army officers seeking to achieve union with Greece, and who were supported by Greece's then military government. Rioting and violence erupted throughout the island as a result, and five days later, Turkey sent in the troops. Claiming it was only there to protect the Turkish Cypriots, Turkey soon controlled about one third of Cyprus.

Of course, the Greek Cypriots saw this as an illegal occupation of their country. Nevertheless, the massive show of force by Turkey effectively partitioned the island. Turkish Cypriots occupied the northern third, whereas the Greek Cypriot community held the southern sector. Two hundred thousand Greek Cypriots were displaced in the action. Under the U.N. cease-fire that followed, Turkey was permitted to retain its military forces in the areas it had captured.

In 1975, the island was legally partitioned into Greek and Turkish territories separated by a buffer zone mined and patrolled by U.N. peacekeepers. In 1983, the Turkish-held area declared itself the "Turkish Federated State of Cyprus," and eight years later, it declared its independence as the "Turkish Republic of Northern Cyprus." Unfortunately, the only country in the world that formally recognized it was Turkey.

Throughout the years that followed, successive attempts to resolve the literal and figurative division of Cyprus were met by successive failures. By the late 1990s, it was estimated that over half of the population of Turkish Cyprus consisted of settlers from Turkey. Turkey continued to keep 35,000 troops in the north.

Peacekeepers

The Turkish north of the island is much poorer than the Greek south, and is politically isolated. It has been subject to U.N. sanctions and economic turmoil.

In 2001, with still no resolution in sight, the U.N. Security Council renewed the United Nation's 36-year mission in Cyprus. Some 2,400 peacekeepers continued to patrol the buffer zone between Greek and Turkish Cypriots. Turkey has also warned that it is not averse to simply annexing the Turkish Cypriot part of the island.

2001, a Cypriot Odyssey

But encouraging signs also emerged in 2001: Turkish Cypriot leader Rauf Denktas crossed to the South for the first time since the Turkish invasion of 1974 to dine with Greek Cypriot leader Glafkos Clerides. It was an unheard of, landmark event.

The dinner foreshadowed what could be real progress in the deadlock for the first time in 25 years. The impetus was, maybe not surprisingly, membership in the European Union—both Cyprus and Turkey wanted to join the EU, and the EU wanted them in. U.N.-sponsored negotiations in 2002 allowed the EU to invite at least the Greek part of Cyprus (which is still called Cyprus) to join the Union in 2004.

Turkey, which also aspires to EU membership, seemed to realize that its chances would be much improved if the Cyprus issue could be resolved. Certainly, if Cyprus were to join the EU as a divided island, with Turkey an occupying power, Turkey's prospects of EU membership would be damaged.

As EU membership for Greek Cyprus approached in 2004, the United Nations put together a reunification plan and submitted it to both sides for a vote. Both had to agree to the referendum for it to take effect. Turkish Cypriots voted in favor, although their leader, Rauf Denktash, opposed the plan. Greek Cypriots rejected the plan, and the country remained divided.

Nevertheless, "Cyprus" joined the EU in 2004, but because Turkey is not yet a member of the EU and Greece is, EU benefits and laws apply only to the Greek Cypriots. Because Turkey so desires EU membership, it may be that the best hope for resolving this conflict is the EU carrot rather than any military stick. However, peace is never easy, and the problems these two sides face are numerous, including ...

- The need for a power-sharing formula.

- Compensation for those who lost land in the division of the island.

- Recognition of injustices done toward each other before partition.

- Fear among the minority Turks that they will again be dominated by the Majority Greeks upon reunification.

So maybe it will be that one thing that is neither Greek nor Turkish, neither West nor East, neither Islamic nor Christian, that can make peace in this land: money.

The Least You Need to Know

- Islamic terrorists killed almost 200 and injured thousands more in the Spanish train bombings.

- They perpetrated the same sort of attack, with similar results, on the London transit system.

- Armenia and Azerbaijan are still at it.

- Greeks and Turks in Cyprus might soon be over it.

Part 6

South America and Latin America

In South America, civil war is the name of the game. Colombia's civil war lasted more than 30 years. In Peru, although the Shining Path has been vanquished, the problems that led to its emergence largely have not. Haiti has been wracked by corruption, Cuba has been ruled by a despot, and other countries in the region have their own problems, too.

23

Colombia in Conflict

In This Chapter

- ◆ Colombia's history of conflict
- ◆ FARC emerges
- ◆ Drug money
- ◆ Peace talks

Colombia is a country of mixed blessings. One of the largest and most populous countries in South America, Colombia, is also a major producer of gold, silver, emeralds, platinum, coal, and oil.

On the other hand, it also has a highly structured class-based society in which the rich families of Spanish descent have gotten demonstrably richer, whereas the indigenous peasants have clearly gotten poorer. This dichotomy has proven to be productive ground for leftist insurgents and guerillas who are funded largely with drug money. Moreover, at the other end of the political spectrum are right-wing paramilitary groups backed by the army and the police. All told, Colombia is a place with more conflict than any one country should have to endure.

Colombia: Maybe "just say no" might work.

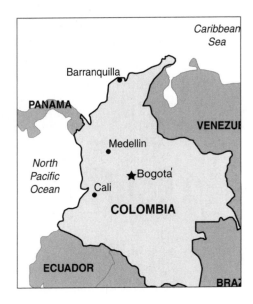

A Conflicted History

In the sixteenth century, Spain began to colonize South America, and the settlement of Santa Fé de Bogotà (subsequently known as Bogotà) became part of the Spanish colony of Peru.

In 1819, the great South American general Simón Bolívar defeated the Spanish, and the Republic of Gran Colombia was formed from the countries that would later become Colombia, Ecuador, Panama, and Venezuela. After only 10 years in existence, Gran Colombia dissolved when Venezuela and Ecuador split off, eventually followed by Panama, leaving the present-day Colombia.

Colombian society has always been split in two—between liberals and conservatives, between the rich and poor, and between indigenous natives and Spanish immigrants.

Reliable Resources

Simón Bolívar was born on July 24, 1783, in Caracas, Venezuela, and he inherited a fortune as a child after his parents died. He traveled extensively throughout Europe as a young man, and later went on to become one of South America's greatest generals. His heroics won independence for Bolivia, Panama, Colombia, Ecuador, Peru, and Venezuela. Bolívar is known as *El Libérator* (The Liberator) and the "George Washington of South America."

Later, more divisions would emerge—between the government and the rebels, between the drug trade and the police, and between the haves and the many have-nots. At times, these various divisions in the country would practically tear it apart.

The first evidence of that occurred between 1899 and 1903, during the so-called "war of the thousand days." It is believed that more than 120,000 people died in this civil war that pitted the right-wing monied class against the leftist poor.

Civil war again erupted in 1948. This time it is estimated that 250,000 to 300,000 were killed during the war. Although many contemporary news accounts label the ongoing Colombian conflict as beginning in the mid-1960s, the roots of Colombia's largest guerrilla group, the Revolutionary Armed Forces of Colombia (FARC), dates back to the peasant armed self-defense movements formed during this civil war: a period known as "la violencia."

Resolution came in 1958 when the Conservative Party and the Liberal Party agreed to form a single party—the National Front. In a move that would portend ill for all Colombia, all other political parties were banned. The agreement concentrated control of the state apparatus and bureaucracies in the hands of elites, and prevented the expression of alternative political projects.

The result was that Colombia became a breeding ground for rebels fighting against the powers that be. Their fight would last into the next millennium.

Guerrilla War

Colombia is in the middle of a deadly, decades-long civil war. The conflict pits the Colombian government against both well-armed, dangerous, violent guerrilla organizations and similarly dangerous, brutal, as well as growing paramilitary forces.

The Guerillas

A 40-year insurgent campaign to overthrow the Colombian government escalated during the 1990s because of increased funds from the drug trade. Although the violence is deadly and widespread, the movement lacks the overall armed strength and popular support necessary to overthrow the government. However, its support is not insignificant. Accordingly, the insurgency is a major issue in Colombia.

As indicated, the roots of the guerrilla movement go back to the civil war of the 1950s, but the emergence of actual insurgent guerilla groups occurred in the mid-1960s, when it was far too evident that Colombia had become a country marked by intense class divisions. The few in the stratified upper classes controlled the country's wealth, power, and resources. There was no middle class. So, the masses of people below increasingly lived in hunger and squalor—a recipe, as we have seen repeatedly, for rebellion.

> **Landmine!**
>
> In 2001, Human Rights Watch decried abuses by Colombian guerillas that included killings of civilians, hostage taking, the use of child soldiers, grossly unfair trials, the "cruel and inhumane" treatment of captured combatants, the forced displacement of civilians, and the use of prohibited weapons, including gas cylinder bombs.

In 1965, the first of these groups, the Leftist National Liberation Army (ELN), was formed, and the Maoist People's Liberation Army (EPL) soon followed in its footsteps. But it was the last group that would become the main player in Colombia's long guerrilla war—the Revolutionary Armed Forces of Colombia, FARC.

> **Peacekeepers**
>
> Bogotá is one of South America's fastest-growing areas. After 1940, large numbers of rural Colombians migrated to Bogotá in search of greater economic opportunities, and the population rapidly grew. It currently stands at more than six million.

Over the past 40 years, FARC has grown into a powerful, well-financed military organization. Although much of this growth has been funded by illicit drug money, there is support for FARC among the peasants because of the lack of government response to the hardships faced by peasant farmers. FARC generally lacks any significant support among Colombia's middle class.

FARC's Beginnings

During the first years of FARC, the guerrillas concentrated on expanding their narrow base. The founders of FARC followed the political lead of the Colombian Communist Party and even by the late 1970s, FARC was a marginal guerrilla force.

However, FARC grew and became bolder in the late 1970s as the army failed to subdue them. This was evidenced best in 1980, when FARC took and occupied the Dominican embassy in Bogotá for 61 days, holding many foreign diplomats as hostages. By the end of the siege, 100 were dead, including the president of the Colombian Supreme Court and 10 other justices.

Nourished by the ever-increasing lack of political and economic opportunity for the working class, FARC had now become "the people's army."

FARC Gets Serious

In the 1980s and 1990s the guerillas became more violent as a means to achieve their ends. Kidnapping and extortion became far more commonplace, and in fact became a significant source of revenue as FARC targeted politicians and rich executives.

Despite its violence against the system (or maybe because of it), FARC continued to gain support in some regions of the country. Armed with the ability to control some territory, maintain a presence in others, and exploit rural unemployment, the group has been able to establish legitimacy and support in various regions of the country.

The growth of the insurgency was no doubt also in part because of the Colombian government's inability, or unwillingness, to deal with the myriad problems in the countryside. Combined with its tacit, if not express, approval of the growing, ruthless rightwing paramilitary groups, the government is largely seen as being equally responsible for the tremendous loss of human lives, possessions, security, and the integrity of the country.

So, although the guerrillas' military growth is at least partially because of their increased ability to generate revenues through drugs, extortion, and kidnapping, it is equally true that they have grown because of their ability to take advantage of cracks in a highly decayed political system that neglects socio-economic needs of the poor.

The Paramilitaries

In response to the leftist insurgents, right-wing paramilitary groups, supported by the government and the ruling classes, also emerged in the 1980s. They wage war not only against the guerrillas, but also anyone suspected of being a guerrilla sympathizer, such as union members, peasant organizers, human rights workers, and religious activists.

Some paramilitary groups have even extended the parameters of the war against the guerrillas to include drug addicts, alcoholics, prostitutes, petty criminals, and the homeless. These paramilitary groups have been accused of gross human rights violations, including rape, murder, and dismemberment.

According to Human Rights Watch, the Colombian military and police actually work with, support, profit from, and tolerate these paramilitary groups, treating them as a force allied to and compatible with their own. The relationship is so intertwined that

- The army and the paramilitaries communicate with one another via radios, cellular telephones, and beepers.

- They share intelligence, including the names of suspected guerrilla collaborators.

- They share fighters, including paramilitary commanders.

- They share vehicles, including army trucks used to transport paramilitary fighters.

- They coordinate offenses together.

As a result, according to Human Rights Watch, 35,000 people have been killed in the fighting during the past 2 decades, and "most of them have been poor civilians accused by the Colombian Army or right-wing paramilitaries of collaborating with left-wing guerrillas." Moreover, Colombia has the highest murder rate, per capita, in the world.

Drugs and Money

What complicates matters in Colombia, what makes it different from other places where conflict thrives, are the vast sums of money that come from the drug trade. Drug money influences everything, and has the potential to corrupt anything is in its path. As such, rebels have more money than their counterparts in other countries, the government has more money to fight them, and the stakes are correspondingly much higher.

The War on Drugs

During the late 1970s and early 1980s, the growing contraband export of marijuana and cocaine became a major source of income for the Colombian economy. Not only did the government begin to get proceeds from illicit drug sales, but so did the leftist insurgents and the paramilitaries. Everyone in the country began to drink from the drug teat.

Enter the United States, deciding that Colombia needed to wean itself from its mother's milk. In 1980, after the election of Ronald Reagan, the United States began its war on drugs. In an attempt to stamp out growing drug use at home and increased production abroad, the Americans began to fund this "war" to the tune of hundreds of millions of dollars. One of the first to receive this largesse was the Colombian government.

In 1984, the Colombian government, aided by the Americans, launched a crackdown on drug trafficking, but it was largely unsuccessful. Drug trafficking continued, and the leftist guerrillas remained. The anti-drug crackdown lost momentum as the drug traffickers and rebels joined forces in some regions.

Part of the problem for Colombia is that the American money goes to support one of the most repressive governments in the hemisphere. The regime then uses this money to crack down on anyone affiliated with the drug trade, including popular leftist guerillas and the poor peasants themselves, who often grow cocoa because it is the only crop that brings in real money. Although the crackdowns might eradicate a bit of the cocaine production, it simultaneously helps to foster more left-wing sentiments and rebellion.

The Medellin Drug Cartel

By the mid-1970s, it had become apparent to American law enforcement that a well-organized effort was exporting illegal drugs into the United States from abroad. Trafficking networks inside the United States, organized from Colombia, were discovered. These networks sold drugs, created and ran stash houses, laundered money, developed distribution networks, and killed their enemies.

The first to dominate this illicit market trade were organized criminal groups headquartered in Medellin, Colombia. The Medellin drug cartel ruled the early drug trade in Colombia.

This network began when Carlos Lehder conceived of the idea of smuggling cocaine into the United States the same way marijuana was smuggled. Specifically, Lehder decided that, rather than hiding small amounts of cocaine in luggage or on airline passengers, large quantities of cocaine could be put on small, private aircraft and flown into the United States.

> **Reliable Resources**
>
> In 1998, the U.S. Congress allocated $290 million in anti-drug aid to Colombia to be spent over the next 3 years. The huge majority of this aid was geared toward purchasing helicopters and weaponry for military and police use in coca-eradication projects. Only $45 million of the aid was earmarked for crop-substitution programs.

To this end, Lehder bought a sizable portion of a Bahamian island about 225 miles southeast of Miami. On this small island, he built an extended airstrip as a refueling stop for the light planes that would be transporting his cocaine to his secret airstrips in the United States.

Willing to use whatever means necessary to achieve his ends, Lehder was the first in what would be a long line of violent criminals from Medellin. In 1984, he was involved in the assassination of Colombia's justice minister, Rodrigo Lara Bonilla. Outraged by the terrorist tactics employed by the Medellin organization, the Colombian government turned Lehder over to the U.S. Drug Enforcement Agency and extradited him to the United States in February 1987. Although Lehder was sentenced to 135 years in federal prison, he soon cooperated in the U.S. investigation of Panama dictator Manuel Noriega and received a reduced sentence in return.

Besides Lehder, the infamous Pablo Escobar also ran the Medellin cocaine cartel. Under Escobar, Medellin became the most dangerous city on Earth. Using bribery, intimidation, and murder to get his way, Escobar created an equally ruthless organization. Informants were bombed, planes were blown up, and bounties were put on the lives of police officers. As many as 2,000 police officers and civilians were murdered each year during the 1990s in Medellin.

In 1992, he escaped from prison and for the next 17 months was the target of the largest manhunt in Colombian history. Finally, in December 1993, Escobar was killed in a firefight with the police at a private residence in downtown Medellin.

The Cali Mafias

With the elimination of most of the major figures in the Medellin groups, drug-trafficking groups in Cali, Colombia, came to the fore. Unlike their predecessors, the members of the Cali cartel avoided obvious acts of violence, instead trying to pass themselves off as legitimate businessmen.

During the early 1990s, members of the Cali drug cartel generated billions of dollars in drug revenues per year operating sophisticated drug trafficking enterprises.

In the 1986 elections, Virgilio Barco Vargas became president of Colombia. Barco vowed to combat the drug cartels. In August 1989, the government arrested more than 10,000 people and confiscated the property of suspected drug traffickers. However, despite numerous successes in intercepting cocaine shipments and the chemicals used to refine the drug, the drug trade remained strong, demand creating supply.

Eventually, however, the combined efforts of the *DEA* and the Colombia authorities paid off when, in June 1995, the Cali mafia began to disintegrate. That summer five leaders of the Cali mafia were arrested, and by September 1996, the remaining kingpins had been captured.

def•i•ni•tion

The **DEA,** or Drug Enforcement Agency, is a unit of the U.S. government that is charged with enforcing drug laws and eradicating illegal drugs. Since 1973, the DEA has grown significantly, especially during the past several years. The DEA has more than 4,000 agents, and its annual budget is roughly $1.5 billion.

> **Reliable Resources** _____
>
> According to Bartleby, "Most of the world's coca is grown in Peru, Bolivia, and Colombia. For the farmers, it is a well-paying crop. They harvest and dry the leaves, which are then processed into coca paste. Cocaine base is extracted from the paste in laboratories. Further processing continues, where the white powder, cocaine hydrochloride, is produced for export. Once in the United States, the cocaine is diluted with ingredients such as lactose, and it is sold or further processed into crack."

The Drug Trade Today

Since then, the drug trade has become more decentralized. Power is now passing to new traffickers. By working with their associates in Mexico, the Colombia drug traffickers remain responsible for most of the world's cocaine production and wholesale distribution.

Peace Efforts

In June 1994, Ernesto Samper Pizano was elected president of Colombia. Like Barco before him, Samper, too, wanted to try and create peace for his country by dealing with the guerillas. FARC and ELN were invited to the peace table, and they accepted that offer. The talks were aimed at the disarmament of, and legislative representation for, the guerrillas.

Breakdown

Despite that hopeful beginning, Colombia entered a political crisis in 1995 after Samper was accused of accepting almost $6 million in campaign contributions from drug traffickers in exchange for leniency. In the meantime, the talks broke down.

Samper's government encountered many difficulties controlling the armed factions within Colombia, and the nation's military was unable to contain the violence.

> **Landmine!** _____
>
> According to the *Denver Post*, "Colombia is the world's largest processor of cocaine. It supplies about 90 percent of the cocaine in the United States and the great majority of cocaine to other international drug markets. Its latest export is heroin, having increased its production by 25 percent in the past few years."

Thus in 1997, leftist guerrillas launched a campaign of violence and intimidation aimed at preventing voters from participating in municipal and regional elections, and paramilitary squads launched a counter campaign of violence, raiding a number of villages and executing individuals suspected of supporting guerrilla activities.

However, prospects of a peaceful settlement to the protracted violence improved. In June 1998, Colombian voters elected Andrés Pastrana, the son of a former Colombian president, who had a law degree and was a fellow at the Center for International Affairs at Harvard as Colombia's new president. Following the election, FARC, ELN, and the United Self-Defense Units of Colombia, a leading right-wing paramilitary organization, all announced their willingness to engage in peace talks with the new government.

Peace Talks

Talks between the Pastrana government and FARC officially opened in January 1999. In October of that year, they signed the "San Francisco Agreement," committing themselves to negotiate a cease-fire. A safe haven for the guerillas, which had been given to them as part of the peace negotiations in 1998, was extended until 2002.

However, peace proved elusive. Both sides walked out and came back to the table several times. The talks struggled on. Cease-fires were followed by ultimatums, which were followed by retractions and declarations. President Pastrana then told the rebels that they had to come up with a viable peace offer or vacate the safe haven (an area twice the size of New Jersey).

FARC's plan was deemed unacceptable, and the long, bloody war—a war marked by civilian death, disappearance, and destruction—was on again.

The Least You Need to Know

- FARC has waged a decades-long struggle.
- Drugs provide money for all sides.
- The war on drugs hurts the neediest in Colombia.
- Peace talks have led nowhere.

24

Hatred in Haiti

In This Chapter

- A brief history of Haiti
- The reign of the Duvaliers
- The coming of Jean-Bertrand Aristide
- The going of Jean-Bertrand Aristide
- The song that never ends

Haiti is a country that has been shattered by conflict, violence, and dictatorship, leaving it among the poorest countries in the Americas.

As a result, Haiti is a country deeply divided. It has a huge wealth gap between the black majority and the mulatto minority (one percent of whom own nearly half the country's wealth). Haiti has the hemisphere's lowest per capita income as well as the highest mortality rate. Furthermore, the country's infrastructure is dilapidated, and drug trafficking has corrupted much of the government.

Haiti deserves better.

Haiti's History

Haiti is also a lush, beautiful, mountainous country with a warm, tropical climate. Its location, history, and culture (epitomized by its traditional music, drumming, and dancing) once made Haiti a desired tourist destination. But the political repression and violence that took root in the last half of the twentieth century killed any desire for people to visit the country.

> **Reliable Resources**
>
> Those of you who have been there know that it is one of the most beautiful countries in the world. It has everything. It is an amazing place. I strongly recommend, whenever you get a chance, that you go to Haiti. I think it was a certain Queen of England who said that after her death, Calais would be found written on her heart. When I die, I think that "Haiti" is going to be found written on my heart.
> —President Franklin Delano Roosevelt; state dinner, October 14, 1943

Land Ho!

Six months after setting sail from Portugal, Christopher Columbus and the Santa Maria ran into a coral reef off the coast of Haiti and sank on Christmas Eve, 1492. Columbus, helped by local Indians, removed the supplies, dismantled the ship's timbers, and proceeded to name the island Hispaniola, or "Little Spain."

In 1496, the Spanish established the first European settlement in the Western Hemisphere at Santo Domingo (now capital of the Dominican Republic). Europeans would dominate the Caribbean for the next 300 years.

Spain's dominance in the Caribbean began to wane when Sir Francis Drake of England attacked the Spanish armada in Hispaniola in 1586. Although Drake failed to secure the island, his raid was part of a pattern of encroachment that gradually diluted Spanish dominance. By the late 1600s, Spain was ready to relinquish control of its colony to the emerging French presence.

> **Reliable Resources**
>
> Columbus returned to Spain in 1493 aboard the *Nina*. The trip was extremely difficult, much of the crew was sick, and four of the six Indians he brought back with him died.

The Slave Trade

Many present-day Haitians are slave descendents. The first-ever slaves were stolen from Africa and sent to the Americas in the sixteenth century. The slave trade slowly grew, but by the middle of the 1600s, African slave labor had become an economic lynchpin for both the colonists and the colonies. In the Caribbean, these slaves were used mostly for sugar production.

In 1791, Haitian slaves began a revolt against their inhumane lives. An uprising in the French West Indian colony of Santo Domingo helped to create what was probably Haiti's first guerrilla leader as a former black slave named Toussaint Louverture led the resistance movement. In 1801, Louverture attacked the French in Hispaniola, defeated them, conquered the island, abolished slavery, and proclaimed himself governor-general of an autonomous government.

On January 1, 1804, the region declared itself a free and independent country. The name of the new Republic, "Haiti," comes from the Creole word *Ayiti*, which is the name given to the land by the indigenous people who live there. It means "mountainous country."

Big Brother

Conflict in Haiti today comes from three places. First, there is the disparity between the elite French mulatto aristocracy and the poor black majority. Second, there is the subjugation of the population by the oft-oppressive military. Finally, because of its proximity to the United States, Haiti has often come under the large thumb of the Americans.

Accordingly, and not for the last time, the United States invaded Haiti in 1915 to protect America's economic interests that the Americans thought had become threatened by increasing black-mulatto friction. The United States stayed in Haiti until 1934, but maintained economic control over the country until almost 1950.

The Duvalier Era: 1957–1986

After a string of military juntas ruled the country, elections were arranged for 1957. The black candidate was a medical doctor who had served as a rural administrator before entering politics. François Duvalier seemed to most to be an honest leader without either a strong ideological motivation or program. They were wrong.

Duvalier's only opponent was the scion of a prominent family. As a result, Duvalier scored a significant victory at the polls. His followers took two thirds of the legislature's lower house and all the seats in the Haitian Senate.

> **Reliable Resources** _____
>
> Voodoo is the major religion of Haiti. It is taken seriously by young and old, rich and poor alike. In voodoo, there are three important categories of other spiritual beings: lwa (spirits), the twins (forces of contradiction—good and evil, happy and sad, and so on), and the dead (souls of one's own family members). Voodoo doctors heal with herbs and faith healing (with the help of lwa and other spirits).

Papa Doc

In 1961, Duvalier, or "Papa Doc" as he was known, replaced the bicameral legislature with a unicameral one. Despite a 1957 prohibition against presidential reelection, Duvalier ran for office again that year and won with an official tally of 1,320,748 votes to 0!

Apparently, winning by so wide a margin was not enough for Papa Doc. In 1964, he declared himself "president for life." His regime, which would become the longest in Haiti's history, was a brutal reign of terror and incompetence:

> **Landmine!** _____
>
> Duvalier had a personal police force called the Tonton Macoutes. Responsible only to Duvalier, they were given license to torture, kill, and extort.

- Political opponents were summarily executed.

- The population was kept in a state of fear by Duvalier's notorious paramilitary organization, the Tonton Macoutes.

- The economy of Haiti deteriorated steadily.

- The illiteracy rate remained at about 90 percent.

Although his rule was marked by political repression, Duvalier was often a popular leader. One reason for this was that his medical experiences in the countryside helped him understand the everyday concerns of the people, including their inclination toward paternalistic authority. In fact, it is that attitude that caused his patients to refer to him as "Papa Doc," a nickname he loved. What Duvalier especially understood was the central role voodoo played in the lives of the black majority population.

Duvalier was rumored to be a houngan, a voodoo sorcerer. In fact, he recruited such sorcerers and incorporated them into the Tonton Macoutes. His public acceptance of voodoo and its practitioners, as well as his reputed practice of magic and sorcery, helped to enhance his popularity and legitimized his otherwise repugnant reign.

> **Peacekeepers**
>
> Although the moniker "president for life" might seem a bit egocentric, in Haiti, no one thought much of it. Each of the previous seven rulers before the Duvaliers also dubbed themselves "president for life."

Duvalier's rule was marked by terror—an estimated 30,000 Haitians were killed for political reasons during his tenure. Duvalier's unrivaled authority led to the megalomaniacal conviction that he was, in his words, the "personification of the Haitian fatherland." Fittingly, before his death in 1971, François Duvalier designated his son, Jean-Claude Duvalier, as Haiti's new supreme leader.

Baby Doc

And so it was that Jean-Claude Duvalier, at age 19, was proclaimed "president for life." But Baby Doc, as he came to be known, cared little for politics, leaving the day-to-day machinations to his father's old cronies, a group known as "the dinosaurs."

What seemed to interest Baby Doc far more than politics was money. Much of his wealth, which amounted to hundreds of millions of dollars, came from the Haitian Tobacco Administration. Baby Doc used this agency as his own private tobacco monopoly. Later, he expanded it to include proceeds from other government enterprises, creating, in effect, a government-sponsored slush fund. Already minimal, public services deteriorated as Jean-Claude and his gang misappropriated millions of dollars from the national treasury.

In 1980, Jean-Claude married a mulatto woman, causing great consternation in the country. One reason his father ruled for as long as he did was because of his support of the black lower and middle classes and his opposition to the established mulatto elite, endearing Papa Doc to the Haitian black majority. But by marrying a mulatto, Jean-Claude appeared to be abandoning this bond. The fact that the wedding cost a reported $3 million didn't help either.

A growing, sweeping discontent with Baby Doc came to the fore in 1983 when Pope John Paul II visited Haiti. The Pontiff declared that "Something must change here," and called for ...

- More equitable distribution of income.

- A more egalitarian social structure.

- More concern for the well-being of the masses.

- More popular participation in public life.

The pope's words galvanized the public and contributed to increased mobilization among the masses. Indeed, Baby Doc's kleptocracy was so enormous that, even in this poorest of nations, his drain on the national treasury was felt throughout the country. The economy was in shambles, public health was in crisis, and Baby Doc fiddled.

Landmine!

Why do other countries hate the United States? Consider this example: African swine fever (ASF) is a highly contagious and fatal disease. ASF plagued pigs in the Dominican Republic in mid-1978. The United States, fearing that the disease would spread to North America, pressured the Duvalier government to slaughter all of Haiti's black pigs and to replace them with ones supplied by the United States. The Haitian government complied, but in doing so, failed to understand that black Haitian pigs were not only a form of "savings account" for peasants because they could easily be sold for cash, but they were also exceptionally well-suited to the rural Haitian environment. The replacement pigs were not.

The first real revolt began in the city of Gonaïves in 1985, when street demonstrators made raids on food-distribution warehouses. By 1986, protests had spread to six other cities. Duvalier then cut food prices by 10 percent, shut down radio stations, and ordered a crackdown by police and army units. However, these moves failed to end the popular uprising. Jean-Claude's wife and advisers, wanting to keep their profitable grip on power, urged him to put down the rebellion at all costs. He did.

But in 1986, with even more mass protests erupting throughout the country, the army decided that it was finally time for the Duvaliers to go. Military conspirators demanded their departure. Left with no bases of support, Jean-Claude and Michele Duvalier departed from Haiti on February 7, 1986, for France. They left behind a country economically ravaged, bereft of functional political institutions, and devoid of self-rule.

In 1988, Leslie Manigat became president, but was soon ousted in a coup led by Brigadier-General Prosper Avril, who installed a civilian government under military control. Elections were called again in 1990.

Election Time

Jean-Bertrand Aristide was born in poverty and raised in a religious atmosphere. At 16, he entered the seminary in Port-au-Prince. He did advanced studies abroad in the Dominican Republic, Great Britain, Canada, Rome, and Jerusalem, and in 1982 he was ordained in the Roman Catholic Church as a member of the Salesian Fathers.

Reliable Resources

Aristide has written 10 books and is fluent in seven languages. He is also an accomplished musician and composer. He plays the guitar, saxophone, organ, drums, clarinet, and piano.

In 1985, Father Aristide was back in Haiti and rose to national prominence through the broadcasts of his sermons on the Catholic station, Radio Soleil. Outraged by what had become of his homeland, Aristide became an outspoken critic of the Duvalier regime. At one startling, defiant mass, Aristide called for change in the country and bluntly criticized the dictatorship of Jean-Claude Duvalier. This mass by Aristide is often cited as one of the sparks that set off the popular uprising and demonstrations that led to the ouster of Duvalier a year later.

After Duvalier's departure in 1986, Aristide led a march in memory of the thousands of Haitians who had lost their lives under Duvalier. The Haitian military then opened fire on the crowd; Aristide bravely continued his live broadcast during the massacre, reaffirming his reputation as a courageous opponent of the corrupt regime.

These sorts of actions earned Aristide the lasting enmity of the army, police, and Tonton Macoutes. In 1988, his church, St. John Bosco, was destroyed by arson.

Jean-Bertrand Aristide, however, clearly was a man who was not easily distracted. In 1990, Haiti prepared for new presidential elections. When Aristide announced his candidacy that fall, it electrified the country. After a 6-week campaign Aristide won, garnering an astounding 67 percent of the vote. He took office in February 1991.

His government began the difficult tasks of cleaning out a corrupt civil service, enforcing tax laws, fighting drug trafficking, and delivering much-needed services. For the first time in a long time, Haiti lived in relative security, with military violence and criminal activity declining. Human rights organizations reported a drop in violations, and the flow of refugees ended. The international community applauded the reforms and pledged funds to the new government.

The Predictable Coup

All of this ended on September 30, 1991, when the Haitian military violently overthrew the Aristide government after only seven months in office. Aristide was forced into exile, first to Venezuela, and then to America.

From October 1991 to June 1992, Joseph Nerette led an unconstitutional regime, and the Haitian military unleashed a horrific campaign of violence, killing more than 5,000 Haitians over three years and forcing tens of thousands to flee their homeland by boat.

By this time, Haiti's problems had made it onto the international radar screen, and overthrowing a legitimate, popularly elected president was not something the international community takes lightly. In June 1993, the United Nations imposed an oil and arms embargo on Haiti. This eventually had the effect of forcing the Haitian military to the negotiating table.

In 1993, a U.N.-brokered agreement established a process for the restoration of both Aristide and constitutional government in Haiti.

But once again, the Haitian military had other ideas. To retain power, the military undertook a campaign of repression and assassination, torture and rape.

As a result, tens of thousands of Haitians began to flee the country. Many attempted to sail into American territorial waters and enter the United States. These so-called "boat people" became both a political and social crisis.

The United Nations and the United States had seen enough. On July 31, 1994, the United Nations adopted a resolution that authorized member states to use "all necessary means" to restore constitutional rule to Haiti, as well as the return of Jean Bertrand Aristide.

Operation Restore Democracy

The United States took the lead in carrying out the U.N. mandate. "Operation Restore Democracy" would foster democracy and reduce the flow of illegal immigrants.

An invasion involving almost 4,000 U.S. army paratroopers was readied. With U.S. troops prepared to immediately enter Haiti, President Clinton dispatched a negotiating team led by former President Jimmy Carter (and including a civilian Colin Powell, retired from the Pentagon) to tell the Haitian leadership that it was time for them to go. In the face of this massive, imminent U.S. invasion, the negotiations proved successful, and the military in Haiti relinquished control of the government. U.S. forces landed unopposed.

Operation Restore Democracy then set about paving the way for the return of civilian rule to Haiti. Its mission was to …

 ◆ Restore democracy.

 ◆ Return Aristide to power.

 ◆ Ensure security.

 ◆ Assist with the rehabilitation of civil administration.

 ◆ Train a police force and judiciary.

 ◆ Help prepare for new elections.

The mission succeeded. Democratically elected government was restored, and emigration was greatly reduced. On March 31, 1995, peacekeeping responsibilities were transferred to the United Nations.

The Legacy of Aristide

On October 15, 1994, President Aristide victoriously returned to Haiti, where he completed his presidential term. One of his first acts was to dismantle the worst parts of the Haitian military. His government also created Haiti's first civilian police force.

With the support of the United Nations, legislative elections were held in 1996. Because he was constitutionally barred from running in successive elections, Aristide watched as Haiti witnessed its first peaceful transition from one democratically elected president to the next.

In 2000, Aristide could legally run again, and he did. Although there were some charges of voter fraud, Aristide won another resounding victory and remained president until a rebellion forced him from power in 2004. Presently he lives in exile in South Africa.

So Just Who Is Aristide, Really?

Yes, Jean Bertrand Aristide has twice been elected president of Haiti and indeed he is, as his supporters claim, the "first democratically elected leader of Haiti." However, on the flip side of the coin, Aristide has also twice been ousted from office and his opponents allege that he became just another corrupt Haitian politician. Indeed, opposition leaders accused the Aristide government of widespread corruption and using violence against opponents.

At the beginning of 2004, as is the wont of this country, violence erupted between government forces and the opposition. Rebel forces captured large swaths of the country and on February 29, 2004, Aristide left the country. The question, however, is—why?

Should I Stay or Should I Go?

The facts surrounding Aristide's departure from Haiti remain in dispute. The only thing that is clear is that on leap year day, 2004, Aristide resigned as president and left his homeland for Africa aboard an American plane. However, Aristide claims (in a lawsuit filed in Paris, no less) that he resigned and left Haiti under duress because France and the U.S. conspired and kidnapped him against his will. Opponents say he left of his own volition.

Whereas the truth may never be known, what is known is that a year after Aristide's departure, several high-ranking members of the Aristide administration were indicted for drug trafficking and other crimes, although to date, Jean Bertrand Aristide has not been indicted for any crime. He remains in exile in South Africa, and his country remains as impoverished as ever.

The Least You Need to Know

◆ Haiti is mired in poverty and corruption.

◆ The Duvaliers ruined the country.

◆ Aristide tried to restore democracy.

◆ The military is loathe to give up power.

◆ Aristide was twice elected, and twice evicted.

25

More Latin and South American Standoffs

In This Chapter

- ◆ Crises in Cuba
- ◆ Peruvian guerrillas
- ◆ Coups in Ecuador
- ◆ Problems in Paraguay

During most of the Cold War, Central and South America were pawns in the superpower struggles. The Soviet Union poured guns and money into America's backyard in an effort to destabilize the region and the United States responded by doing the same for mostly right-wing dictatorships. The result was a virtual standoff.

A by-product of those efforts was that the region had far too many weapons readily available for any would-be rebel. Insurgencies abounded.

South America struggles with insurgencies.

Castro's Cuba

The most obvious example of Cold War conflict in the Americas is Cuba. What was once a thriving resort destination became the focal point of international intrigue, and practically the cause of global thermonuclear war.

Rebel Yell

Cuba has always been a place where revolution has thrived. In 1933, an uprising known as the "revolt of the sergeants," led by Fulgencio Batista, took over the country.

The new revolutionary government, although it lasted but 100 days, engineered lasting and radical changes in Cuba:

- ◆ It created the 8-hour workday.

- ◆ It established a Department of Labor.

- ◆ It opened the university to the poor.

- ◆ It granted peasants the right to the land they farmed.

- ◆ It gave women the right to vote.

- ◆ It reduced the electric rates by 40 percent.

Reliable Resources

In 1946, famed mobster Lucky Luciano called a summit in Havana. Attendees at the Hotel Nacional meeting included the who's who of mobsters—Meyer Lansky, Frank Costello, Tommy Lucchese, Vito Genovese, Joe Bonanno, Santo Trafficante Jr., and Moe Dalitz. Among the topics discussed was the assassination of fellow gangster Bugsy Siegel. Coincidentally, Frank Sinatra made his singing debut in Havana that year.

One of President Franklin Roosevelt's advisors, Sumner Wells, called these changes "communistic" and "irresponsible," and the U.S. government refused to recognize the new government. But one person who liked the new Cuban government was mobster Meyer Lansky, who met with Fulgencio Batista and forged a friendship and business relationship that would last three decades.

In 1938, Batista legalized the Cuban Communist Party, and the country adopted a new constitution in 1940. The document protected individual and social rights, supported full employment and a minimum wage, extended social security, called for equal pay for equal work, and outlawed the huge plantations known as *latifundias* (which were synonymous with economic inequality).

Fidel Castro

In 1953, rebel leader Fidel Castro led a revolt in which 100 men and women attacked the Moncada army barracks near Santiago de Cuba. The attack was a failure. Castro was arrested and sentenced to 15 years in prison. Two years later, the government called for a general amnesty, and Castro was released. However, revolution was now in Cuba's blood, and Castro was its new leader.

> **Reliable Resources**
>
> On December 10, 1959, the Hotel Riviera opened in Havana. It cost $14 million, and most of the money was supplied by the Cuban government to its American owner Meyer Lansky. The floorshow in the Copa Room was headlined by Ginger Rogers. On opening night, Lansky complained that Rogers "can wiggle her ass, but she can't sing a goddamn note."

Four years later, on January 1, 1959, Castro's revolutionary forces took control of Havana. Che Guevara and Camilo Cienfuegos led the rebels into the capital, and Fidel Castro arrived about a week later. One of the first acts of the new Cuban government was to reinstate the Constitution of 1940, which had been suspended by General Batista in 1952.

Originally, Castro was not a Communist, but circumstances forced him into the Soviet camp. After the revolution, Cubans with money feared they would lose their holdings and defected mostly to the United States. This in turn caused a drain on an already poor economy. Castro went to the United States for economic aide. He was turned down. So in order to keep what assets remained in the country, Castro decided to nationalize some of Cuba's businesses, and in the process some U.S. businesses were taken over. The United States suddenly became anti-Castro.

def•i•ni•tion

A **trade embargo** is a prohibition by a government on certain or all trade with a foreign nation. By preventing both imports and exports with that country, an embargo can sometimes be an effective way to punish one's enemies.

Castro then did the logical thing—he met with Soviet foreign minister Anasta Mikoyan and secured a $100 million loan. The Soviets, happy to have a beachhead practically in the United States, became Castro's benefactor. And that is how Castro's regime became a Communist one. The United States followed this by imposing a *trade embargo* on Cuba, and the stage was set for conflict.

Cuba and the United States

From 1960 on, the United States and Cuba engaged in a prolonged, drawn-out, multi-faceted conflict. America was threatened by the Communist presence a mere 90 miles from its border, and Cuba was afraid of its huge neighbor to the North. The result was a relationship that careened from invasion to embargo to near irrelevance.

The first confrontation, as mentioned in Chapter 16, was the Bay of Pigs. The disastrous failed invasion set the stage for many problems between the United States, Cuba, and the Soviet Union. Certainly the Cuban missile crisis can be traced to the failed Bay of Pigs invasion and the subsequent increased Soviet military support for Castro. Similarly, around the globe, U.S. prestige was hit hard, and the glow quickly came off the Kennedy administration. Kennedy's first foray into foreign affairs was an unmitigated disaster.

> **Peacekeepers**
>
> The CIA tried to get rid of Castro for years. It tried to kill him using poisoned pens, fatal bacteria, and deadly capsules. It also tried to embarrass him by putting a powder in his shoe that was supposed to make his beard fall out. It's surprising that they didn't slip him an exploding cigar!

Of course, the next confrontation was the nuclear missile crisis. On October 16, 1962, John F. Kennedy called a secret meeting of his closest advisors at the White House. Late the night before, the CIA had produced detailed photos identifying Soviet nuclear missile installations being constructed on Cuba.

After 13 tense days, the crisis was resolved, but not before an already bad relationship had grown much worse. After the missile crisis, Cuba became a constant problem and threat to America. Never big enough to fret over too much, but always strategic enough to be concerned about, Cuba remained a problem for every U.S. president thereafter.

Throughout the 1970s, the relationship played itself out both near and far. Locally, Cuba provided support for rebel movements throughout Latin America. And outside the Western hemisphere, it participated in a number of extracurricular activities.

For example, in 1978, at the request of the Ethiopian government, thousands of Cuban troops—supported and led by Soviet and East German officers—helped repel a Somali invasion of Ethiopia. In response, U.S. Secretary of State Cyrus Vance stated that he could not foresee the normalization of relations with Cuba because of the presence of Cuban troops in Africa.

Tensions increased in the 1980s under conservative, anti-Communist President Ronald Reagan. Reagan instituted the most hostile policy against Cuba since the Bay of Pigs. Despite conciliatory signals from Cuba, the new U.S. administration …

- Announced a tightening of the embargo.
- Began four weeks of exercises in the Caribbean, with the stated intent of "sending a message to Cuba."

- ◆ Reinstituted a travel ban.

- ◆ Prohibited U.S. citizens from spending money in Cuba.

- ◆ Allowed a 1977 fishing accord to lapse.

The Fall of Communism

The fall of communism throughout most of the globe in the late 1980s had a profound impact on Cuba. Without its Soviet sponsor, Cuba's economy faltered markedly, and its ability to intervene elsewhere declined correspondingly. In 1991, all Soviet troops left Cuba, and Castro was finally on his own. Emigration from the island, already a problem, jumped dramatically as people tried to escape any way they could.

In 1992, the U.S. Congress passed the Cuban Democracy Act, which prohibited trading with Cuba by foreign-based subsidiaries of U.S. companies, traveling to Cuba by U.S. citizens, and sending money to family in Cuba.

At this time, 70 percent of Cuba's trade with U.S. subsidiary companies was in food and medicine. Many claimed the Cuban Democracy Act was thus in violation of international law and United Nations resolutions that food and medicine cannot be used as weapons in international conflicts.

In 1994 at least 35 men, women, and children died at sea when their boat, en route to Florida, sank 7 miles out of Havana. Castro then declared an open migration policy. The United States, which had always welcomed Cuban refugees, was not prepared for what came next. Thirty thousand Cubans set sail from Cuba bound for the United States. Some made it, many did not, and others were picked up by the U.S. Coast Guard and taken to the U.S. naval base in Guantanamo Bay. A migration agreement was thereafter reached between the United States and Cuba, which allowed for a minimum of 20,000 immigrants per year.

Reliable Resources

Guantanamo Bay, originally a vacation resort, was leased to the U.S. Navy in 1898. The terms of the lease are contained in three documents—two agreements and a treaty. The lease calls for Washington to pay rent. Set a century ago at 2,000 gold coins a year, it is now worth just over $4,000. The lease can only be voided by a mutual agreement or abandonment of the land by the United States.

Yet even so, mass migration attempts continued to flummox both countries. In late 1999, the most celebrated of these immigrants, Elián Gonzalez, was rescued at sea after the boat he was on capsized, killing his mother and 10 others. On June 28, little Elián was returned home to Cuba.

Somehow, some way, Castro survived it all. He survived more than four decades of U.S. embargos and conflicts. He survived Khrushchev, Brezhnev, Gorbachev, and Yeltsin. He survived the fall of the Berlin Wall. However, whether his revolution will survive the many expatriates who loathe Castro is another matter altogether.

Indeed, there are many wealthy Cuban expatriates living in south Florida today who would love the opportunity to remake Cuba once Castro dies—men and women with both political clout and financial wherewithal. The possibility of a war over Cuba after Castro dies is very real.

Peru's Problems

Communism is a philosophy that attracts people who want to help the poor. Its altruistic belief of "from each according to his abilities, to each according to his needs" seems to be a panacea in a troubled world.

Yet even though communism never worked and it brought economic ruin to almost every place it was tried, it somehow remained a potent political philosophy. This has been as true in Peru as anywhere else.

def•i•ni•tion

Communism is political system in which property is held in common. Based on the works of Karl Marx, and interpreted by Vladimir Lenin, communism's aim is to overthrow capitalism by revolutionary means and to establish a classless society. Communism must be distinguished from socialism, which seeks similar ends but by evolution rather than revolution.

A Not-So-Shining Path

Founded in 1970 by Abimael Guzmán Reynoso, Peru's Shining Path was supposed to be an orthodox Marxist-Leninist offshoot of the Peruvian Communist Party. But in 1980, the group turned to terrorism and became nothing more than another bloodthirsty, power-hungry group. By the 1990s, Shining Path was considered by many to be the most dangerous and violent terrorist organization in the world.

The group derives its name from Mariategui, an avowed Marxist, who once stated that Marxism was a "shining path to the future." The goal of this organization was the destruction of the existing Peruvian government in favor of an Indian-run socialist system. Shining Path waged a bloody battle for the ensuing 13 years.

Shining Path was able to garner some popular support, mostly among students, teachers, the unemployed, and peasants in more rural areas where the government's reach was weaker.

Funding for the group came primarily from robberies and other crimes, although a significant revenue source was the "tax" that Shining Path extorted from businesses and individuals. Recruits came from well-established indoctrination programs that frequently targeted young teenagers who are more easily molded into fanatical terrorists.

Between 1989 and 1992, Shining Path's terror campaign shook the foundation of the government in the capital of Lima. But the Peruvian state did what states do—it struck back.

Martial Law

In 1992, Peruvian President Alberto Fujimori used the ongoing crisis with the rebels to suspended congress and the courts and declared emergency rule to combat corruption and Shining Path terrorism. This act endowed his administration with the power to operate much more aggressively against the guerrillas.

Fujimori cracked down hard on Shining Path. His Special Intelligence Group, a small elite police unit, uncovered a trail of clues that would eventually lead them to the head of Shining Path, Abimael Guzmán Reynoso. Between the emergency rule and the work of the special police units, Guzmán was eventually located, arrested, and sentenced to life in prison.

In addition, aside from giving the president protracted dictatorial powers, the net result of Fujimori's emergency rule was the capture of more than 2,500 additional Shining Path terrorists. In 1993, more than 1,000 Peruvian terrorists were convicted on various charges, including Shining Path Regional Chief "Comrade Albino," who was, in 1995, convicted of ordering the murders of more than 100 people and sentenced to life in prison.

Even with the arrests, it is unlikely that Shining Path will disappear completely from Peru's political stage. However, given its vastly reduced size, any conflict it creates should be much less severe.

If Peruvians have anything to fear these days, it might be their own government.

Human Rights Abuses

In 2000, after 10 years in office, Fujimori ran for election a third time. This time, the outcome was much less certain. His National Intelligence Service was blamed for harassing opposition candidates, the press, the courts, and the electoral bodies in an effort to secure Fujimori's reelection. It worked. Fujimori was officially reelected, but his new government was deemed illegitimate from the start.

At his inauguration, the Lima police fired tear gas on thousands of protestors. Then the opposition party staged a walkout, as it believed that Fujimori's was an unconstitutional government.

Furthermore, according to Human Rights Watch, Fujimori subjected his actual or potential critics to legal harassment and character assassination. Through his influence over the courts and the taxation office, Fujimori had secured the support of several television channels and radio stations previously critical of him. Bogus criminal accusations were launched against independent media.

Reliable Resources

Ancient Peru was the seat of several prominent Andean civilizations—most notably that of the Incas, whose empire was captured by the Spanish conquistadores in 1533.

On November 13, 2000, Fujimori left Peru to attend the Asia-Pacific Economic Cooperation forum in Brunei. On November 17, he travelled from Brunei to the home of his ancestors, Japan. Facing continued ridicule and upheaval at home, Alberto Fujimori submitted his resignation as president—by fax.

Coup of a Kind

If Africa is the king of coups and attempted coups, South America must follow close behind. These countries seem to attract rebellion, insurgency, and government takeovers.

Ecuador

Ecuador's capital of Quito was once a center of the Inca Empire. It also has some of the best-preserved early colonial architecture on the continent.

Ecuador was long an agrarian country, until oil was discovered there in the 1960s. This resulted in rapid growth and brought about progress in health, education, and housing. The bad news is that this oil wealth also fueled inflation and boosted consumer imports, which in turn increased foreign debt.

Even worse, as is the case throughout much of South America, the traditionally dominant Spanish-descended elite gained far more than the indigenous peoples during the boom years. Sixty percent of the Ecuadorian population lives in poverty, and most of those are native Indians.

All this has led to a lot of instability in the political arena:

- In 1987, the president was kidnapped and beaten up by the army.

- In 1995, the vice president sought political asylum in Costa Rica so as to escape charges of corruption.

- In 1997, the president was deposed on the grounds of mental incapacity.

In 2000, a coup occurred when the head of the armed forces in Ecuador announced the formation of a three-man council to take over the country. The military chief said that the council would be made up of himself, an indigenous Indian leader, and a former Supreme Court judge. According to the leader of the coup, he did what he did "to work against corruption."

Paraguay

Unlike much of South America, Paraguay has a racially homogeneous population; 95 percent of Paraguayans are people of mixed Spanish and Native American descent. Paraguay is also unique in that it experienced the region's longest dictatorship, under Alfredo Stroessner, who ruled the country for 35 years until 1989.

What makes Paraguay like much of the rest of South America, however, is the large wealth gap, with an estimated 60 percent of urban and 80 percent of rural dwellers living below the poverty line.

Such need has created much political instability:

- In 1989, although Stroessner was deposed in a coup, his military-backed Colorado Party won a majority in the first free multiparty elections.

- In 1998, even though allegations of fraud abounded, Colorado Party candidate Raul Cubas was elected president.

- In 1999, President Raul Cubas ordered tanks to the streets of the Paraguayan capital of Asunción after protesters demanded his removal from office.

- In 1999, President Cubas did in fact resign in the wake of the assassination of Vice President Luis Maria Argana.

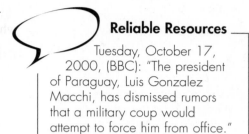

Reliable Resources

Tuesday, October 17, 2000, (BBC): "The president of Paraguay, Luis Gonzalez Macchi, has dismissed rumors that a military coup would attempt to force him from office."

In 2000, rebels staged a coup attempt. They attacked parliament with tanks and took over several radio stations, calling for the overthrow of the government.

The coup attempt was quickly put down, and 75 people were detained or arrested in connection with it. Most of those arrested were members of the state security forces. They were said to be supporters of the country's former army commander, General Lino Oviedo, who was blamed for the uprising. A state of emergency was put in place throughout Paraguay.

There have been 45 coups or attempted coups in Paraguay in the past 100 years.

The Least You Need to Know

- Cuba was the focus of some of the most important conflicts in the twentieth century.

- Peru has successfully battled communist guerillas.

- Ecuador is a politically unstable place where attempted coup d'états occur frequently.

- Paraguay, too, is a country beset by political instability.

Part 7

North America

Although it might seem at first glance that North America is probably the most peaceful place on the planet, that would be a false impression. To begin with, Mexico is in flux. With a large drug trade, the loss of power by the ruling PRI, and an active rebellion in the southern state of Chiapas, Mexico has many problems to contend with. By the same token, Canada has been dealing with its own separatist movement in Quebec.

But by far the largest place of conflict is the United States. September 11 merely reinforced the fact that the United States is a nation that has not been unwilling to engage in war and conflict, angering many countries in the process. Combined with its history of poor race relations, the United States is a place simmering with conflict.

Chapter 26

Life in These United States

In This Chapter

- The making of a superpower
- The Cold War
- Proxy wars
- The War on Terrorism
- The ugly residue of slavery

In the past half century, the country that has engaged in the most wars, incidents, conflicts, missions, and violent events has been the United States. Sometimes it was the victim; sometimes the aggressor. But usually, it was in the thick of things.

Part of this has to do with the Cold War and the eventual success of the West. Ending up as the only superpower made the United States both a bully and a target. Part of it also has to do with race relations in the giant country—conflict breeds from within as well as from without.

The United States was long protected by two great oceans.

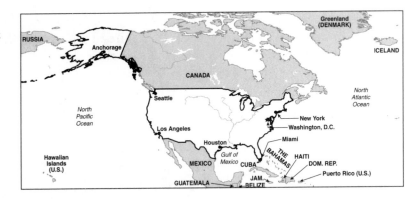

A Star Is Born

Prior to World War I (or as it was known at the time, the Great War), the United States was an emerging industrial society more concerned with its own problems (recovering from slavery and the Civil War) than international relations. World War I changed all that.

There They Go Again

World War I began in 1914 when Archduke Francis Ferdinand of Austria-Hungary was assassinated by a Serbian Nationalist. The causes of the war were, needless to say, far more complicated than that. The main reason for the war was brewing economic, nationalistic, imperialistic, territorial, and economic rivalries among Germany, France, Great Britain, Russia, and Austria-Hungary.

> **Landmine!**
>
> Americans were also convinced to enter the war because, they were repeatedly told, it would be "the war to end all wars."

The war pitted a powerful alliance fronted by Italy, Germany, Austria-Hungary, and Romania against the Allies—France, Great Britain, and Russia. The neutrality of the United States was first imperiled after the Germans sank the *Lusitania* in 1915. The next year, Germany announced that it would begin unrestricted submarine warfare in an effort to break British control of the seas. In protest, the United States broke off relations with Germany, and on April 6, 1917, it entered the war.

America's entry into the war proved to be decisive, both for the war and for America. On the war front, American participation meant that the Allies now had new, enormous industrial and manpower resources at their disposal. President Woodrow Wilson was able to convince a skeptical American public that war was in its best interest by insisting that the war "would make the world safe for democracy."

Although American entry neither made the world safe for democracy nor ended all wars, it did tip the scale in this war in favor of the Allies. An armistice in their favor was signed on November 11, 1918.

Practically every country, save one, was severely depleted by the war. For the European participants, World War I proved to be a bloody, expensive, exhausting campaign. It ruined economies, and the number of dead and injured was unbelievable: about 10 million died, and 20 million were wounded.

Reliable Resources

The use of chemical weapons is nothing new. In the Middle Ages, a flammable composition known as "Greek fire" (sulfur, naphtha, and quicklime) was used in war. Germans used chlorine and mustard gasses against the Allies in World War I.

For United States, however, the war was different:

♦ One of America's blessings is that it is geographically isolated from much of the rest of the world. When wars break out, it is difficult for them to spread to North America. World War I, having been fought in Europe, devastated Europe, not America.

♦ Because the United States entered so late, it lost far fewer men.

♦ The economic push predicated by the war forced the United States to industrialize much more rapidly than it probably would have.

♦ Finally, because the United States made the difference, it left the war as, if not the king of the hill, one of the kings of the hill.

This newfound American might was soon challenged by the Great Depression (1929–41). Although the policies of President Franklin Delano Roosevelt's New Deal administration did much to mitigate the worst effects of the depression (and to restore a sense of confidence to the American people), a complete economic recovery was not achieved until the government began to spend heavily for defense in the early 1940s.

World War II

History does indeed have a way of repeating itself, and it did in the late 1930s. Once again, France, Great Britain, and Russia found themselves at war with Germany. Once again, they risked losing if the United States failed to enter, and the American public was skeptical about getting involved in European entanglements.

One person who was not skeptical was President Roosevelt. Roosevelt understood that democracy was truly threatened by the powerful rise of Hitler and his fascist Nazi regime. The German juggernaut had quickly overrun Poland, France, and much of the rest of Europe. Its ally Japan had done the same in Asia. All that stood between German *hegemony* and freedom was a battered, but brave, Britain, and a poor, but large, Russia. FDR was unwilling to let America stay on the sidelines while the world careened toward darkness.

def•i•ni•tion

In politics, **hegemony** is the overwhelming influence and authority of one country over another country or countries.

So, in the late 1930s and early 1940s, Roosevelt quietly prepared America for the war he knew was coming. He was aided greatly in his efforts when, on December 7, 1941, Japan attacked Pearl Harbor. The United States entered the war the next day.

When the war ended about three and a half years later, there were but two kings of the hill left standing. In the East, the Soviet Union, though bruised and battered, emerged as the dominant force from Eastern Europe to Asia. And in the West, the United States once again left a war mightier than it had been before it entered.

So conflict and the United States go hand in hand. If it were not for war, the United States would not have become a superpower.

Fighting the Good Fight

The Cold War created even more opportunity for the United States to build its empire, as well as promote democracy and capitalism. Although the Korean War was a virtual standoff (see Chapter 13), neither helping nor hurting American dominance, Vietnam was another matter altogether.

Quagmire

On July 8, 1959, two U.S. military advisors, Major Dale Buis and Sergeant Chester Ovnand, were killed in South Vietnam. They were among the first American soldiers killed in the Vietnam War. Before it was over 14 years later, another 58,000 Americans would die there.

The United States entered into Vietnam slowly, and with much trepidation. However, as the war escalated, the United States often believed that it had no choice but to continue to fight there, incorrectly assuming that losing South Vietnam to Communist North Vietnam would endanger democracy throughout Asia.

The first salvo, insofar as the Americans were concerned, occurred in 1961 when Soviet Premier Nikita Khrushchev pledged support for "wars of national liberation" throughout the world. His statement greatly encouraged Communists in North Vietnam to escalate their armed struggle to unify Vietnam.

That same month, John Fitzgerald Kennedy was inaugurated as the thirty-fifth U.S. president. Kennedy, who was a genuine World War II hero, was keenly aware that the Soviets posed a direct threat to American interests. In his inaugural address, JFK declared that, "We shall pay any price, bear any burden, meet any hardship, support any friend, oppose any foe, to ensure the survival and the success of liberty." In private, outgoing President Eisenhower told Kennedy, "I think you're going to have to send troops to Vietnam."

The Kennedy administration's initial policy was to wage a limited war to attempt to force a political settlement. So that year, he secretly sent 400 American Green Beret "special advisors" to South Vietnam to train South Vietnamese soldiers.

The Kennedy administration failed to understand several things about Vietnam, namely …

- The will of the North Vietnamese to "win at any cost" (as Ho Chi Minh put it).

- That the U.S. military was unprepared to fight a guerilla war half a world away.

- That the American public would not support a war in which it did not feel its national interests were at stake, and that was the feeling about Vietnam.

These were lessons that would be learned much too late.

Guns or Butter

In 1963, Kennedy was assassinated in Dallas, and Lyndon Johnson inherited the war. Johnson was nothing if not a testosterone-driven egomaniac and was not about to lose. By the end of that year, 16,300 American military advisors would be shipped off to Southeast Asia. By the end of 1964, the number of American troops in South Vietnam was 23,000. (There were an estimated 170,000 North Vietnamese fighters.)

The war escalated sharply after Johnson's 1964 win. By 1965, 1,000 tons of bombs were being dropped by the United States on the Vietcong, and an astounding 125,000 Americans went to war. Not coincidentally, that same year, 15,000 students marched on Washington in opposition to the war.

By the end of 1966, troop levels had reached 400,000, and Johnson requested an additional half billion dollars to wage war. But the United States, like any other country, did not have unlimited funds. When a country decides to buy guns, it usually must forgo butter. As Reverend Martin Luther King said at the time, "The pursuit of this widened war has narrowed the promised dimensions of domestic welfare programs, making the poor white and Negro bear the heaviest burdens both at the front and at home."

Landmine! ⎯⎯⎯⎯⎯

On March 1, 1968, Clark Clifford became the new U.S. secretary of defense. The very first thing he did was to conduct an intensive study of the entire situation in Vietnam. Clifford concluded that there was neither a concept nor any overall plan anywhere in Washington for achieving victory in Vietnam.

By 1968, opposition at home to the war in Vietnam had hit a crescendo. LBJ couldn't run from the fact that he had led the United States into quicksand from which it could not easily escape. Yet he still shocked the world when he announced on March 31, 1968, "I shall not seek, and I will not accept, the nomination of my party for another term as your president."

Although President Johnson was not Vietnam's first casualty, he certainly was one of its most tragic. By the time Richard Nixon was elected president in November 1968, troop levels had reached 500,000 and 1,000 young Americans were being killed every month.

It would take another four years for the United States to finally end its bitter folly in Vietnam, and not before it had also invaded neighboring Laos and Cambodia. Yet somehow with a straight face, Nixon was able to announce, on January 23, 1973, that an agreement had been reached ending the war—an agreement which would "bring peace with honor."

In response to the overbroad authority granted to LBJ in the Gulf of Tonkin Resolution, on November 7, 1973, Congress passed the War Powers Act, requiring the president to obtain the support of Congress within 90 days of sending American troops abroad.

The Fifty-Third Hostage

The taint of Vietnam damaged both America's psyche and its image around the globe. A country once thought to be impregnable had been brought to its knees by a band of guerrilla warriors. Maybe America wasn't so tough after all.

Certainly this belief came home to roost in Iran. There, in 1979, the Islamic Fundamentalist revolution overthrew the Shah, and on November 4, militant Iranian students proved that the United States might in fact be a *paper tiger* when they overtook the United States embassy in Teheran.

def•i•ni•tion

A **paper tiger** is a country that is seemingly dangerous and powerful but is in fact timid and weak. The phrase was first used by Mao Tse Tung to describe the United States: "U.S. imperialism seems quite powerful, but in reality it isn't. It is very weak politically because it is divorced from the masses of the people and is disliked by everybody and by the American people too. In appearance it is very powerful, but in reality it is nothing to be afraid of: It is a paper tiger."

The Iranian Hostage Crisis occurred after the exiled Shah's admission to the United States for medical treatment. As a result, a crowd of about 500 seized the American embassy. Of the approximately 90 people inside the embassy at the time, 52 remained in captivity until the end of the crisis.

President Jimmy Carter, although a decent and honorable man, also seemed, if not incompetent, at least incapable of solving the crisis. He first attempted to free the hostages using a variety of nonviolent means: applying economic pressure by halting oil imports from Iran, as well as freezing Iranian assets in the United States. He also began several diplomatic initiatives to free the hostages, all of which proved fruitless.

In the end, Carter's own presidency was taken hostage by the Iranian "students" (many of whom were not students at all). He had become, in effect, the fifty-third hostage.

The Tiger Meows

With nothing else working, Carter reluctantly, but finally, concluded that he had to try the military option. The problem was that the hostages likely weren't all being held in the same spot. Where they were held was the middle of Teheran, making a rescue mission all the more difficult.

Reliable Resources

When we opened that door, we were taken over immediately. The Iranians swarmed in. One guy looked at me and said, "Walk out the door." So I walked out the door. Two guys grabbed me, one on either side, put my hands behind my back, and tied my hands. They had a long nylon rope that they used to tie us up. After my hands were tied, this guy tried to cut the rope with a knife. The rope slipped and he gouged me, stabbed me in the back. I said, "Ouch!" And he said, "Oh, I'm sorry. I'm sorry. I didn't mean to hurt you!"

—Bill Belk, embassy communications officer

Nevertheless, on April 16, 1980, President Carter met with his foreign policy staff in the White House Situation Room. Also present was Colonel Charles Beckwith, a veteran who had created the elite Delta Force. The Joint Chiefs of Staff had recommended Beckwith to lead a rescue mission.

The plan was this: Beckwith's 132-man team would arrive in Egypt, the staging area for "Operation Eagle Claw." The team would then fly to an island off the coast of Oman. From there, they would fly to Desert One, a staging area in the Iranian desert, 200 miles from Teheran, where they were to rendezvous with eight helicopters dispatched from the USS *Nimitz*.

The helicopters would refuel at Desert One before proceeding with the Delta Force team to mountains about 65 miles southeast of Teheran. The following night, the rescue team was to enter Teheran in four trucks. The rescuers would then infiltrate the embassy and free the hostages. The helicopters would then fly in, pick them all up, and deliver them safely to an airfield outside Teheran.

Peacekeepers

Secretary of State Cyrus Vance, who opposed the rescue mission from the beginning, resigned after it was over.

What happened instead was this: Beckwith and his men reached Desert One as planned, but a short time later, a bus carrying Iranian civilians happened into the area, and were taken into custody. Then a fuel truck and a pickup appeared in this area that was supposed to be quite remote. The fuel truck was destroyed, but the driver of the pickup escaped.

The helicopters were due at 11:30 P.M., but were late. One of them had lost rotor blade pressure and was forced to land. The remaining helicopters flew into a dust storm, as another lost its gyroscope and turned back. The remaining six reached Desert One two hours late. Once there, it was discovered that another one of the choppers had lost its hydraulic pump and could not take off.

That left five copters: one less than the minimum needed to carry out the plan. Beckwith was forced to scrub the mission. Bad turned to worse when, as the helicopters and transport planes began to depart, one of the choppers collided with one of the planes. The helicopter exploded into flames and eight men died.

444

Back in the United States, the continued failure to resolve the crisis contributed to Ronald Reagan's defeat of Jimmy Carter in the presidential elections of 1980. After the election, with the assistance of Algerian intermediaries, successful negotiations began. On January 20, 1981, just hours before Reagan's inauguration, a final deal was struck. The United States released almost $8 billion in Iranian assets, and Jimmy Carter brought every one of the hostages back home alive after 444 days in Iranian detention just as Reagan was being sworn in.

War by Proxy

As president, Ronald Reagan was far more bellicose than Jimmy Carter. He ramped up the Cold War to heights it hadn't seen in 20 years. And by extension, he led the United States into a series of proxy wars, especially in the Caribbean, where he felt America's security was being threatened by Soviet assistance to various Marxist guerilla groups. The United States was back on familiar ground—war mode.

Sandinista!

In 1979, a Marxist revolution led by the Sandinistas ousted the Somoza dictatorship in Nicaragua. In one of his first acts, Reagan authorized the CIA to overthrow the Sandinistas. William Casey, the CIA director, arranged with Argentine military officials to begin training an opposition group known as the Contras, using U.S. weapons and money.

Reagan tried to drum up support for the Contras within the United States by referring to them as "the moral equivalent of our founding fathers." The CIA received $50 million for training programs.

But it turned out that the Contras were typical South American thugs. The group resorted to hit-and-run tactics aimed primarily at women and children. Horatio Arce, chief of Contra intelligence, stated, "We attack a lot of schools and health centers.

We tried to make it so that the Nicaraguan government cannot provide social services for the peasants." As word of these sorts of tactics spread, American support of the Contras diminished.

In 1984, for the first time in Nicaragua's history, free elections took place. The Sandinistas received 69.2 percent of the vote. As a result, in the United States, Congress passed the Boland Amendment, barring U.S. actions to overthrow the Sandinistas.

Stuck but not dismayed, the Reagan administration utilized Oliver North to sell arms to Iran and use the profits to fund the Contras. The resulting "Iran Contra scandal" almost brought down the Reagan White House. Ironically, the Sandinistas were eventually driven from office, but not by guns—they were voted out some time later by the Nicaraguan electorate.

Grenada

On October 13, 1983, the Grenadian Army and former Deputy Prime Minister Bernard Coard led a bloody coup d'état in Grenada. Because Coard was a Marxist and because nearly 1,000 American medical students were then in Grenada, Washington was deeply troubled by the events.

On October 25, 1983, the United States attacked and invaded Grenada. The initial assault consisted of some 1,200 troops. Heavy fighting continued for several days, but as the invasion force grew to more than 7,000, the Grenadian Communists either surrendered or fled. Although scattered fighting continued for a few more days, the island quickly fell under American control. By the first of the year, U.S. troops went home and a pro-American government took power.

Panama

In 1968, General Omar Torrijos led a coup in Panama that allowed blacks and the poor to obtain a share of power in the traditionally European-dominated Panama. Torrijos was killed in a plane crash in 1981, and by 1983, Manuel Noriega had become the ruler. Noriega was a Torrijos ally, as well as a friend of U.S. intelligence.

The United States was content to let Noriega run Panama, and its vital canal, as long as he abided by Washington's ways. And he did, for the most part. That he was a known drug trafficker mattered little; in fact, the U.S. government had known that Noriega was involved in drug trafficking since at least 1972, when the Nixon administration considered assassinating him. Yet he stayed on the CIA payroll.

When Noriega began to sow his oats and act more independent than the United States wanted, especially insofar as the Contras went, he became expendable. In December 1989, the United States invaded Panama, capturing Noriega, and brought him back to the United States on drug charges. The U.S. invasion also had the effect of restoring power to the rich white elite that had been displaced by the Torrijos coup, just in time to ensure a friendly government for the administrative changeover of the Panama Canal on January 1, 1990.

Reliable Resources

In 1903, Panama and the United States signed the original Panama Canal Treaty, which allowed the United States to build and operate a canal connecting the Pacific Ocean with the Caribbean Sea through the Isthmus of Panama. On September 7, 1977, a new Panama Canal Treaty was signed by President Torrijos of Panama and President Carter of the United States that transferred full control of the canal to Panama on December 31, 1999. The United States, by far, uses the canal more than any other country in the world.

The Once and Future King?

Conflict from abroad hit the shores of America for the first time on September 11, 2001. Although, as can be seen herein, the country should have been used to war and conflict, it was not. September 11 was a body blow precisely because all the conflict the United States had engaged in for almost 100 years had happened abroad. It was antiseptic conflict.

September 11 was different. Occurring as it did, not only in America, but also in its most powerful and important cities (Washington, D.C., and New York), the terrorist attacks made the United States feel vulnerable like nothing had before, save for Pearl Harbor.

Yet the attacks should not have been a surprise. Not only had the United States been imposing its will upon lesser countries since at least 1945, but also al-Qaeda had declared war on the United States two years earlier. It was hubris that shielded U.S. foresight of the attacks.

The resulting War on Terror certainly poses risks and potential rewards for the United States. On one hand, it is an opportunity to make the world safer, and despite acting in its own self-interest (as all countries do), there is no small streak of puritanical idealism that runs in Yankee blood. It might surprise the rest of the world that the United States thinks that by attacking terrorists in other sovereign nations, it is making the world a better place for everyone.

The risks are numerous. The first is that the United States might end up being an even larger target. People in countries that might have otherwise ignored America might decide it deserves to be put in its place. Alternatively, others might conclude that the success of the September 11 attacks proved that the United States might be a paper tiger after all. Either way, being the international policeman is dangerous when so many people don't like the police.

The last risk is the most serious. International relations really is not that much different from "king of the hill." The British were once the king, and for a short while, it was the Germans. Both got knocked off the hill. The Soviets were half king for a while, until they got knocked down.

Today, the United States stands alone as king of the international hill. Given that the object of the game is to knock the other guy off and ascend yourself, you can rest assured that someone, somewhere, is making plans to knock America off its pedestal. That is how the game is played.

A Shameful History

Conflict for the United States not only comes from without, but it also has a large race-relations problem stemming from slavery.

Slavery in the United States

During the course of the slave trade, which began in the United States in the seventeenth century, millions of Africans were stolen from their homes and families in Africa and forcibly shipped to America.

Although the European, American, and African slave traders and the politicians, businessmen, and slave owners who supported them did not intend to put into motion a chain of events that would create a brutal and costly civil war, they did.

In all, more than 600,000 people died as a result of the Civil War and its efforts to end the "peculiar institution" of slavery. In the 2 days it took for the Battle of Gettysburg, for example, more than 50,000 soldiers died. Before the war was over, probably the greatest president the United States had ever had, Abraham Lincoln, was assassinated.

Reliable Resources

Lincoln's pre-presidential life:

1832—Lost job.

1833—Failed in business.

1834—Elected to Illinois state legislature.

1835—Sweetheart died.

1836—Had nervous breakdown.

1846—Elected to Congress.

1848—Lost renomination.

1854—Defeated for U.S. Senate.

1856—Defeated for nomination for vice president.

1858—Defeated for U.S. Senate again.

1860—Elected president.

Of course, the end of the war did not end discrimination toward blacks. Throughout the south, *Jim Crow* laws were enacted to keep the blacks at bay. And even though the United States attempted to make amends of sorts by constitutionally outlawing discrimination based on race, creed, or color in the Thirteenth, Fourteenth, and Fifteenth Amendments, changing racist attitudes proved to be very difficult.

def•i•ni•tion

Jim Crow laws barred African Americans from access to voting and employment, as well as to public places such as restaurants, hotels, and other facilities.

We Hold These Truths to Be Self-Evident

In the 1950s and 60s, African Americans began to demand the rights guaranteed them in the Constitution. Both peacefully, through the leadership of Dr. Martin Luther King, and violently, through leaders like Malcolm X, millions of black Americans confronted the white structures that subjugated them.

Many words were said, and far too much blood was shed before laws and—more importantly—attitudes changed. Although the country certainly has made a lot of progress in the area of race relations, an ugly vein of racism remains in the mountain that is America.

According to the Southern Poverty Law Center, in the year 2004, there were 762 active "hate groups" in the United States, categorized as Ku Klux Klan, Neo-Nazi, Racist Skinhead, Christian Identity, Black Separatist, and Neo-Confederate. These groups, with names such as Aryan Nations, Underground Skinhead Action, and the American Nazi Party, are committed to conflict and resistance.

Despite such groups, credit must be given where credit is due. In America, great strides toward equality have been sought and undertaken. No, this conflict is not over, but it is healing. Martin Luther King seemed to be speaking the dreams of many when he said, on August 28, 1963:

> I have a dream that one day this nation will rise up and live out the true meaning of its creed: 'We hold these truths to be self-evident: that all men are created equal.' I have a dream that one day on the red hills of Georgia, the sons of former slaves and the sons of former slave owners will be able to sit down together at a table of brotherhood. I have a dream that my four children will one day live in a nation where they will not be judged by the color of their skin but by the content of their character.

The Least You Need to Know

- Wars made the United States a superpower.

- The war in Vietnam was a mistake from its inception.

- Throughout the 1980s, the United States engaged in several proxy wars.

- The War on Terrorism is a double-edged sword.

- The residue of slavery is an ugly one, although progress can be seen.

Chapter 27

Problems for America's Neighbors

In This Chapter

- ◆ Mexico
- ◆ The Zapatistas
- ◆ Canada
- ◆ The Québécois

Although North America might seem to be a place of relative peace and quiet, it is not. Not only is the most warring nation on Earth, the United States, there, but also its neighbors have their own internal conflicts and problems that are magnified by their proximity to their superpower neighbor.

Viva Mexico!

In the early part of the twentieth century, the legendary peasant leaders Pancho Villa and Emiliano Zapata successfully fought for reform in Mexico. Because of this, the 1917 Mexican constitution contained several provisions concerning worker rights and land reform—ideas that would dominate Mexican politics for years to come.

North America is not as peaceful as it seems.

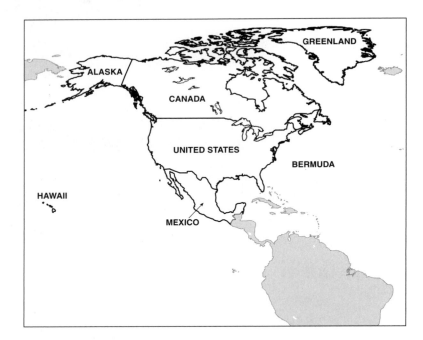

Reliable Resources _____

Mexico's reputation for festive fun is well founded. Most months contain a major national holiday or fiesta, and practically every other day is a local saint's day or town celebration. Carnaval is held in late February or early March. Mexico's most characteristic fiesta is *the Día de los Muertos* (the Day of the Dead), held on November 2.

But not until the presidency of Lazaro Cardenas in 1934 would the revolutionary ideas of Zapata and Villa become part of the government's agenda. The most dramatic proof of this occurred in 1938 when Cardenas nationalized British and U.S. oil firms.

Cardenas was a radical in other ways, too. Most important, he created a political revolution that would last for 70 years. Cardenas cobbled together a coalition of the three broad sectors of Mexican society: the peasants, the unions, and the public employees. He renamed his party the Institutional Revolutionary Party (PRI) in 1946, and it remained the ruling party of Mexico for the rest of the millennium.

Problematically for the country, Mexican presidents after Cardenas began to use the PRI's power for control rather than popular participation. As a result, Mexico became a stable, if undemocratic, nation in which power and corruption became a basic element of politics.

The most dramatic evidence of this occurred during the 1960s, which were a time of social unrest in Mexico as they were in many other places around the world. In 1968, Mexican students began to clamor. The two main sources of discontent were the slow progress made in fulfilling the promises of the Mexican revolution (1910–1920) of eliminating poverty and inequality and the limited levels of democracy. The students were determined to take advantage of the international attention devoted to Mexico during the Mexico City Olympic Games to express their frustration and criticize the government, as well as to demand democratic reforms and social justice.

> **Landmine!**
>
> Despite its vast oil wealth, Mexico remains a very poor country. Rural areas are generally neglected, and huge shantytowns surround the major cities. Many young, poor Mexicans risk crossing the border to the United States in search of a job.

On October 2, 15,000 students marched through the streets of Mexico City and into the central square—known as Plaza de Taltelolco. But this peaceful student demonstration turned bloody in what came to be remembered forever as the Taltelolco massacre. Without any warning, the army began to fire against the unarmed student protestors. The massacre was indiscriminate, killing people who were at the plaza for reasons unrelated to the protest. It is estimated that more than 300 people were killed, hundreds were injured, and several thousand were arrested.

This event typifies conflict in Mexico. It is neither condoned nor allowed. The right-wing PRI often uses brute force to keep the masses of poor peasants in line.

Growing Militarization in Mexico

Needless to say, strong-arming factions of the military are nothing new to Latin America. But they have grown especially worrisome in Mexico, especially in light of its poverty and urgent social needs. In spite of an economic crisis in 1995, the Mexican government paid an estimated $2.2 billion to the United States that year for military purchases, a 40 percent increase over 1993 expenditures.

Why the increase? There are three reasons.

Cocaine, It's Running All Around My Brain

The first reason for the dramatic growth of the army and right-wing paramilitary groups in Mexico has to do with the drug trade. Marijuana, heroin, and cocaine trafficking have reached ever-higher levels in Mexico over the past 20 years. Under pressure from the United States, the Mexican government is making a serious effort to control the problem, and a significant problem it is:

- Roughly 70 percent of South American cocaine and 80 percent of its marijuana comes from Mexico into the United States.

- Mexican drug cartels bring in approximately $50 billion a year from drug sales in the United States.

- It is estimated by some in Mexico that between 70 and 80 percent of the police force has been influenced by drug money.

Landmine!

The Mexican army currently deploys more than 20,000 soldiers in counter-narcotics operations, including eradication and interdiction efforts. The majority of civilian complaints of army abuses have involved troops participating in counter-narcotics operations.

To overcome the problem of corrupt and abusive police forces, U.S. military advisors began to push for military involvement in Mexican anti-narcotic activities. In a 1995 anti-narcotic plan, President Zedillo mandated a military role in drug interdiction. Subsequently the Mexican army began to take control of numerous provincial police forces and, in 1997, an army general was appointed to serve as Mexico's drug czar.

Landmine!

The drug czar was fired after 10 weeks for alleged involvement with the drug cartels.

There have been some successes in the drug war. Several major figures in the cartels have been captured and prosecuted. According to an observer of the U.S.-Mexican drug scene, "In 1996, Mexican officials reported 2 consecutive record years in eradicating nearly 20,000 acres of marijuana and poppy crop: much of this owing to military search-and-destroy missions in the mountainous areas where these crops are grown."

> **Landmine!**
>
> Why do other countries hate the United States? Consider the "drug war." American complicity in drug trafficking is unquestionable. Whereas an estimated 70 percent of all cocaine and 40 percent of all heroin on American streets has traveled through Mexico, in Mexico's view, it is equally true that 100 percent of all these substances travel through the United States. To blame Mexico for drug imports when the United States can claim even less success is seen as utter hypocrisy.

Good Cop, Bad Cop

The second reason for Mexico's increased militarization relates to the aforementioned corruption in Mexican law enforcement. It is said by some that local law enforcement has the choice to either cooperate with the traffickers or face death.

In response to this dilemma, the government began to use the army to deal with the drug runners. But the problem with this solution is that the military is equally corruptible: General Jesús Gutiérrez Rebollo, head of the National Institute to Combat Drugs, was fired from his post in 1996 for taking bribes from the godfather of Mexico's largest drug cartel.

Stand Up for Your Rights

The final reason for Mexico's growing militarization is an increasing disaffection with the federal government. Dissatisfaction in poor, rural areas of southern Mexico especially may indicate the potential for armed rebellion.

Paradise Lost

In the state of Chiapas, high atop a distant mountain, sits an idyllic little town inhabited by friendly Indians wearing colorful garb. A sort of Shangri-La, San Cristobal de Las Casas is the sort of place travelers yearn to discover. Its cafés surround the central square, art galleries line its cobblestoned streets, and jazz wafts through the air—or at least it used to. (I was there in 1988, and it was an amazing place.)

The Zapatista National Liberation Army staged an uprising in idyllic San Cristobal de Las Casas on, not coincidentally, January 1, 1994, the day the North American Free Trade Agreement (NAFTA) took effect. A guerrilla group, which was previously unknown to the public, the Zapatistas—under the leadership of articulate pipe-smoking poet "Subcommandante Marcos" (later revealed to be a former university lecturer)—announced a long list of demands. Among them were demands for reforms in health care, land distribution, an opposition to NAFTA, and better education for the indigenous Mayan population.

Landmine!

NAFTA began on January 1, 1994. It removed most barriers to trade and investment among the United States, Canada, and Mexico. Under NAFTA, all nontariff barriers to agricultural trade between the United States and Mexico were eliminated. In addition, many tariffs were eliminated immediately, with others being phased out over periods of 5 to 15 years.

The 12-day fight between the Zapatistas and the government left an estimated 145 dead and hundreds arrested. Incidents of torture and forced confessions were reported during and after arrests.

The rebellion took the country by surprise. In Mexico, dominated as it had been by the ruling PRI and as militarized as it had become, armed rebellion had not been a common occurrence. This was especially true during the Cold War, when social, economic, and cultural problems in Mexico—especially as perceived by the left—were neglected. Said one Zapatista rebel, "If you brought up those problems in the 80s, you were immediately labeled pro-Communist, or a puppet of the Soviet Union." Given Mexico's proximity to the United States, such a label was heresy.

When the Cold War ended in the 1990s, Mexico's many social problems began to come to the fore. And unlike other armed rebellions in Latin America, this one was media savvy. The Zapatistas used the news media, books, and the Internet to lobby for local autonomy and economic development for a people they felt had long been neglected by the federal government.

After the rebellion had been quashed, the government signed a cease-fire agreement with the Zapatistas. But even so, the next year, the Mexican army launched a military offensive against them. The Mexican government hadn't bought all those arms for nothing. But the attack failed to defeat the Zapatistas, and Mexico faced strong international criticism.

Yet the government wanted to contain the rebels, so rather than attack them outright, it sponsored paramilitary groups who terrorized on its behalf. These paramilitaries focused especially on the civilian population in an attempt to undermine support for the Zapatista rebellion. Even so, the Zapatistas, and what they stood for, would not go away.

The Zapatista rebellion, in fact, signaled the beginning of a dangerous time for Mexico. Later that year, 1994, presidential candidate Luis Donaldo Colosio was murdered. As a result, the election was won by PRI candidate Ernesto Zedillo. The stock market plunged later that year, and the peso lost a third of its value. The next year, former President Carlos Salinas was forced into exile after his brother Raul Salinas was connected with Colosio's murder.

> **Reliable Resources**
>
> In Mexico, troop size has grown 15 percent since 1994, and the military budget continues to rise at a rate of about 16 percent per annum.

Clearly change was in the air. In 1997, for the first time since its inception in 1929, the PRI lost parliamentary elections. In December, 45 Indians were killed by paramilitary gunmen in a Chiapas village. The incident caused an international outcry, and President Zedillo began an investigation. The governor of Chiapas then resigned, and peace talks with the rebels started up again, although they would break down at the end of the year.

Pandora's Box

Even though the two sides eventually reached an agreement of sorts on greater autonomy for the indigenous Mayans of Chiapas, the insurgency in the southern part of Mexico escalated. A different group, the leftist Popular Revolutionary Army (EPR), also attacked government troops.

These guerrillas stated that their purpose was "to overthrow the anti-popular, anti-democratic, demagogic, and illegitimate government which panders to national and foreign capital interests." The group targeted police stations, government offices, and military installations.

> **Peacekeepers**
>
> According to CNN, "In the tourist markets of San Cristobal de Las Casas today, Zapatista souvenirs are everywhere. You can find Zapatista dolls, key chains, and even T-shirts emblazoned with Zapatista slogans."

The Zapatistas and the EPR are apparently not alone. It is estimated that as many as eight different armed rebel groups might be operating throughout Mexico.

Presidente Fox

The most dramatic change in Mexico in 50 years occurred in July 2000 when opposition party candidate Vincente Fox was elected president, the first opposition candidate ever to do so. His Alliance for Change party beat the institutional PRI by just more than 1 percent. The election of Fox was a mandate for change. One of Fox's first acts was to address issues raised by the Zapatistas.

At Fox's urging, the Mexican parliament passed a bill increasing the rights of indigenous people. But Subcommandante Marcos rejected the bill, saying it would leave the Indian population worse off than before. Marcos declared that "the uprising in Chiapas will continue."

Oh Canada!

Other than, say, New Zealand, Canada might seem to be about the most peaceful place on Earth. But that is a misconception. Would it surprise you to learn that the country came within a hair of disintegrating in 1995?

To understand how this could have happened, you need to travel back in time 500 years, to the earliest explorations of North America by the Europeans.

New France

In 1524, an Italian navigator named Giovanni da Verrazzano was sponsored by King François I of France to explore the New World. Verrazzano explored the American east coast between Florida and Newfoundland, and he named these new lands "Nova Franca." In 1529, his brother Girolamo created a map of the area, and he called the area "Nova Gallia." Over time, the name "Nouvelle-France" (New France) became the norm to identify French possessions of Northeastern America.

French influence really began in earnest when, in 1608, Samuel de Champlain established the first permanent French settlement in North America in Quebec City. Unlike much of the rest of Canada, or North America for that matter, Quebec became a French-speaking Catholic region. More important, over the next 150 years, it became a major battleground in the fight between England and France for control of the New World.

The Québécois

The roots of the modern conflict can be directly traced back to 1759. That year, General James Wolfe's British forces routed the French at the Battle of the Plains of Abraham and Quebec City fell to the British. At the Treaty of Paris four years later, France surrendered its North American colony. The residents of Quebec City, the Québécois, numbering about 70,000 then, suddenly became British subjects.

Peacekeepers

The Treaty of Paris was signed in February 1763 and ended the "Seven Years War." The treaty decreed to England all of Canada and all the great interior east of the Mississippi, except for the port of New Orleans.

Although the British were not overbearing, with the British army came English-speaking settlers. Threatened by this foreign occupation and their foreign tongue, the Québécois came to believe their very existence was in danger. This belief continued throughout the nineteenth century as the British minority dominated the French majority in Quebec.

Resentful of their diminished status and disturbed by the increasing number of English-speaking immigrants, a number of Québécois took up arms against the British in 1837. The rebellion failed, and there were no further nineteenth-century rebellions in Quebec.

In 1867, modern Canada was created when the provinces of Quebec, Ontario, Nova Scotia, and New Brunswick confederated under the British North America Act. The new constitution guaranteed the rights of French Canadians. Section 133 of the Act permitted the use of French in …

- The Quebec legislature.

- Quebec courts.

- The Quebec parliament.

In order to hold on to their French origins, the Québécois became, possibly, more French than the French. For the next century, Québécois nationalism grew, as did its Catholicism. Yet even so, their English-speaking countrymen quickly began to dominate commerce in major Quebec cities like Montréal.

The Québécois in the Twentieth Century

The era between 1950 and 1965 became known as the "quiet revolution" in Quebec. It was a time of social transformation as Quebec moved from a rural, religious society to a more modern, urban one. Things that had traditionally distinguished the Québécois—their religion and rural lifestyle—were vanishing. The French language became, seemingly, the only difference between Quebec and the rest of Canada.

But even so, Quebec refused to assimilate with the rest of Canada. Instead, it led to an increase in nationalism, as well as a newfound desire for separatism and independence. In 1968, the "Parti Québécois" emerged, advocating self-rule for Quebec. It was led by Rene Lévesque.

Reliable Resources

We are Québécois. What that means first and foremost—and if it need be, all that it means—is that we are attached to this one corner of the earth where we can be completely ourselves; this Quebec, the only place where we have the unmistakable feeling that "here we can really be at home." Being ourselves is essentially a matter of keeping and developing a personality that has survived for three and a half centuries. At the core of this personality is the fact that we speak French.

—1968 speech by Rene Lévesque

At the same time, other, more radical groups began the requisite terror campaign. Bombing public places and kidnapping high-profile Canadian and British officials, the radicals dramatized the emergence of French-Canadian nationalism. In 1970 alone, for example, the Front de Libération du Québec kidnapped James Cross, the British high commissioner in Montreal, and murdered Pierre Laporte, the Canadian minister of labour.

Peacekeepers

One of the Parti Québécois' first moves was to pass a French-only law, even though French had already been made the sole official language of Quebec in 1974. Bill 101, the French Language Charter, reflected the Québécois' fear of becoming a minority in their own province.

In 1976, the Parti Québécois came to power in Quebec on the promise of holding a referendum on sovereignty, and the issue of separation was finally put to Quebec voters in 1980: 59.5 percent voted against independence for Quebec.

Attempting to quell Quebec's dissatisfaction, Canada created a new constitution in 1982 that recognized the "distinctiveness" of Quebec. The Québécois weren't mollified, though; Quebec was the only Canadian province not to approve the reformed constitution.

In 1995, the issue of Quebec's independence was put before the voters again, and this time lost by only one percent. As a result, it became quite clear that this conflict was not going away any time soon.

Lesson Learned

What is interesting is how differently the Canadians dealt with its separatist movement than other countries. In almost every other country discussed throughout this book, when the desire of one people to be free surfaces, some radical group emerges from its ranks, ready to kill and maim anyone in their way. The government then usually becomes correspondingly repressive by arresting, murdering, and torturing the rebels.

In Canada, however, the issue was dealt with in a civilized manner. Yes, there were some wanton acts of murder, but by and large, both the Québécois and the Canadians have handled the issue of Quebec separatism responsibly and civilly. There were no death squads. There were no paramilitary crackdowns. Rather, the issue was put to a vote, of all things.

In that, they are a model for the rest of us.

The Least You Need to Know

- ◆ Mexico is becoming increasingly militarized.
- ◆ The Zapatistas are demanding rights in Chiapas.
- ◆ The roots of modern conflict in Canada can be traced to 1759 when the French residents of Quebec City became British subjects.
- ◆ The Québécois have been demanding independence in Canada.

Chapter 28

Give Peace a Chance

In This Chapter

- ◆ Is change possible?
- ◆ The United Nations
- ◆ The Olympic movement
- ◆ The Nobel Peace Prize
- ◆ Nongovernmental organizations
- ◆ Peace in our time

To read about so many conflicts and so much death, hatred, and animosity can be depressing. It is truly shocking what people do to one another in the name of some ideology, ethnicity, or for power.

But progress, too, is possible. Conflicts do get resolved and people can learn to live with one another. It should be comforting, then, to realize that although the bad guys get the most press, there are far more good guys than bad.

Change Is in the Air

No, it is not easy to make peace. You do not make peace with your friends; you make peace with your enemies. It is not an appetizing thought for most people. Yet evidence abounds that people do it all the time and that peace and progress are possible.

The Abolition of Slavery

Once, the African slave trade was one of the largest businesses in the world. Starting in about 1500, slaves were imported to the Western Hemisphere until the nineteenth century. In the United States, the importing of slaves was outlawed by Congress in 1808.

But the United States was actually only a small player in the overall slave trade that brought roughly 10 million Africans west. The numbers broke down this way:

◆ The United States imported about 650,000 slaves before 1808, or roughly 7 percent of the overall number of slaves.

◆ The Caribbean and Brazil imported the largest percentage of the 10 million African slaves—73 percent.

◆ The rest of South America accounted for 17 percent.

Slaves sold for about $1,500 in 1850, or in year 2005 dollars, about $18,000. They brought in an annual rate of return of about 10 percent. So the slave trade, in today's terms, would be a multibillion dollar enterprise.

And even though it was clearly abhorrent and repugnant, the slave trade lasted for more than 300 years. By the time the United States was ready to go to war over the issue, slavery had become an ingrained institution that kept the rural south economically viable in relation to the more industrial north.

What should encourage us all is that despite its vast economic underpinnings, despite racism and hatred, despite the fact that it was big business, more important was that slavery was disgusting and wrong. In a world in which money means so much, and morals often amount to so little, that is no small thing.

By the end of the nineteenth century, slavery had been all but abolished in the Western Hemisphere (although it certainly thrived, and thrives, in other parts of the world). And it was not just the institution that was ended; it was the idea that people's lives could literally be bought and sold that was also eradicated.

If we can end that idea, is it not impossible to conclude that other ideas—such as hunger, war, or racism—could similarly be done away with? Sure, it sounds pie in the sky, but so did the abolition of slavery to that black field hand slaving in Mississippi in 1825.

Ding Dong, the Witch Is Dead!

The Soviet Union cast a giant, dark cloud over most of Europe for the last half of the twentieth century. It was, according to Ronald Reagan, "an evil empire," and certainly there was plenty of proof to back up that assertion:

◆ Soviet forced-labor camps were first established in 1919. By 1934, the Gulag had several million inmates.

◆ Josef Stalin was one of the greatest tyrants of all time, killing 20 million of his own countrymen.

◆ On April 13, 1943, Germans discovered the mass graves of several thousand officers of the former Polish army murdered on Stalin's orders.

◆ In 1968, Alexander Dubcek in Czechoslovakia set out to reform his Warsaw Pact country. For the first time since 1948, the Czech government proclaimed the legitimacy of basic human rights and liberties and objected to the persecution of people for their own political convictions. In response, the Soviets, on August 20, 1968, invaded Czechoslovakia, ending the so-called "Prague spring."

By the 1980s, the Soviet Union had seemingly become a monolithic empire determined to keep its satellites of Albania, Bulgaria, Hungary, East Germany, Poland, Rumania, and Czechoslovakia in check at any cost.

What no one expected was that a visionary man of peace would come to lead the Soviet Union. Mikhail Gorbachev concluded that something had to change in the USSR, and he instituted a so-called "Sinatra doctrine" that allowed the Warsaw Pact countries to do things their way.

That small opening was all that was needed. In the fall of 1989, Hungary decided to open its

Reliable Resources

General Secretary Gorbachev, if you seek peace, if you seek prosperity for the Soviet Union and Eastern Europe, if you seek liberalization: Come here to this gate! Mr. Gorbachev, open this gate! Mr. Gorbachev, tear down this wall!

—Ronald Reagan, remarks at the Brandenburg Gate, West Berlin, Germany, June 12, 1987 border with East Germany, heretofore a completely isolated country. That decision, that little crack in the iron curtain, was all the people of Eastern Europe needed to break free and eventually topple modern communism.

Hungary's decision to open its East German border allowed East Germans to enter Hungary, and then enter Austria, and finally land in West Germany, reuniting with long-lost loved ones. What started out as a trickle of refugees quickly became an unstoppable flood of change that swept through Eastern Europe with surprising swiftness.

Here's how it played out in Germany. After weeks of discussion in East Germany about a new travel law, and after mass demonstrations against the government, a member of the East German government was asked—at 6:53 P.M. on November 9, 1989, at a press conference—when the new travel law would come into force. He stammered, "Well, as far as I can see … straightaway, immediately."

Thousands of East Berliners stormed to the border crossings. At the Berlin Wall, the people demanded that the border be opened, and at 10:30 P.M. it was opened. That was the end of the Berlin Wall. An onrush of East Berliners streamed into West Berlin over, around, and through the wall. Wild celebrations erupted in both countries throughout the night. The Berlin Wall had fallen, and Eastern Europe would finally be free of the yoke of communism and Soviet repression.

Reliable Resources

According to one participant, the night went like this: "Perhaps 7,000 people were pressed together, shouting, cheering, clapping. We pushed through the crowd. From the East German side we could hear the sound of heavy machines. With a giant drill, they were punching holes in the wall. Every time a drill poked through, everyone cheered. People shot off fireworks and emergency flares and rescue rockets. Many were using hammers to chip away at the wall. There were countless holes. At one place, a crowd of East German soldiers looked through a narrow hole. We reached through and shook hands. The Germans were drunk with joy."

Again we see that progress is possible, and peace is achievable. It seemed to many people that the mighty Soviet Union was insurmountable and would dominate Eastern Europe forever. What few expected was that it would fold like a house of cards.

If the evil empire could be defeated and freedom could be restored to its seven satellites, what else is possible? What other evils in this world can be eradicated?

Middle East Peace

If you want more proof that the impossible is possible, consider the Middle East. In the modern world, no two countries have gone to war against each other more often than Israel and Egypt. Yet these bitterest of enemies found a way to create peace for their people.

What it took is not all that different from what it took in the Soviet Union—brave, bold leaders who were willing to take a risk in hopes of a higher return. Menachem Begin and Anwar Sadat both risked ridicule at home, and in Sadat's case, his decision to make peace probably cost him his life.

Reliable Resources

Peace is more precious than a piece of land.
—Anwar Sadat

By the same token, Sadat and Begin personify what is needed if the world is to ever be a more peaceful place: the power to make a change, the understanding that change is necessary, the realization that peace is not easy, and the willingness to lead people and change minds.

That last aspect, the ability to change minds, might be the most important ingredient of all. By and large, people are creatures of habit and indoctrination. Serbs are taught to hate Bosnians. Israelis are taught to hate Arabs. It takes a leader of extraordinary courage to lead his people down a new path and to teach them a new way of thinking.

The people of Israel and Egypt were fortunate to have once had men like that in charge. One can only wonder what, say, Yasser Arafat could have done had he taken a page out of the Sadat playbook.

Northern Ireland

Peace also requires a people who are willing to change. In Northern Ireland, the Catholics and Protestants got so tired of war that they concluded that peace had to be better. Doing so meant that they had to give up age-old animosities and beliefs about each other—not an easy thing to do, either.

But it is to their everlasting credit that they are trying.

The United Nations

One of the very first efforts to create a world of greater tolerance and more understanding occurred in 1899 at the International Peace Conference. The Conference, held in the Hague, worked on methods for settling crises peacefully, preventing wars, and codifying rules of warfare. It adopted the Convention for the Pacific Settlement of International Disputes and established the Permanent Court of Arbitration.

def•i•ni•tion

When a person (or country) wants to stay out of foreign affairs and international relations, the person is said to be an **isolationist**; someone who wants their country to remain isolated. In this rapidly shrinking, interconnected world, isolationists are becoming dinosaurs.

Reliable Resources

Mankind has grown strong in eternal struggles, and it will only perish through eternal peace.

—Adolf Hitler

The immediate forerunner of the United Nations was the League of Nations, the brainchild of President Woodrow Wilson. The League of Nations was established in 1919 under the Treaty of Versailles "to promote international cooperation and to achieve peace and security." But it was doomed to failure when an *isolationist* United States refused to join, and it ceased its activities after failing to prevent World War II.

In 1945, at the conclusion of World War II, representatives from 50 countries met in San Francisco to draw up the United Nations Charter. The charter was signed on June 26, 1945, by the representatives from the 50 countries. Poland, which was not represented at the conference, signed it later and became one of the original 51 member states.

The United Nations officially came into existence on October 24, 1945, when the charter had been ratified by China, France, the Soviet Union, the United Kingdom, the United States, and by a majority of other signatories.

The purpose behind the United Nations was to help stabilize international relations and give peace a more secure foundation. Indeed, peacekeeping has become one of its most vital functions. This function is critical in an oft dangerous world. As the organization puts it:

United Nations peacekeepers—military personnel in their distinctive blue helmets or blue berets, civilian police, and a range of other civilians—help implement peace agreements, monitor cease-fires, create buffer zones, or support complex military and civilian functions essential to maintain peace and begin reconstruction and institution-building in societies devastated by war.

Member states voluntarily provide troops and equipment—the United Nations has no army or civilian police—for which they are compensated from a special peacekeeping budget.

The peacekeepers' strongest "weapon" is the impartiality with which they carry out their mandate. But peacekeeping is dangerous business; more than 1,650 U.N. peacekeepers have died in the performance of their duties since 1948.

Maybe even more impressive is that since 1945, the United Nations has negotiated 172 peaceful settlements of various conflicts. Similarly, the United Nations has enabled people in many countries to participate in free and fair elections, including those held in Cambodia, Namibia, El Salvador, Eritrea, Mozambique, Nicaragua, South Africa, Kosovo, and East Timor. It also provides electoral advice, assistance, and monitoring of results.

The United Nations promotes peace in many other ways, too:

- The U.N. Development Programme (UNDP) designs and implements projects for agriculture, industry, education, and the environment. It supports more than 5,000 projects with a budget of $1.3 billion.

- By investigating individual complaints of human rights abuses, the U.N. Human Rights Commission has focused world attention on cases of torture, disappearance, and arbitrary detention and has generated international pressure to be brought on governments to improve their human rights records.

- The United Nations, through the International Atomic Energy Agency, helps minimize the threat of nuclear war by inspecting nuclear reactors in 90 countries to ensure that nuclear materials are not diverted for military purposes.

- More than 30 million refugees fleeing war, famine, or persecution have received aid from the U.N. High Commissioner for Refugees since 1951.

- U.N. agencies have worked to make safe drinking water available to 1.3 billion people in rural areas since 1990.

- A 13-year effort by the World Health Organization resulted in the eradication of smallpox from the planet in 1980. In 1974, only 5 percent of children in developing countries were immunized against major diseases. Today, as a result of the efforts of UNICEF and WHO, there is an 80 per cent immunization rate, saving the lives of more than 3 million children each year.

(Source: UN: Major Achievements of the UN; www.un.org/aboutun/achieve.htm)

> **Reliable Resources**
>
> The United Nations and its related agencies have won the Nobel Peace Prize an amazing eight times:
>
> 1950—U.N. Middle East mediator
>
> 1954—U.N. Refugee Agency
>
> 1961—U.N. secretary general
>
> 1965—UNICEF
>
> 1969—U.N. Labour Agency
>
> 1981—U.N. Refugee Agency
>
> 1988—U.N. peacekeepers
>
> On December 10, 2001, the United Nations and its Secretary General, Kofi Annan, received the Nobel Peace Prize on the hundredth anniversary of the venerated award.

That the U.N.'s work has been successful, and that peace can in fact find a way, is seen in a 2005 report stating that between 1992 and 2004, armed conflicts around the world declined by more than 40 percent. Genocide and human rights abuses declined even more. The reason for this dramatic decline, as outlined in the first-ever Human Security Report, is two-fold:

- The collapse of the Soviet Union reduced funds, and the need, for proxy wars across the globe.
- The end of the Cold War freed the U.N. to finally and properly do its job, according to the study's author, professor Andrew Mack.

International Humanitarian Law

Another international movement that is a very encouraging sign for a more humane world is that of international humanitarian law (IHL). It may surprise you to learn that war is illegal. The Charter of the United Nations states that the threat or use of force against other States is unlawful and so, since 1945, war has no longer been an acceptable way to settle conflicts between states.

Yet even so, armed conflicts are permissible under international law under a few circumstances:

◆ In self-defense

◆ During a civil war

◆ To maintain or restore international peace and security

And as you have seen throughout this book far too much, war is still a fact of life. As such, there emerged a need for rules which limit the effects of war on civilians. That is the goal of IHL, with the Geneva Conventions as its primary expression, along with an important body of resulting law: 6 major treaties with more than 600 articles place restrictions on the use of violence in wartime.

According to Hans-Peter Gasser, IHL can be summarized in a few principles:

◆ Persons who are not taking part in hostilities, or who no longer are, shall be protected and treated humanely. They shall be given appropriate care, without any discrimination.

◆ Captured combatants shall be treated humanely. They shall be protected against all acts of violence, especially torture. They have the right to a normal judicial procedure.

◆ No superfluous injury or unnecessary suffering shall be inflicted on the opponent.

◆ Neither civilian populations nor civilian objects shall be the target of military attacks.

According to Gasser, "these principles give expression to what the International Court of Justice has called 'elementary considerations of humanity,' and serve to remind us that even in war, there should be dignity."

Going for the Gold

International understanding can occur in other ways as well. The modern Olympic Games do much to promote world peace by bringing countries together in the spirit of friendly rivalry. By so doing, the Olympics prove time and again that there are many ways to interact internationally, war being just one of them.

The first Olympic Games were held in 776 B.C.E. At first, the sprint was the only event. Events such as the discus and javelin throw were added later. These ancient Olympic Games were held for more than 1,000 years but were abolished in 394 C.E.

The Games were revived in 1896. As Baron Pierre de Coubertin, the father of the modern Olympic movement put it, "The idea of the revival of Olympic Games was the logical culmination of a great movement. The nineteenth century saw the taste for physical exercises revive everywhere. At the same time, the great inventions—the railways and the telegraph—abridged distances. People intermingled and have learned to know each other better."

In fact, the symbols that we associate with the Olympics were all chosen as symbols of peace and international understanding:

◆ The colored rings were conceived of by Baron Pierre de Coubertin. Each of the five rings symbolizes one of the five continents. The intertwining of the five rings symbolizes the conjunction of the continents during the Games and represents the ideal of international peace and brotherhood.

◆ The flame symbolizes purity. It lights the way for the athletes, showing them the importance of creating a lasting unity for all humankind.

◆ The festivities associated with the Games symbolize a united community of people who come together peacefully from different societies. Despite their various backgrounds, they all can contribute to a peaceful coexistence between nations.

A Noble Prize

The Nobel Peace Prize is one of the world's great honors. That the Nobel Committee honors peacemakers so is critical because it symbolizes just how important peacemaking is in this modern world.

The Nobel Peace Prize has been hailed as "the greatest honor a man can receive in this world." Since 1901, when the first Peace Prize was handed out, recipients have included Theodore Roosevelt, Albert Schweitzer, and Mother Teresa.

A popular misconception is that Alfred Nobel, as the inventor of dynamite, established the prize to assuage his guilt. But the truth is that the money Nobel made from dynamite came mostly from peacetime applications. In 2005, the prize was worth just about $1.3 million.

The Nobel Peace Prize honors people who are dedicated to peace and human rights in a world that at times seems to honor neither.

Nongovernmental Organizations

Nongovernmental organizations (NGOs) are increasingly playing a vital role in peacekeeping and education throughout the world and should be a cause of optimism. NGOs are (usually) international nonprofit organizations working in conjunction with local peoples to create a better world. They perform a variety of critical peacemaking functions:

◆ **An early warning system.** Because of their close work with local communities, NGOs are in a position to alert people of potential breakdowns in a country's government or among relations among domestic groups.

◆ **Human-rights monitoring.** NGOs play an important role by gathering information, sending out fact-finding missions, and so on.

◆ **Community building.** NGOs play an important role in strengthening social systems by building needed infrastructure, working on public health, and training local leaders, for example.

◆ **Education.** This is a traditional role for NGOs and helps bring about conflict resolution.

Peace in Our Time

One reason there is so much war and conflict in the world today is that people are identifying themselves ever more narrowly. Thus, for example, although they lived in relative peace and harmony when they identified themselves as one nation, when Yugoslavs splintered into five separate subnationalities, they were free to war upon each other precisely because there were now "others."

When a group identifies with some religion or country, it is far too easy to conclude that anyone not of that identity is the enemy:

◆ Arabs and Jews can hate each other.

◆ Islamic fundamentalists can hate Westerners.

◆ Hutus can murder the Tutsis who live next door.

Interestingly, people in one's own group usually get a pass for actions that, if done by the others, would be cause for revenge. Thus, for example, it is considered to be valid self-defense to Palestinians when one of their own blows up a bunch of Israelis. However, that same action is thought to be murder when an Israeli kills Palestinians (and vice versa).

For all its faults, one reason the United States is as stable as it is, is that constitutionally it is illegal to identify people because of their race or color. This doesn't mean that it doesn't happen, but it does mean that people in that heterogeneous society tend to think of themselves as Americans first and their subset nationality second. When you expand the scope of your identity, there are fewer people to blame and more people on your side.

Changing that narrow sort of thinking is exactly what creates peace. The United Nations, by fostering peaceful relations between countries, endeavors to change the way people think. The Olympics, by showing people competing peacefully, does the same thing.

When Israel and Egypt chose peace, it not only required their people to think differently, it also required brave leaders who were willing to take a risk on new and unpopular ideas. The leaders needed to, in fact, lead. When those living in Northern Ireland are willing to put aside their longstanding differences and animosities, they light the way for people in the rest of the world to change the way they think about their enemies, too. Enemies are not a requirement.

So one way to create a more peaceful world is for people to expand the scope of who they think they are, as well as to change the way they think about who they are. Noted futurist and inventor of the geodesic dome, Buckminster Fuller, did not consider himself a Californian (though he lived there), nor an American (though he lived there, too). He considered himself an "Earthian." It might seem idealistic, but killing others becomes far more difficult when they can be identified as part of your group.

Imagine how much less war there would be if more people expanded their identity similarly. If we can end slavery, if we can topple totalitarianism, if bitter enemies can learn to live in peace, if leaders can forge a new path, there is no telling what the planet Earth can do. The good guys can still win.

The Least You Need to Know

- The end of slavery and the fall of the Soviet Union prove that the impossible can be made possible.

- Difficult peace treaties also prove that progress is possible.

- The United Nations does much good, if often unheralded, work.

- The Olympics and the Nobel Peace Prize foster peace in their own way.

- Identity causes conflict.

- The good guys can still win.

Appendix A

For More Information

This section provides a bibliography of the resources that have provided invaluable information and insights during my research for this book. If you are interested in learning more about any of the conflicts listed in this book (historical or otherwise), or about various peace efforts underway throughout the world, these resources should prove useful.

Bibliographical Information

The World Wide Web is an invaluable resource for all kinds of information. The following links provide a good starting point for general information and facts about the countries discussed in this book.

Allafrica.com
www.allafrica.com
African news.

Center for Defense and International Security Studies
www.cdiss.org/hometemp.htm
Provides information about a wide range of defense and security issues relevant to both the United Kingdom and the international community.

Country Reports
www.emulateme.com/alphanationtext.htm
A site devoted to the history of every country on Earth.

Crisis Web
www.crisisweb.org/
Anticipating and understanding conflicts.

Flashpoints
home.earthlink.net/~vehicool/countries-conflicts/countries-conflicts.html
Links to conflict briefings.

Global Issues that Affect Everyone
www.globalissues.org
This site provides a gateway to all kinds of global issues that ultimately affect us all.

Human Rights Watch
www.hrw.org
A good resource if you want to learn more about human-rights violations and abuses worldwide, including in the United States.

National Defense Council Foundation
www.ndcf.org/
Yearly updates of world conflicts.

Political Africa
www.africapolitical.com/
All Africa, all the time.

The BBC News Service
news.bbc.co.uk/
A great international news resource; the BBC search engine allows you to look up various countries—stories about them, background facts, and so on.

The Central Intelligence Agency's World Fact Book
www.cia.gov/cia/publications/factbook/index.html
An excellent overview of all countries.

The Federation of American Scientists
www.fas.org/man/dod-101/ops/war/
Great background information about world conflicts.

The History Guy
www.historyguy.com/
A good source for more information about new and recent conflicts, listed country by country.

The United Nations
www.un.org/
Everything you need to know about the United Nations.

Timetable of the History of Cuba
www.historyofcuba.com
Cuban history in a nutshell.

Unrepresented Nations and Peoples Organization (UNPO)
www.unpo.org
Provides a forum for occupied nations, indigenous peoples, minorities, and even oppressed majorities who currently struggle to regain their lost countries and preserve their cultural identities.

Online Encyclopedias

Here is a list of search engines that are good for quick background checks and facts about countries and historical events or definitions of terms.

ebooks.whsmithonline.co.uk/

lexicorient.com/e.o/index.htm

www.bartleby.com/65/

www.encyclopedia.com/

www.humanitas-international.org/

www.lexisnexis.com

www.m-w.com/

www.onwar.com

www.pbs.org/wgbh/buildingbig/index.html

www.slider.com/index.htm

www.wikipedia.com

www.worldatlas.com

Web Bibliography

This section provides a chapter-by-chapter listing of the articles and links that provided invaluable insights and facts for my account of the state of world conflicts.

Chapter 1, "The World at War"

Council for a Livable World. "Foreign Aid and the Arms Trade: A Look at the Numbers." www.clw.org/cat/foraid/faidexe.html

Crossett, Barbara. "Kofi Annan's Astonishing Facts!" *The New York Times.* September 27, 1998.
www.teachingforchange.org/News%20Items/un%20data.htm

Deen, Thalif. "Inequality Primary Cause of Wars, says Annan." InterPress Third World News Agency, September 9, 1999.
www.hartford-hwp.com/archives/27a/052.html

Fritz, Walter. "Peace Between Nations."
www.anice.net.ar/intsyst/peace.htm

Georgieff, Anthony. "Swedish Report Emphasizes Role of Poverty in War." Radio Free Europe/Radio Liberty.
www.rferl.org/nca/features/2000/06/F.RU.000620135251.html

Keegan, Sir John. "Eliminating the Causes of War."
www.pugwash.org/reports/pac/pac256/keegan.htm

Rummel, R. J. *Power Kills: Democracy as a Method of Nonviolence.* Transaction Publishers: 1997.
www.hawaii.edu/powerkills/

Chapter 2, "East Is East, and West Is West"

Anon. "Attack on the USS Cole." Yemen Gateway.
www.al-bab.com/yemen/cole1.htm

Anon. "World Trade Center." PBS Online
www.pbs.org/wgbh/buildingbig/wonder/structure/worldtrade.html

Armstrong, Karen. "The True, Peaceful Face of Islam." *Time.* October 1, 2001. Vol. 158 No. 15.
www.time.com/time/magazine/printout/0,8816,175987,00.html

Glossary of Islamic Terms and Concepts.
www.usc.edu/dept/MSA/reference/glossary.html

The International Policy Institute for Counter-Terrorism has put together the Osama bin Laden and al-Qaeda page, which provides an extensive listing of al-Qaeda-related reports and articles.
www.ict.org.il/articles/bombings.cfm

Islam: Empire of Faith. Companion website to the PBS film of the same name.
www.pbs.org/empires/islam/index.html

Symon, Fiona. "The Roots of Jihad." BBC News, Tuesday, October 16, 2001.
news.bbc.co.uk/hi/english/world/middle_east/1603178.stm

Chapter 3, "The War on Terror"

About.com War on Terrorism: usgovinfo.about.com/library/blattack.htm

Aljazeera: english.aljazeera.net/HomePage

The British Broadcasting Company Online:
news.bbc.co.uk/1/hi/in_depth/world/2001/war_on_terror/

Cable News Network: War Against Terrorism:
www.cnn.com/SPECIALS/2001/trade.center/

Clark, Richard, *Against All Enemies: Inside America's War on Terror.* (Free Press, 2004).

Washington Post War on Terrorism: www.washingtonpost.com/wp-dyn/nation/
specials/attacked/

Wikipedia: en.wikipedia.org/wiki/War_on_terror

Chapter 4, "The Middle East Mess"

Anon. "Camp David: Historic Moments." BBC News, Monday, July 10, 2000.
http://news.bbc.co.uk/1/hi/world/middle_east/827488.stm

Anon. "Failure of the Oslo Accords."
www.globalexchange.org/campaigns/palestine/oslo.html

Bard, Mitchell. "The Lebanon War." The Jewish Virtual Library.
www.us-israel.org/jsource/History/LebanonWar.html

Beinin, Joel. "Camp David II." MERIP Press Information Notes, July 26, 2000.
www.merip.org/pins/pin26.html

Camp David Accords. September 17, 1978. The Camp David agreements, annexes,
exchange of letters, 17 September 1978.
www.mfa.gov.il/mfa/go.asp?MFAH00ie0

Isseroff, Ami. "A Brief History of Israel and Palestine."
www.mideastweb.org/BriefHistory.htm

Lee, Roger. "The History Guy: Arab-Israeli Wars: Suez/Sinai War (1956)."
http://www.historyguy.com/suez_war_1956.html

Chapter 5, "Israel and Palestine Struggle for Peace"

British Broadcasting Company Online:
news.bbc.co.uk/hi/english/static/in_depth/world/2001/israel_and_palestinians/
timeline/, and news.bbc.co.uk/2/hi/middle_east/default.stm

Columbia University: Middle East and Jewish Studies:
www.columbia.edu/cu/lweb/indiv/mideast/cuvlm/peace.html

Israel-Palestine Center for Research and Information: www.mideastweb.org/
briefhistory.htm

Middle East Research and Information Project:
www.merip.org/palestine-israel_primer/toc-pal-isr-primer.html

Wikipedia: en.wikipedia.org/wiki/Israeli-Palestinian_conflict

Chapter 6, "Iraq I: The Rise and Fall of Saddam Hussein"

Butt, Gerald. "Saddam Hussein Profile." BBC News, Thursday, January 4, 2001.
news.bbc.co.uk/hi/english/world/middle_east/newsid_1100000/1100529.stm

CNN Special Report. "The Survival of Saddam Hussein."
www.cnn.com/SPECIALS/2001/gulf.war/unfinished/war/index4.html

Columbia Encyclopedia. "Iran-Iraq War."
www.bartleby.com/65/ir/IranIraq.html

Hooker, Richard. "Mesopotamia: The Sumerians."
www.wsu.edu:8080/~dee/MESO/SUMER.HTM

Jews for Justice in the Middle East. "The Origin of the Palestine-Israeli Conflict."
www.mediareviewnet.com/JewsForJustice.htm

Kuwait Information Office, "History of the Kuwait-Iraq Border Dispute."
www.kuwait-info.org/Gulf_War/history_Kuwait_iraq_border_dispute.html

Malowany, Matthew. "Defiance in the Desert."
www.cbc.ca/news/indepth/iraq/index.html#backandhistory

VanDoodewaard, William. "Islam United? A Comparison of Shi'ite and Sunni Belief
and Practice."
www.rim.org/muslim/shiite.htm

Chapter 7, "Iraq II: Ground Zero for the War on Terror"

British Broadcasting Company Online:
news.bbc.co.uk/1/hi/in_depth/middle_east/2002/conflict_with_iraq/default.stm

Cable News Network: www.cnn.com/SPECIALS/2003/iraq/

Clark, Richard, *Against All Enemies: Inside America's War on Terror.* (Free Press, 2004).

Institute for Policy Studies, www.ips-dc.org/iraq/primer.htm

The New York Times: www.nytimes.com/pages/world/worldspecial/

Wikipedia: en.wikipedia.org/wiki/Iraq_War

Yahoo! News: p143.news.scd.yahoo.com/fc/World/Iraq

Chapter 8, "Sudan: A Land Divided"

AllAfrica.com: allafrica.com/sudan/

Anon. "Sudan: A Historical Perspective."
www.sudan.net/society/history.html

Astill, James. "Osama: The Sudan Years." The *Guardian*, October 17, 2001.
www.guardian.co.uk/g2/story/0,3604,575396,00.html

Broder, Jonathan. "How *real* terrorists do it."
www.salon.com/june97/news/news2970609.html

CIA World Fact Book: www.cia.gov/cia/publications/factbook/geos/su.html

Darfur Information Center: www.darfurinfo.org/

Davis, Karen. "Slave Trade Thrives in Sudan."
www.s-t.com/daily/02-98/02-22-98/a02wn011.htm

Wikipedia: en.wikipedia.org/wiki/Sudan

en.wikipedia.org/wiki/Darfur_conflict

en.wikipedia.org/wiki/Janjaweed

Chapter 9, "Hot Spots in Northern Africa"

Aljazeera: english.aljazeera.net/

British Broadcasting Company Online:
news.bbc.co.uk/1/hi/world/middle_east/4308823.stm

Out There News. "Egypt: All under wraps until recently."
www.megastories.com/islam/world/egypt.htm

Chapter 10, "Death Around the Horn"

FAS. "Ethiopia / Eritrea War."
www.fas.org/man/dod-101/ops/war/eritrea.htm

Human Rights Watch. "Mengistu Haile Mariam."
www.hrw.org/press/1999/nov/mengitsu.htm

Milner, Kate. "Flashback 1984: Portrait of a famine." BBC News Online,
April 6, 2000.
news.bbc.co.uk/hi/english/world/africa/newsid_703000/703958.stm

Chapter 11, "Insanity in West Africa"

Anon. "Country profile: Liberia." BBC News, May 20, 2002.
news.bbc.co.uk/hi/english/world/africa/countryprofiles/newsid1043000/1043500.stm

Anon. "Q&A: Sierra Leone's hostages" BBC News, August 10, 1999.
news.bbc.co.uk/hi/english/specialreport/1999/01/99/sierraleone/newsid252000/252822.stm

Anon. "Snapshot of issues surrounding Clinton's Nigeria visit." CNN,
August 25, 2000.
http://news.bbc.co.uk/hi/english/world/americas/newsid756000/756309.stm

Blunt, Elizabeth. "The Guinea conflict explained." BBC News, February 13, 2001.
news.bbc.co.uk/hi/english/world/africa/newsid_1167000/1167811.stm

FAS. "Movement of Democratic Forces in the Casamance (MFDC)."
www.fas.org/irp/world/para/mfdc.htm

Human Rights Watch. "Sierra Leone Rebels Violating Peace Accord."
www.hrw.org/press/1999/aug/sierra3008.htm

Rupert, James. "Nigerian Ruler Dies After Brutal Reign." *Washington Post,*
June 9, 1998.
www.washingtonpost.com/wp-srv/inatl/longterm/nigeria/stories/abacha060998.htm

Chapter 12, "Struggles in Central Africa"

Anon. "Angola."
home.earthlink.net/~vehicool/countries-conflicts/Angola-web/Angola_briefing_main.html

Anon. "Rwanda genocide inquiry to end in 2004." BBC News, December 7, 2001.
news.bbc.co.uk/hi/english/world/africa/newsid_1691000/1691954.stm

British Broadcasting Company Online:
news.bbc.co.uk/1/hi/world/africa/country_profiles/1070265.stm

British Broadcasting Company Online:
news.bbc.co.uk/1/hi/world/africa/country_profiles/1076399.stm

Chadwick, Alex. "Coltan Mining and Eastern Congo's Gorillas."
www.npr.org/programs/re/archivesdate/2001/dec/20011220.coltan.html

Human Rights Watch. "Leave None to Tell the Story: Genocide in Rwanda."
www.hrw.org/reports/1999/rwanda/index.htm#TopOfPage

Internet Movie Database: www.IMDB.com

Pearce, Justin. "Landmines: War's deadly legacy." BBC News, January 29, 1999.
news.bbc.co.uk/hi/english/special_report/1999/01/99/angola/newsid_264000/264223.stm

Washington Post:
www.washingtonpost.com/wp-dyn/articles/A175282005Feb11_2.html

Chapter 13, "All in the Family: North and South Korea"

Anon. "Profile: Kim Jong-il." BBC News, April 2, 2002.
news.bbc.co.uk/hi/english/world/asia-pacific/newsid1907000/1907197.stm

Anon. "Kim Dae-jung: Dedicated to reconciliation." CNN, June 14, 2001.
www.cnn.com/2001/WORLD/asiapcf/east/06/12/bio.kim.daejung/

Cable News Network: www.cnn.com/SPECIALS/2003/nkorea/

FAS. "Korean War."
www.fas.org/man/dod-101/ops/korea.htm

Online Newshour: www.pbs.org/newshour/bb/asia/northkorea/

Schnabel, James F. "United States Army in the Korean War: Policy and Direction: The First Year."
www.army.mil/cmh-pg/books/p&d.htm

Chapter 14, "Enter the Dragon: China"

Anon. "China-Taiwan History." PBS Online News Hour, March 7, 2000.
www.pbs.org/newshour/bb/asia/china/china-taiwan.html

Anon. "What You Need to Know About the Chinese Occupation of Tibet."
www.freetibet.org/info/basics.htm

Holland Sentinel Archives. "Leaders who ordered Tiananmen crackdown feared arrest."
www.thehollandsentinel.net/stories/010701/new_Leaders.html

Human Rights Watch. "China: Human Rights Concerns in Xinjiang."
www.hrw.org/backgrounder/asia/china-bck1017.htm

Macan-Markar, Marwaan. "Asian governments seen exploiting September 11."
www.thinkcentreasia.org/News/news012.html

O'Hanlon, Michael. "Can China Conquer Taiwan?"
www.brook.edu/dybdocroot/views/articles/ohanlon/2000fallIS.htm

Smith, Charles R. "Rand Report Warns of Conflict with China." Newsmax.com, June 20, 2001.
www.newsmax.com/archives/articles/2001/6/19/205940.shtml

Chapter 15, "Cain and Abel: India and Pakistan"

British Broadcasting Network Online:
news.bbc.co.uk/1/hi/world/south_asia/1430367.stm

Dhar, L. N. "An Outline of the History of Kashmir."
www.koausa.org/Crown/history.html

FAS. "Jammu and Kashmir."
www.fas.org/irp/world/india/threat/kashmir.htm

Kumar, Radha. "Sovereignty and Intervention: Opinions in South Asia."
www.pugwash.org/reports/rc/como_india.htm

Ramana, M. V. and A. H. Nayyar. "India, Pakistan and the Bomb."
www.sciam.com/2001/1201issue/1201ramana.html

Sahay, Tara Shankar. "India ready to take on Pakistan at two levels."
www.rediff.com/news/2001/dec/21parl.htm

Spaeth, Anthony. "India: Piercing the Armor." *Time*. September 11, 1995.
www.time.com/time/international/1995/950911/india.html

The Legacy Project. "India-Pakistan Partition."
www.legacy-project.org/events/display.html?ID=10

Chapter 16, "Religious and Ethnic Animosity in Indonesia"

www.acehtsunami.org/

Anon. "Dayaks broaden violent campaign in Borneo." CNN, February 26, 2001.
www.cnn.com/2001/WORLD/asiapcf/southeast/02/26/indonesia.killing02/

Arthurs, Clare. "Irian Jaya: A troubled history." BBC News, January 1, 2000.
news.bbc.co.uk/hi/english/world/asia-pacific/newsid_587000/587064.stm

Australia Broadcasting Company: www.abc.net.au/ra/news/infocus/s1438843.htm

British Broadcasting Company Online: Bali bombing
http://news.bbc.co.uk/1/hi/in_depth/asia_pacific/2002/bali/

FAS. "Timor."
www.fas.org/man/dod-101/ops/war/timor.htm

Frontline: www.frontlineonnet.com/fl2218/stories/20050909001905500.htm

Karon, Tony. "Megawati: The Princess Who Settled for the Presidency." *Time*.
July 27, 2001.
www.time.com/time/pow/article/0,8599,169130,00.html

Linder, Diane. "Ethnic Conflict in Kalimantan." ICE Case Studies.
www.american.edu/projects/mandala/TED/ice/kaliman.htm

McCarthy, Terry. "Chaos in the Islands." *Time*. January 17, 2000.
www.time.com/time/asia/magazine/2000/0117/indonesia.ambon.html

Nugent, Nicholas. "Roots of Sulawesi Conflict." BBC News, December 20, 2001.
news.bbc.co.uk/hi/english/world/asia-pacific/newsid_1719000/1719964.stm

U.S. Committee for Refugees. "Political History of Aceh."
www.refugees.org/news/crisis/indonesia/aceh.htm

Wikipedia: en.wikipedia.org/wiki/2002_Bali_terrorist_bombing

en.wikipedia.org/wiki/Abu_Bakar_Bashir

Chapter 17, "More Asian Atrocities"

Anon. " Country Profile: Burma." February 25, 2002.
news.bbc.co.uk/hi/english/world/asia-pacific/countryprofiles/
newsid_1300000/ 1300003.stm

Anon. "Guide to Philippines conflict." BBC News, December 6, 2001.
news.bbc.co.uk/hi/english/world/asia-pacific/newsid_1695000/1695576.stm

Anon. "Sri Lanka: The ethnic divide." BBC News, May 16, 2000.
news.bbc.co.uk/hi/english/world/south_asia/newsid_514000/514577.stm

Anon. "Sri Lanka: An unwinnable war?" BBC News, April 27, 2000.
news.bbc.co.uk/hi/english/world/southasia/newsid_620000/620631.stm

British Broadcasting Company Online:
news.bbc.co.uk/1/hi/world/asia-pacific/3955543.stm

CIA World Fact Book: www.cia.gov/cia/publications/factbook/geos/np.html

Global Security: www.globalsecurity.org/military/world/war/thailand2.htm

Gregorius, Arlene. "World: Asia-Pacific Profile: Aung San Suu Kyi." BBC News,
July 29, 1998.
news.bbc.co.uk/hi/english/world/asia-pacific/newsid_140000/140955.stm

Horn, Robert. "Burmese Democracy Leader Faces New Threat." *Time.*
November 28, 2000.
www.time.com/time/asia/features/news/2000/11/27/burma.suu_kyi.html

Huang, Cheng-China. "Diaoyutai Islands Dispute."
www.american.edu/projects/mandala/TED/ice/DIAOYU.HTM

Iyer, Pico. "Woman of the Year: Corazon Aquino." *Time.* January 5, 1987.
www.time.com/time/special/moy/1986.html

Kelly, Todd C. "Vietnamese Claims to the Truong Sa Archipelago."
www.hawaii.edu/cseas/pubs/explore/v3/todd.html

Powell, Leigh. "Spratly Islands Dispute."
www.american.edu/TED/SPRATLY.HTM

Wikipedia: en.wikipedia.org/wiki/Nepal

en.wikipedia.org/wiki/Communist_Party_of_Nepal_%28Maoist%29

Chapter 18, "Trouble in the Stans"

Asia Times: www.atimes.com/atimes/Central_Asia/GC26Ag03.html

British Broadcasting Company Online: news.bbc.co.uk/2/hi/asia-pacific/3143462.stm

Frontpage magazine: www.frontpagemag.com/Articles/ReadArticle.asp?ID=14115

Global Security: www.globalsecurity.org/military/world/war/tajikistan.htm

Jihad Watch: www.jihadwatch.org/archives/001730.php

Mother Jones magazine: www.motherjones.com/commentary/columns/2000/09/rall3.html

Rashid, Ahmed. *Jihad: The Rise of Militant Islam in Central Asia.* (Penguin Books, 2003).

Time magazine: www.time.com/time/europe/webonly/europe/2000/09/malashenko.html

Whole Earth magazine: www.wholeearthmag.com/ArticleBin/173.html

Wikipedia: en.wikipedia.org/wiki/Tulip_Revolution

Chapter 19, "The Balkan Mess"

Simpson, Bob. "Milosevic's Yugoslavia." BBC News.
news.bbc.co.uk/hi/english/static/in_depth/europe/2000/
Milosevic_yugoslavia/croatia.stm

FAS. "Operation Deliberate Force."
www.fas.org/man/dod-101/ops/deliberate_force.htm

Judah, Tim. "Milosevic's legacy." BBC News June 30, 2001.
news.bbc.co.uk/hi/english/world/europe/newsid_1415000/1415683.stm

U.S. State Department Report. "Ethnic Cleansing in Kosovo: An Accounting."
www.state.gov/www/global/human_rights/kosovoii/document.html

Wood, Paul. "The downfall of Milosevic." BBC News April 1, 2001.
news.bbc.co.uk/hi/english/world/europe/newsid_1204000/1204857.stm

Chapter 20, "The Russian Bear"

Anon. " Destination Guantanamo Bay." BBC News, December 28, 2001.
news.bbc.co.uk/hi/english/world/americas/newsid_1731000/1731704.stm

Anon. "Arrests follow failed Paraguay coup." BBC News, May 20, 2001.
news.bbc.co.uk/hi/english/world/americas/newsid_756000/756309.stm

Anon. "The first bloody battle." BBC News, March 16, 2000.
news.bbc.co.uk/hi/english/world/europe/newsid482000/482323.stm

British Broadcasting Company Online:
news.bbc.co.uk/1/shared/spl/hi/world/04/russian_s/html/1.stm

Cable News Network: www.cnn.com/2004/WORLD/europe/09/04/russia.school/

CBS News: www.cbsnews.com/stories/2004/09/04/world/main641167.shtml

Miller, Sarah K. "Crisis in the Caucasus; History of the conflict in Dagestan."
www.infoplease.com/spot/dagestan1.html

Valasek, Tomas. "Demystifying the Role of Islam in the Former Soviet South."
www.cdi.org/weekly/1999/issue33.html

Valasek, Tomas. "The Changing Face of the Chechnya War." Weekly Defense Monitor,
July 13, 2000.
www.cdi.org/weekly/2000/issue28.html

Chapter 21, "Northern Ireland Imbroglio"

Anon. "Ireland's Troubled History."
www.washingtonpost.com/wp-srv/inatl/longterm/nireland/overview.htm

Anon. "The Honorable George J. Mitchell."
www.us-irelandalliance.org/aboutmitchell.html

USA Today: www.usatoday.com/news/world/2005-07-28-ira_x.htm

Chapter 22, "Smoldering European Conflicts"

Anon. "Country profile: Armenia." BBC News, March 8, 2002.
news.bbc.co.uk/hi/english/world/europe/country_profiles/
newsid_1108000/1108052.stm

Anon. "Terrorist handbook reveals 'secret of success.'" BBC News, May 21, 2001.
news.bbc.co.uk/hi/english/world/monitoring/media_reports/
newsid_1343000/_1343250.stm

Anon. "Turkey foresees Cyprus settlement." BBC News, January 8, 2002.
news.bbc.co.uk/hi/english/world/europe/newsid_1749000/1749138.stm

British Broadcasting Company Online:
news.bbc.co.uk/1/hi/in_depth/europe/2004/madrid_train_attacks/default.stm

British Broadcasting Company Online:
news.bbc.co.uk/1/hi/in_depth/uk/2005/london_explosions/default.stm

FAS. "Nagorno-Karabakh."
www.fas.org/man/dod-101/ops/war/nagorno-karabakh.htm

Housden, Tom. "Cyprus: Years of division." BBC News, January 15, 2002.
news.bbc.co.uk/hi/english/world/europe/newsid_1760000/1760565.stm

"Q&A: Cyprus conflict explained." BBC News, January 15, 2002.
news.bbc.co.uk/hi/english/world/europe/newsid_1761000/1761585.stm

Wikipedia: en.wikipedia.org/wiki/March_11,_2004_Madrid_attacks

   en.wikipedia.org/wiki/7_July_2005_London_bombings

Chapter 23, "Colombia in Conflict"

Anon. "Country profile: Colombia." BBC News, May 1, 2002.
news.bbc.co.uk/hi/english/world/americas/country_profiles/
newsid_1212000/1212798.stm

Anon. "The Colombian Drug Cartels."
gangstersinc.tripod.com/Car.html

Human Rights Watch. "Colombia."
www.hrw.org/wr2k1/americas/colombia.html

Meza, Ricardo Vargas. "The Revolutionary Armed Forces of Colombia (FARC) and the
Illicit Drug Trade."
www.tni.org/drugs/pubs/farc.htm

Chapter 24, "Hatred in Haiti"

Anon. "Country profile: Haiti." BBC News, March 19, 2002.
news.bbc.co.uk/hi/english/world/americas/country_profiles/
newsid_1202000/1202772.stm

Anon. "Profile of H.E. Mr. Jean-Bertrand Aristide: President of the Republic of Haiti."
www.haiti.org/aristide-bio.htm

Aristide.org: aristide.org/

FAS. "Operation Uphold Democracy."
www.fas.org/man/dod-101/ops/uphold_democracy.htm

Sorre, Lucio. "Christopher Columbus."
www.castellobanfi.com/features/story_3.html

Wikipedia: en.wikipedia.org/wiki/Jean-Bertrand_Aristide

Chapter 25, "More Latin and South American Standoffs"

Anon. "Arrests follow failed Paraguay coup." BBC News, May 20, 2000.
news.bbc.co.uk/hi/english/world/americas/newsid_756000/756309.stm

Anon. "Country profile: Ecuador." BBC News, March 7, 2002.
news.bbc.co.uk/hi/english/world/americas/country_profiles/newsid_1212000/1212882.stm

Anon. "Peru's Fujimori resigns effective Tuesday, leaving Peru to debate a transition government." CNN, November 20, 2000.
www.cnn.com/2000/WORLD/americas/11/20/peru.fujimori.03/

Anon. "Timeline: Ecuador." BBC News, March 21, 2002.
news.bbc.co.uk/hi/english/world/americas/newsid_1212000/1212826.stm

Anon. "Timeline: Paraguay." BBC News, March 21, 2002.
news.bbc.co.uk/hi/english/world/americas/newsid_1224000/1224216.stm

Human Rights Watch. "Peru."
www.hrw.org/wr2k1/americas/peru.html

Izaguirre, Carlos Reyna. "Shining Path in the 21st Century: Actors in Search of a New Script."
www.hartford-hwp.com/archives/42a/016.html

Chapter 26, "Life in These United States"

Chomsky, Noam. "The Invasion of Panama."
www.zmag.org/chomsky/sam/sam-2-05.html

CNN. "Vietnam." (Episode script).
www.cnn.com/SPECIALS/cold.war/episodes/11/script.html

Kennedy, Bruce. "Dien Bien Phu 1954 battle changed Vietnam's history."
www.cnn.com/SPECIALS/cold.war/episodes/11/spotlight/

King, Martin Luther Jr. "The Casualties of the War in Vietnam."
www.stanford.edu/group/King/speeches/unpub/
670225-001_The_Casualties_of_the_War_in_Vietnam.htm

Chapter 27, "Problems for America's Neighbors"

Anon. "The Beauty of Resistance."
www.globalexchange.org/campaigns/mexico/chiapas/communities/diary1.html

Anon. "Mexico; A chronology of key events." *Time.* March 21, 2002.
news.bbc.co.uk/hi/english/world/americas/newsid_1210000/1210779.stm

Anon. "So You Wanna Know about Quebec Separatism?"
www.soyouwanna.com/site/pros_cons/quebec/quebec.html

Cummings, Joe. "Drugs, Rebellion, and Mexico's Militarization."
www.mexconnect.com/mex_/travel/jcummings/jcdrugsmiltariz.html

Robberson, Tod. "Rebels Show Flair for Communicating." *Washington Post,*
February 9, 1994.
www.washingtonpost.com/wp-srv/inatl/longterm/mexico/overview/keymarcos.htm

Whitbeck, Harris. "Mexico faces ironies of post-Cold War rebellion." www.cnn.com/SPECIALS/cold.war/episodes/18/then.now/

Chapter 28, "Give Peace a Chance"

Gasser, Hans-Peter. "International humanitarian law and the protection of war victims." www.ICRC.org

"History of the United Nations." www.un.org/aboutun/history.htm

"Major Achievements of the United Nations." www.un.org/aboutun/achieve.htm

"United Nations Peacekeeping: Some questions and answers." www.un.org/Depts/dpko/dpko/ques.htm

Books

If you prefer a more traditional way of browsing for information and insights about the human path of war and conflict, check out these books.

Clark, Richard. *Against All Enemies: Inside America's War on Terror.* (Free Press, 2004).

Grenville, J. A. S. *A History of the World in the 20th Century.* Cambridge, MA (Harvard University Press, 2000).

Halberstam, David. *War in a Time of Peace.* (New York: Scribner, 2001).

Kozodoy, Neal. *The Mideast Peace Process: An Autopsy.* (San Francisco: Encounter Books, 2001).

Mandela, Nelson. *The Long Walk to Freedom: The Autobiography of Nelson Mandela.* (New York: Little Brown & Co., 1995).

Mitchell, George J. *Making Peace.* (Berkeley: University of California Press, 2001).

Shlaim, Avi. *The Iron Wall: Israel and the Arab World.* (New York: W.W. Norton & Co., 2001).

Tolstoy, Leo. *War and Peace.* (New York: Viking Press, 1982).

Tzu, Sun. *The Art of War.* (Oxford, England: Oxford University Press, 1984).

Index